Legislating
the Courts

Judicial Dependence

in Early National

New Hampshire

John Phillip Reid

Northern Illinois University Press

DeKalb

© 2009 by Northern Illinois University Press

Published by the Northern Illinois University Press, DeKalb, Illinois 60115

Manufactured in the United States using postconsumer-recycled, acid-free paper

All Rights Reserved

Design by Shaun Allshouse

Library of Congress Cataloging-in-Publication Data

Reid, John Phillip.

Legislating the courts : judicial dependence in early national New Hampshire /
John Phillip Reid.

   p.   cm.

Includes bibliographical references and index.

ISBN 978-0-87580-387-6 (clothbound : alk. paper)

1. Judicial power—New Hampshire—History. 2. Judicial independence—
New Hampshire—History. 3. Justice, Administration of—New Hampshire—
History. 4. New Hampshire—Politics and government—18th century.

5. New Hampshire—Politics and government—19th century. I. Title.

KFN1628.R45 2008

347.742′012—dc22

2008013478

for Sarah Barringer Gordon
of the University of Pennsylvania

Contents

LEGISLATING *the* COURTS

Introductory Note

Americans lawyers are so fond of legal platitudes, they turn them into slogans. "At present it will be sufficient to remark," St. George Tucker confidently observed in 1803, "that no citizen of Virginia can be prejudiced either in his person or his property, by any of the government of this commonwealth, (or of the United States) so long as the judiciary departments of those governments, respectively, remain uncorrupt, and independent of legislative or executive control. But whenever the reverse of this happens, by whatever means it may be effected (whether *fear* or *favour*) liberty will be no more, and property but a shadow."[1] In the twenty-first century it seems to be a given among American lawyers that the independence of the judiciary has always been a fundamental constitutional principle and that judicial independence has existed since the adoption of the original state constitutions. They could be wrong. What is not wrong is to put attention on state judiciaries. American histories of judicial independence invariably begin with origins in the federal courts and pay slight or no heed to what was happening in the states. That is a mistake. The framers and ratifiers of the United States Constitution, and the congressmen who adopted the Judiciary Act of 1789 creating the national courts system, may have had some slight experience with British imperial tribunals, but the legal world in which they had lived for the past two decades had been dominated by local courts. They did not think of judicial "independence" as nineteenth-century American lawyers would. They thought of it as it was understood in the late eighteenth century—on the state level of government.[2]

Legal thought in the 1780s and 1790s had been formed by the American Revolution. The colonists had rebelled against the mother country not to be independent of the British crown or to be free of English legal theory but to escape direct rule by Parliament in which they were not represented and whose powers were rapidly becoming "arbitrary," unchecked by constitutional restraints.[3] To create a new government, all that people of some states had to do, John Adams advised, was adopt "[a] plan as nearly resembling the government under which we were born, and have lived, as the circumstances of the country will admit." That meant a government that was a copy of the mother country's, with a representative legislature and "independent judges." For many Americans, however, separation from Great Britain introduced a new political element, republicanism, changing how they thought of the judiciary. Some people understood that republicanism espoused a government not of the will and pleasure of rulers but of law, with the judges as the guardians of that law and the watchdogs of liberty against the rulers. For a majority, by contrast, republicanism implied government by consent, or, as James Madison explained, "a government which derives all its powers directly or indirectly from the great body of the people." Consent of the people, the Massachusetts General Court had resolved in 1776, is government's "only foundation," meaning that "every act of Government, every exercise of sovereignty against, or without the consent of the people, is injustice, usurpation, and tyranny."[4] For political theorists who interpreted the doctrine of consent broadly, all officers of the state, including the judiciary, were answerable to the people, and in constitutional theory the term, "the people," did not refer to those citizens who possessed the right to vote but to the representatives whom they elected to the legislature. It followed that state legislatures had the right—in some situations they had the duty to supervise the people's servants, including the judiciary—to limit judicial tenure, restrict appellate jurisdiction, and prevent judges from usurping the law-deciding functions of juries.

This study recounts the struggles in the early republic of two extremes of republican political theory for domination over American law and of the judiciary that was caught between them. At one end were those who wanted a government of law defined and administered by men educated in the common-law jurisprudence of England, making rulings and applying principles without regard for the politics of the day. Against them, at the other extreme, were people who mistrusted the law of professional lawyers and wanted all law to originate from republican institutions, whether law-applying jurors or law-creating legislators. The contest was conducted in all the American jurisdictions with varying intensity. In Massachusetts it was largely concluded by the end of the first decade of the nineteenth century. In Georgia it lasted into the 1840s. "It took a decade of experience under the state constitutions," Jack Rakove recently pointed out, "to expose the . . . danger that so alarmed Madison in 1787: first, that abuse of legislative power was more ominous than arbitrary acts of the executive"; and "second, that the true problem of rights was less to protect the ruled from the rulers than to defend minorities and individuals against factious popular majorities acting through government." Gordon Wood called the change in political thinking that led people to accept the judiciary as a republican institution, "a remarkable story." It was, "One of the great political and cultural transformations in American history," he concluded, "and it was accompanied by one of the great propaganda efforts in our history: to get people to believe that judges appointed for life were an integral and independent part of America's democratic governments—equal in status and authority to the popularly elected executives and legislatures—was an extraordinary accomplishment."[5]

In no other state were the competing theories of judicial republicanism more evenly matched during the early years of the republic than in New Hampshire. Yet, for the first three decades or more, it must have seemed to the lawyers of New Hampshire that the victory had gone to the populist side. In 1776 the legislature promulgated America's first written constitution without any semblance of judicial independence. It has been suggested that New Hampshire's revolutionaries adopted a constitution without separating judicial, legislative, and executive powers, because, unlike the larger states of Massachusetts and Virginia where lawyers took the lead, New Hampshire's organic act was drafted by merchants, physicians, clergymen, and farmers.[6] That supposition does not wash, just as it is wrong to claim that "[c]onstitutional government began in America when this New Hampshire constitution of 1776 was signed into law."[7] Constitutional government was present from the very beginning of English settlement on the continent. The first settlers of Massachusetts-Bay, the colony from which New Hampshire law originated,[8] had not only insisted on being governed by the rule of law; they also forced their rulers to apply its maxims rather rigidly, much against the magistrates' own concepts of Christian governance.[9] What was new in 1776, when New Hampshire began the epoch of written constitutions, was the emergence of a revisionist constitutional theory that elevated the judiciary into a separate branch or power of government. New Hampshire legal thought was then not ready to go so far as to embrace the notion of separate governmental branches. At most it divided the body politic into two parts, the legislative and the executive, and in actuality into one, the legislative. The judiciary was perceived as a subordinate function of the executive, or the crown.[10] That traditionalist view had been explained by Bunker Gay, the Congregational pastor of the town of Hindsdale, when preaching in 1771 at the opening of the courts in and for the county of Cheshire. "Even at this Distance," he said of the colony's judiciary, "our *Judges* reflect the King's Image: They hold a *regal Office*: They execute a *kingly* Power, perform *princely* Duties, and dispense *royal* Blessings." Put more simply, the judiciary was part of the executive branch.[11]

Surprising as it may seem today, some New Hampshire jurisprudents in 1776 believed that Gay's two branches were two too many. The more "republican" theorists wanted no branches at all. John Sullivan was one. He was perhaps the most influential man in the colony and a lawyer to boot. He was the leader of New Hampshire's rebellion from Great Britain, not only a representative from the colony to the Continental Congress but generally credited at the time with committing the first overt act of treason against the crown. He led men from Durham and Portsmouth in December 1774 against the king's troops stationed in Fort William and Mary, appropriating over one hundred barrels of gunpowder the royal army wished to keep out of American hands, and, in a memorable act of contempt, had his law student tear down the British standard. At the time when New Hampshire legislators were drafting that first American constitution, Sullivan was serving as a brigadier general under George Washington at the siege of Boston. Assuming a role in shaping the constitution, he wrote a directive to the framers, admonishing them not to create a government with distinct branches. "That Government which admits of contrary, or clashing Interests, is imperfect, and must work its own Ruin," he warned.

> When ever one Branch has gained a Power sufficient to over-rule or destroy the other: and the adding a third, with a Seperate & distinct Interest, in Immitation of the British Constitution, so much celibrated, by those who understanding nothing of it, is only like two contending Powers, calling in a third, (which is unconnected in Interest) to keep the other two in Awe, till it can gain Power sufficient to destroy them both. And I may almost venture to prophesy, that the Period is at Hand, when the British Nation will too late discover the Defects of their much boasted Constitution, and the Ruin of that Empire evince to the World the Folly and Danger of establishing a government consisting of different Branches, having Seperate and distinct Interests.[12]

General Sullivan's reputation as a lawyer did not equal his prestige as a political leader. In fact, he was not a very competent lawyer, unless we judge him by the lax standards of eighteenth-century New Hampshire. Yet he was good enough not to have been taken in by the legal fatuities of Tom Paine. He was not espousing Paine's constitutionalism, which John Adams called "foolish."[13] Nor was he anticipating the sarcasm of a better lawyer than himself, Patrick Henry, who, twelve years later, would dismiss the checks and balances of the proposed federal constitution as "incompatible with the genius of republicanism," and would mock the proponents of the constitution for "your specious imaginary balances, your rope-dancing, chain-rattling, ridiculous ideal checks and contrivances."[14] Sullivan, rather, was urging New Hampshire to take the new experiment with republicanism to logical extremes by trusting the people. Instead of writing a constitution on the British model, he was telling the drafters it was better, and safer, to frame a document vesting all power in a single authority, the people, whose policies and directives would be made known by their instrument of government, the elective legislature. To do so, he admitted, would be to go contrary to current constitutional wisdom. English constitutional theory—principles endorsed by most Americans—had long taught that concentrating power in one institution, or what then was called one "interest," unchecked and without restraining balances, would inevitably lead to that "interest" exercising arbitrary power. To introduce competing interests as checks and balances restraining one another, besides risking chaos and conflict within the body politic, was unnecessary. In the new republic that New Hampshirites were creating, the danger of arbitrariness could best be avoided not by separate institutions checking one another but by electing representatives frequently.[15] People voting often was the best shield for protecting popular rights from power. Separate branches of government served to divide and become rival spheres of authority. "[N]o Danger can arise to a state from giving the People, a free & full Voice in their Government," Sullivan contended. "[W]hat are called the Prerogatives of the Crown, or Checks upon the Licentiousness of the People, are only the Children of ambitious, and designing Men, no such Thing being Necessary."[16]

Sullivan's constitutional philosophy won the day. The New Hampshire Constitution of 1776 contained no separate branches of government and no checks on the exercise of official power. All authority was concentrated in one institution, the legislature. Far from being constitutionally independent, the judiciary was hardly recognized at all. To the extent that it existed, it was at the will and pleasure of a majority of legislators, and, as Chief Justice Charles Doe later summed up, the Constitution of 1776, "consolidated power, military, civil, executive, judicial, legislative, and indeterminate" in the legislature.[17]

This study is concerned with judicial events in New Hampshire during the early decades of American independence. Although it does not relate happenings in the other states, it should be kept in mind that the story is representative of what was occurring in all American jurisdictions, except the federal. New Hampshire's history of the struggle for judicial separatism is not unique; it is, though, richer in details and more evenly balanced between political forces favoring judicial autonomy and political forces opposing judicial autonomy than were most other jurisdictions. Just about every attack upon the judicial system that occurred anywhere also occurred in New Hampshire.[18] There were, to be sure, manifest differences. The attacks by radical Republicans of the Jeffersonian persuasion were not nearly as intense or popular in New Hampshire as they were in Pennsylvania. In North Carolina and, especially, Georgia, the subordination of the judiciary to the legislature lasted much longer and was conducted in a much more hostile manner than in New Hampshire. Yet, if written large, the judicial history of New Hampshire would mirror much of the judicial history of most other early-republic states.

In most of the early states, legislative controls over the judiciary were more openly direct than in New Hampshire. Some constitutions put judges immediately under legislative supervision by limiting judicial terms from one to seven years, and in many cases these judges were elected by the legislators, not appointed by the executive. Republicanism was the reason. Short terms with election and reelection voted by the same lawmakers who set rates of compensation and paid their salaries made judges more dependent than independent. The purpose was not to control the judiciary but to put a check on its lawmaking by having it answerable to the most republican branch of government.[19]

Tenure during good behavior, the foundation of judicial independence in the mother country since 1701, and one of the most persistent demands of American whigs during the pre-revolutionary controversy with Great Britain, no longer was constitutionally necessary, some radical Republicans claimed, now that American states were all republics. "[W]e have no hereditary monarch" and "those who appoint the judges do not hold their offices for life," BRUTUS reasoned. "The same arguments, therefore, which will conclude in favor of the judges's offices for good behavior, lose a considerable part of their weight when applied to the state and condition of America."[20] Influenced by the Massachusetts Constitution of 1780, New Hampshire was one of the jurisdictions that did not place high-court judges under the legislature's supervision by limiting their tenure, except for a rule that none serve beyond the age of seventy years.[21]

One of the most direct and frequently implemented ways that legislatures supervised judges in the era of the early republic was to control what they could read in court and what they could cite or quote as authority. New Hampshire was one of the first jurisdictions to enact these statutes, but its legislature was by no means as active as Pennsylvania's, where bills were introduced at several sessions to restrict the reach of judges and curtail the activities of the courts. One Pennsylvania law passed in 1810 on regulating citations and confining the search for new law made it unlawful for lawyers and judges "to read or quote in any court in this Commonwealth, any British precedent or adjudication" pronounced subsequent to the Declaration of Independence.[22] The thrust of these laws is often misunderstood. They were not enacted, as sometimes guessed, because English law, supposedly based on monarchical and feudal principles, was unsuited for the new republic, or because American judges and lawyers, due to their professional training, were likely to be overinfluenced by English precedents simply because they were English, or they would adopt any principle enunciated by an English court due to its Englishness. Some of these explanations were considerations supporting most legislation but not the motivations of the political policy makers or of the more knowledgeable opponents of the common law. They sponsored such legislation to stifle the reception of English ways of thinking about law, a growing likelihood once American jurisdictions, both federal and state, began to publish the decisions of their highest courts.[23] To allow state judges to cite English precedents and quote English judicial opinions as authority was to allow the methodology of the common law to seep into American jurisprudence, a methodology that made judges' pronouncements and decisions a source of law equal to—possibly more persuasive and usually more comprehensive than—ordinary legislation enacted by elected representatives in the legislative branch of the government. It was that methodology of making common law, as much as any particular rules or principles of English law, that the statutes forbidding citation or reading of English books and precedents were intended to prevent.

If it were asked what is the greatest difference between the institutional and constitutional givens of the judiciary of the early republic and that of today, the answer could well be what Christine A. Desan has labeled "legislative adjudication." "The world in which legislatures exercised the authority to interpret public law has been virtually lost," she writes of the difference. "Law, legality, and legal authority have not always been synonymous with the reasoning produced by courts."[24] During colonial and early republic times, legislatures not only authorized payments of claims made against the government; they also adjudicated them, ruling on their validity, determining the state's liability, and then passing bills appropriating awards to claimants named in the resolutions.[25]

Legislative adjudication, Desan discovered, "remained vital in the new republic because early Americans attributed to their political representatives a very different authority to define the political economy than the one we now assume." A rule readily accepted by judges in all jurisdictions that have been studied was that the legislature was the correct tribunal for hearing and redressing contract claims against the government. One compelling reason was the strength of the sovereign-immunity doctrine, forcing even federal courts to respect legislative adjudication. The "sovereign-immunity doctrine guaranteed that the courts had only as much authority to hear claims against the government as delegated to them" by Congress or the state legislatures.[26] As a result, "[i]n the early days of the republic, claims for money against the United States were regarded as financial questions for Congress and not legal questions for the courts. Private claimants were accustomed to pressing their claims in the legislative hall rather than in the courthouse," at least until the Civil War. "The role of the federal judiciary, therefore, was limited to enforcing the decisions of Congress with respect to claims."[27]

During the era of the early republic, when state courts enjoyed more prestige than federal courts, legislators in most states practiced a more extensive form of legislative adjudication than did Congress. Research has not determined the extent to which legislators adjudicated private claims in some American jurisdictions, but in New England the practice extended well beyond the resolutions of financial and contractual claims against the government.[28] It encompassed much of private litigation, including lawsuits in which final judgments had been decreed by constituted courts of law and that today would be considered fully adjudicated.[29] During colonial times, legislatures in Massachusetts-Bay and Rhode Island had been not only the source of statutory law for those provinces but were also their highest courts, frequently exercising appellate jurisdiction and sometimes even original and concurrent powers.[30] In Connecticut the legislature, like those in other New England states, was part of the judiciary, as Justice William Paterson pointed out in a decision still memorable on other grounds. "The Constitution of *Connecticut* is made up of usages, and it appears that its Legislature have, from the beginning, exercised the power of granting new trials," he explained, concurring in *Calder v. Bull*. Even after 1762, when it granted the Superior Court authority to overturn jury verdicts and order new trials, the legislature continued to review judicial judgments. "[I]t appears, that the Legislature, or general court of *Connecticut*, originally possessed, and exercised all legislative, executive, and judicial authority," Paterson summed up, "and that, from time to time, they distributed the two latter in such a manner as they thought proper; without parting with the general superintending power, or the right of exercising the same, whenever they should judge it expedient."[31]

The Connecticut legislature did more than adjudicate "certain exigencies." It granted equitable relief, intervened in probate proceedings, and, as Paterson said, set aside judgments duly rendered by courts and juries, both civil and criminal. In one instance, Connecticut lawmakers even annulled a sentence of death, claiming that the presiding judge, Zephaniah Swift, had conducted the trial outside his circuit, ignoring the terms of court that the legislature had mandated by statute. Swift replied that even if he had committed an error, the legislature exceeded its authority, raising objections that would have been more persuasive in late nineteenth- or twenty-first century law than in the law of 1795. The power to set aside judicial judgments "will give them a discretionary right to interpose in all cases decided by courts of law," he warned. "It will break down the judiciary, and destroy the system of jurisprudence. There can be no law but the sovereign will of the legislature; for if they can annul and vacate one judgment, they can all, and may thus exercise an absolute and uncontroulable power over all the rights of the people."[32] Swift was correct on one point. In the era of the early republic, legislatures were not only supreme: some were sovereign.

The Connecticut legislature may have been constitutionally supreme, but by the standards of other New England states it was not judicially overactive. Connecticut stood between Rhode Island where adjudicated verdicts were overturned less frequently (though for a longer period, almost to the Civil War), and New Hampshire, where the legislature reversed jury verdicts so often that lawmakers had a name for the process: it was called "restoring to law."[33]

Much has been made of New Hampshire's practice of restoring, by legislation, litigants to their law, but it was not different from what was done in some other states, especially in the northeast, although in New Hampshire restorations were enacted often enough that they acquired a formal procedure, giving the legislature, at some sessions, the appearance of being an appellate court.[34]

Throughout the nineteenth century, New Hampshire lawmakers were surprisingly active controlling the judiciary in yet another regard, marking law at the end of the eighteenth and beginning of the nineteenth centuries with quite different norms from those of twentieth- and twenty-first-century constitutional law and, in some regards, also placing New Hampshire law outside the mainstream of constitutional practice in other states during the period of the early republic. New Hampshire's legislators, in unison with the executive department, removed judges they wanted off the bench from the state's highest court, twice legislating out of office judges belonging to the political party just defeated in the most recent election. What is striking is that in all of New Hampshire's history, they did not oust a single judge by impeachment. Compare that record with Pennsylvania's, where impeachment was the procedure of choice for clearing the bench of objectionable personnel.

The antijudicial, anticommon-law, antibar politics of Pennsylvania during the earliest years of the nineteenth century were more extreme than were similar politics in any other state. Opponents of courts and lawyers were able to mount attacks against the judiciary and the legal profession that were more threatening, at least temporarily, than were similar movements in other jurisdictions, not because they were more extreme in their political and negative programs but because the radicals of Pennsylvania were remarkably well organized, and the state constitution had few restraints on experimentation or change, opening a door for radical innovation. The first Pennsylvania constitution was adopted in 1776. That was a year, Gordon Wood has explained, when American political theory was teeming with competing ideas, "but it was in Pennsylvania that the sense of excitement and experimentation attained its greatest intensity. And it was in Pennsylvania that the most radical ideas about politics and constitutional authority voiced in the Revolution found expression."[35] Virtually all authority was vested in a unicameral legislature, and that legislature was the government. The president had few powers except appointments to office, which was shared with a Council, and the judiciary was not constituted as a separate branch of government.

A recent summing up of the objectives of Pennsylvania's legal radicals at the turn of the eighteenth century into the nineteenth concluded that they sought "to provide democratic legal and political structures and jurisprudence that would replace the independent judiciary and judicial review and expunge the common law from American life." The political theory was classical republicanism—that "the will of the people ought to rule" and that an independent judiciary was an obstacle to popular control.[36] Although their legal reforms—directed against both the common law's methodology of arriving at decisions and the practice of law as a profession —are the aspects of their politics that today are the most striking, their program of judicial impeachments was what attracted the attention of contemporaries. One point arousing special interest at that time was that the Pennsylvania legislature clearly claimed the right to impeach judges for political reasons alone. As early as 1776, the first year of independence, it impeached Francis Hopkinson, the revolutionary pamphleteer and the leading political satirist of the early republic. That was a notable start but only a start. When the "constitutionalists" of Pennsylvania, after a decade of political struggle, replaced the Constitution of 1776 with the Constitution of 1790, the change did not have a discernable effect on legislative impeachments of the state's judiciary—certainly not as much as would have been expected. After all, the organic law of few states underwent such drastic changes as did that of Pennsylvania when the radical-republican first Constitution of 1776 was replaced by a more balanced and restrained second constitution in 1790. As the historian of this "counter-revolution" explained, "[t]he essential features of the new Constitution were a bicameral legislature, a single executive with a check on the law-making activities of the assembly, tenure of judges during good behaviour, and fixed salaries for the judiciary." The enhanced constitutional standing did not shield the judges from the wrath of the legislators or from the Republican Party that, when elected to office, followed the lead of the national Jeffersonians and made impeachment the instrument for ridding the courts of Federalists. Professors John A. Ferejohn and Larry D. Kramer summed up the politics when pointing out that in 1803, Pennsylvania judges were impeached and removed from office for "'misdemeanors' amounting to dubious rulings from the bench."[37]

The new constitution demonstrated the difference it could make when, in 1799, Thomas McKean was elected governor. He could not stop the impeachments, but he could keep judges from being addressed from office, and he could veto antijudiciary legislation. Checking the assembly's authority to control the judiciary may have been McKean's most lasting impact on the governance of Pennsylvania. Although he had been chief justice of the state from 1777 to 1799, it may also have been his most important contribution to American common-law jurisprudence. The election of 1806 was even more bitter than the usual Pennsylvania political contests. The campaign that year, James Hedley Peeling pointed out, was conducted "against judges, lawyers, learning, and all signs of aristocracy. . . . Chief among the grievances against the Governor were . . . his wholesale vetoes [and] refusal to dismiss obnoxious judges on address of the legislature." McKean's jurisprudence has been so little studied that it is impossible yet to evaluate his impact on the development of American law: how much he helped move it away from legal theories that challenged and threatened common-law reception, such as republicanism, Christianity, or neighborly common sense, toward a jurisprudence of professional training, common-law reception, and judicial autonomy.[38] It is possible that—had he not been governor and had the governorship not been vested in 1790 with the power to veto legislation—Pennsylvania would have become the one American jurisdiction to experiment with a noncommon-law jurisprudence, the state that could have proven to the nation whether or not republican law could be successful in a commercial and industrial society. Once his career is studied from the perspective of legal theory and legal history, it may be concluded that McKean was the common lawyer who, as governor, prevented the experiment with radical law and kept the Pennsylvania legal system within the mainstream of American law.

During the period of the early republic, the New Hampshire legislature never seemed to have doubted its authority to remove judges at will, but it only once resorted to the cumbersome impeachment procedure. If a majority of both houses "addressed" the governor to remove a judge, and if he and the Council agreed, the judge was out.[39] New Hampshire legislators had an even simpler method if they wanted to be rid of all the judges. They just "legislated" them out of office—no matter that they enjoyed constitutional tenure of good behavior. Before the story being told in the following chapters concludes, New Hampshire's legislature will twice legislate out of office all the justices of the high court by simply repealing the statute that had created the tribunal, thus establishing another court in its place, to which the governor and Council appointed different justices. The old bench was out. A new one was in.

State judges during the era of the early republic appreciated the constitutional reality that they had nothing to gain by opposing legislative supremacy. Certainly the judges of Virginia's Court of Appeals understood the facts of judicial life. When legislated out of office they accepted the inevitable: they protested and then they resigned. That year, 1788, the Virginia General Assembly reorganized the state's judiciary, abolishing the Court of Appeals and creating new tribunals. The judges objected, informing the legislature that they considered the statute "incompatible with their independence."[40] After all, whether the legislators intended it or not, "[t]he direct operation of this law is the amotion from office of the whole bench of judges of appeals," a removal, they said, that violated the constitution. Although a violation of the constitution, it was a violation that was not significant as a matter of law. At that time an unconstitutional statute was not void. It was, rather, valid law. Unconstitutionality, a historian of the court, Margaret Nelson, observed, was a problem only the Assembly could resolve. "The judges," she pointed out, "expressed the hope 'that the present infraction of the Constitution may be remedied by the legislature themselves; and thereby all further uneasiness should be prevented.' In case the legislature did not correct the error, they saw no other alternative for a decision between the legislature and judiciary than an appeal to the people."[41] Even when dealing with an unconstitutional statute, the Virginia judges of the 1780s did not think of judicial equality. If a statute was in fact unconstitutional, any problems created by that unconstitutionality could be corrected only by the General Assembly.

The judges who were removed wanted both to uphold judicial independence, as it was then understood, and to avoid a confrontation they could not win no matter how persuasive their legal position might be. Seeing no judicial solution, the members of the court who had been legislated from office took the practical way out. Although "protesting every invasion of the judiciary establishments, or any deprivation of office in that line in any other mode than as pointed out in the constitution," they nevertheless did "of their mere free will . . . resign their appointments as judges of the court of appeals"—that is, as the court was abolished, they "resigned" their commissions.[42]

By reorganizing Virginia's court system, the General Assembly had imposed heavy new burdens upon the judiciary without any increase in pay. Those new duties, the judges claimed, also made the act unconstitutional. Again the argument was that the changes threatened their independence. The reasons were a bit of a stretch. Increasing obligations without increasing salaries, the judges contended, was tantamount to removing from office those who could not afford to pay the additional expenses that the extended travel would require.[43] These consequences, even though not intended by the legislators, the judges resolved, amounted to legislating them from office. The added tasks, in fact, created "a new office," they claimed, "the labour of which would greatly exceed that of the former: without a correspondent reward." It was, in fact, so blatant "an attack upon the independency of the judges, that they thought it inconsistent with a conscientious discharge of their duty to pass it over."[44]

The argument was forced. The judges were too ready to plead loss of judicial independence. The statute undoubtedly cost something—the new court sessions and circuit travel were financially expensive—but the law's provisions did not add up to an attack upon independence. Even so, the judges made their case. The General Assembly repealed part of the offending law, creating a separate court and reassigning the judges new circuits.[45] It was one of the few occasions during the period of the early republic that an appeal for judicial autonomy received a favorable response from a legislature.

The General Assembly of Georgia quite likely would have paid the judges no heed. The concept of judicial independence had little standing in that state's jurisprudence. For one thing, no institution could speak with a single voice on the judiciary's behalf for there was no appellate or high court. The Constitution of Georgia did not permit one; correction of errors was left to the Superior Court of the county where an alleged error had originated. Because experience soon proved that, with no appellate jurisdiction, conflicts could arise between county courts, leaving Georgia law contradictory, confused, uncertain, and unpredictable, the Judiciary Act of 1799 had provided for an annual gathering of the judges "to determine upon such points as may be reserved for argument and which may require a uniform decision." That process hardly amounted to an appellate court, yet there was a possibility that it might have created more law than the political leaders of Georgia were willing to tolerate. In 1801 the act of two years earlier was repealed, and all motions for review and other appeals were to be taken no higher than the presiding judge of each county.[46]

When the United States Supreme Court, in the *Chisholm* case,[47] promulgated a rule of constitutional law that angered many Georgians, the state's House of Representatives passed a bill declaring that any person aiding in carrying out the decision should be "guilty of felony and shall suffer death, without benefit of clergy, by being hanged."[48] Constitutional historians generally interpret this bill as an instance of state sovereignty trying to get the best of federal authority, a clash between the state and national governments. It should just as accurately be described as a conflict between branches of government, with the legislature asserting supremacy over the judicial. The Assembly was just doing what was traditional legislative practice in Georgia—lawmakers putting judges down, warning them not to be presumptuous.

When the judges of Georgia were told their place, it was always a place somewhere beneath the legislators. In January 1815, four Superior Court judges, meeting in convention, declared certain state statutes unconstitutional. By Georgia judicial standards the decision was startlingly presumptuous, both for disobeying the act of 1801 forbidding conferences to settle conflicts in law and for telling the legislature that the courts would not enforce duly enacted statutes that the judges ruled violated some provision of the state constitution. When the General Assembly met in December, the delegates restated the Georgia doctrine of legislative supremacy—if not supremacy in all aspects of state government, certainly legislative supremacy over the judiciary. The judges were told they had passed the line beyond their authority in at least three respects. First, they had "pretended" to meet in convention, where any decisions they agreed on were likely to make new rules of law. Second, they "assumed" a prerogative that was not judicial when they held that a statute had violated the constitution and, as a result, had made rulings beyond their constitutional competency, for in Georgia the authority to rule on the constitutionality of legislation belonged exclusively to the two houses of the General Assembly. And, third, they forgot that only members of the legislature who constitutionally could fathom "public opinion" could express it. The resolutions passed by the General Assembly condemning the judges are worth much greater attention than they have received from constitutional historians. They are surely some of the most exact claims to supremacy over the courts ever voted by an American legislature. Although the drafters of the resolutions tried to tone down their hostility, they were unable to hide the fact that they were keeping the judiciary to a decidedly subordinate place in Georgia's constitutional pecking order. "Whereas," the lawmakers asserted, four judges of the Superior Court, did

> assemble themselves together in the city of Augusta, pretending to be in legal convention, and assuming to themselves . . . the power to determine on the constitutionality of laws past by the General Assembly of this state; and . . . did . . . declare certain acts of the Legislature . . . to be unconstitutional and

void—And whereas the power of the said Judges to convene is absolutely denied by this Legislature, and the more extraordinary power of determining
upon the constitutionality of acts of the state Legislature, if yielded by the
General Assembly, whilst it is not given by the Constitution or laws of the
state, would be an abandonment of the dearest rights and liberties of the people, which we, their representatives, are bound to guard and protect inviolate;

   Be it therefore resolved, That the members of this General Assembly view
with deep concern and regret, the aforesaid conduct of the said judges in so il-
legally assembling themselves . . . and they can not refrain from an expression
of their entire disapprobation of the power assumed by them of determining
upon the constitutionality of laws regularly passed by the General Assembly,
as prescribed by the constitution of this state; we do therefore most solemnly
declare and protest against the aforesaid assumption of powers as exercised by
the said Judges; and we do, with heartfelt sensibility deprecate the serious and
distressing consequences which followed such decision; yet we forbear to look
with severity on the past, in consequence of Judicial precedents, calculated in
some measure to extenuate the conduct of the Judges; and hope that for the
future this explicit expression of public opinion will be obeyed.[49]

The resolutions had the facts right in one respect. Public opinion in
Georgia supported legislative supervision of the judiciary. When adopting
the state constitution, the people had made legislative supremacy the constitutional rule. Georgia judges were not appointed with life tenure. They
were elected by the two houses of the General Assembly for three-year
terms, providing the legislators frequent opportunities to examine their
jurisprudence and reprove any judge who showed tendencies of
independence.[50] Even with that degree of control, occasional attempts to
impeach judges who decided cases that did not jibe with current political
policy occurred.[51] It is revealing of popular attitudes in early Georgia that
the Constitution of 1798 had conferred tenure "during good behavior" on
the justices of the relatively unimportant "inferior courts." Fourteen years
later the constitution was amended, and their tenure was reduced to terms
of four years. We can wonder if "good behavior" implied to Georgians too
much judicial independence.[52]

Surely the most striking fact in the judicial history of Georgia is that for
fifty-six years following the adoption of the Constitution of 1789, the state
had no supreme court. More than any other state, Georgia was guided by
extreme Jeffersonian legal theory, or what has elsewhere been called "republicanist" jurisprudence.[53] It appears that Georgia did not trust a supreme
appellate tribunal from which judges could promulgate law. Only the
elected representatives of the people should make law in a republic, not
lawyers.[54] It was not until 1835 that Georgians amended the state constitution and authorized "a supreme court for the correction of errors" in both
law and equity. But even at that late date, Georgia was not ready for tenure
at good behavior. Judges of the court were to be "elected by the legislature

for such terms of years as shall be prescribed by law," that is, the justices were secure only for as long as the General Assembly said—and as long as it did not change its mind.[55]

A supreme court may have been authorized in 1835, but in Georgia constitutional authorization did not mean legislative creation. The constitutional amendment may have allowed a court but did not end political opposition, which remained strong—at least in the General Assembly if not among the populace. Several bills were introduced into the legislature to institute a court, but all were defeated until 1845. It was then, ten years after the constitutional amendment had been enacted, that a supreme court was approved. Georgia now had an appellate tribunal. The authorized number of justices were appointed, appeals were filed and argued, but the opposition continued. So much, in fact, that Joseph Henry Lumpkin, the first presiding judge, became apprehensive that he might be legislated out of office. Four years later he recalled "that when the Court Bill was passed in 1845, a large majority of the people were decidedly hostile to it. To secure its enactment, by accommodating its provisions to the wishes of all, it contained inherent defects, well calculated to insure its miscarriage." It was difficult to "obtain the service of suitable men, under these circumstances, to fill the offices. . . . Who was willing to risk what little reputation he might have acquired by a lifetime of toil, to be crushed, perhaps forever, beneath the superincumbent ruins of a fallen fabric?"[56] Lumpkin and his supreme court survived. He would become the state's first chief justice and preside during the Civil War, into an era when Georgia no longer could afford the anachronism of republicanist or Jeffersonian legal theory.

Judicial politics of the Georgia style were the exception, not the norm, in the early republic. New Hampshire was nearer the norm, for during that period it was more evenly divided than most other states—divided not only politically but jurisprudentially, between Republicans and Federalists, Jeffersonians and Hamiltonians, republicanists and receptionists. More than most of its sister states, New Hampshire's politics were balanced between those political forces championing legislative supremacy and those political forces working for judicial autonomy.

The Legislative Constitution

By 1790, after only a few months in office, New Hampshire's delegation to the lower house of the first United States Congress had become an embarrassment to the state. Its three representatives had not gotten along. The "misunderstandings" that existed between these congressmen upset their colleagues from other New England states, and, as a result, AN ELECTOR wrote to a Portsmouth newspaper that not only was the influence of New Hampshire thereby lost but so was the weight of all New England.[1]

Samuel Livermore had been the only member of the delegation who took part in congressional debates, the only one to speak up and defend the state, especially the interests of New Hampshire's two most influential centers of commerce, the towns of Portsmouth and Exeter.[2] Political opinion around the state concluded that the two other congressmen should be replaced with more assertive men. As there were no party organizations, the selections were made by statewide consensus. "The phrase 'being a candidate,' has not the same meaning here as at the southward," one of the new congressmen wrote six years later to his future wife, a native of Maryland. "It means with you a person who expresses a desire for office, solicits votes, perhaps treats the electors. Here it only means a person *talked of* for an office; not by himself or particular connections, for in that case he certainly would not be elected."[3]

The man most *talked of* that year was Jeremiah Smith, "a gentleman of good character in the country." The thirty-one-year-old Smith was, a supporter wrote; "a Lawyer—[who] in his profession is highly esteemed, not only for his law knowledge, but on account of the rectitude of his heart, & most excellent talent for dispatching business with propriety."[4] What was meant by "in the country" was that Smith lived in Peterborough, about as far into the interior of the state as you could go in those days and hope to find a person known on the seacoast, where most of the voters lived. Because New Hampshire elected its congressmen "at large," geography was as important as reputation, and Smith was elected, receiving the highest number of votes after Livermore.[5]

He may have been comparatively young, a lawyer for only four years, living in the relative isolation of Peterborough, but as his election proved, he was already known throughout New Hampshire. Service in the state's House of Representatives had given him acquaintances from all over the state. Perhaps due to his personal charm and continuous, rapid-fire humor, not common characteristics among dour New Hampshire Yankees, some people thought him Irish. Actually he was Scotch-Irish, the economically dominant ethnic group in Peterborough, among whom his father was one of the most prominent. During the Revolutionary War, his father had permitted him to leave Harvard College to serve in New Hampshire's militia, on condition he keep out of combat. Disobeying his parent's wishes and his captain's orders, Smith fought in the battle of Bennington, was caught in an ambush, and wounded. He finished his collegiate years at Rutgers, in New Jersey, and then studied for the bar in the offices of three different Massachusetts lawyers.[6] Throughout the remainder of his life Smith would be one of the best-known men of New Hampshire, highly respected for his intellect and legal learning but admired most for his humor and personality. Forty-six years after he had been admitted to law practice, a chronicler of the town of Exeter wrote that Jeremiah Smith "combines the solid talents of jurist and statesman, with uncommon readiness and brilliancy in conversation."[7]

Less than a year after Smith's admission to the bar, he was in touch with William Plumer, destined to become both his best friend and his most bitter critic. Born in Newburyport, Massachusetts, Plumer grew to manhood in the town where he would live for the remainder of his life, Epping, in New Hampshire's most southern county, Rockingham, the only county on the seacoast. Although five months older than Smith, Plumer, who had spent a few years as an itinerant Baptist preacher, did not apply for admission to the bar until a year after Smith. Apparently told that the more influential members of the practicing Rockingham bar opposed his application to the court, and that Smith had also encountered opposition that he had overcome, Plumer wrote to Smith for advice on how to proceed. Smith replied that when he let it be known he was applying, lawyers in Hillsborough County had told him to continue his studies. "[B]ut my age, circumstances, & especially when I adverted to the *character & pretensions* of those already admitted, determined me to waive all ceremony & apply directly to the Court. Which I did at the adjournment, & was admitted by their unanimous voice. This bold stroke gave great umbrage as you have undoubtedly heard."[8] Plumer also feared whether the bar was so crowded there would be no business for a new lawyer. Smith assured him he would have clients. "I hate a monopolizing spirit," Smith wrote, congratulating him, "and although the profession seems somewhat crowded at present, the harvest small, and the laborers very many, yet I cannot help thinking that there is room for as many good characters as may be disposed to enter into the profession." He also introduced the always serious, even dour, Plumer to a touch of his humor. "[A]s if the humiliating circumstance of barely asking for admission into such a brotherhood were not enough," he complained of the Hillsborough bar, "'Tis devilish provoking to be denied admittance into *bad* company."[9]

Plumer would not find law practice any more congenial than had Smith. He would make his mark in politics, not in law, occupying in time the highest offices in New Hampshire, except for the judicial, and becoming the most important and, perhaps, the most popular man in the state. And with good reason: in a republican age and a republican society, he was the most republican of men.

Both men relished their relationship and the affection that they felt for one another. Although it would eventually be cherished more by Smith than by Plumer, in the beginning the friendship meant as much to one as to the other. "A man ought not to commit himself indiscriminately to every one who professes a friendship for him," Plumer explained in 1791, when Smith and he were leading an effort to rewrite the New Hampshire constitution. "But an honest mind may surely find at least *one* congenial soul to whom he may unbosom himself with perfect security." For him Smith was that congenial soul. "A friend I trust you are, & through life will continue to be whatever disagreement in opinions, connections & circumstances may happen. Should a *coolness* ever happen to us (which I pray Heaven never may) your letters to me shall not be communicated to your injury. To this conduct I shall religiously adhere. I shall write you *freely* on men & measures, & in return shall expect the same of you."[10]

In that first letter, the one telling Plumer about how he had been admitted to practice, Smith had been the first to reach out his hand in friendship. "I should be wanting in benevolence," he assured Plumer, "if I had not a disposition to do you every service in my power; & tho' I have not the pleasure of a particular acquaintance, you will give me leave to say, that I feel interested in your welfare, & heartily wish you success." Ten years later, after he had decided to resign from Congress and take up residence in Exeter, only a few miles from Plumer's home, Smith knew the friendship would become even closer. "I shall have the pleasure of seeing you in Exeter," he wrote, "& of telling you in person how much I feel myself obliged by your very friendly endeavors to promote my interest & happiness & of assuring you how much I am your affectionate friend."[11]

Of the many strands tying together the professional and personal friendship between Plumer and Smith, none was more binding than their shared

Jeremiah Smith

William Plumer

Arthur Livermore

determination to reform the judiciary of New Hampshire. When still a law student, Plumer had had the prescience to grasp that the courts might perform a role for the governance of America that would be strikingly new in common-law constitutionalism. "If our elective government is long supported, it will owe its existence to the Judiciary," he told a fellow student. "That is the only body of men who will have an effective check upon a numerous Assembly." This expectation grew over time. "An able upright judiciary is the bulwark and support of the best and most valuable rights of man," he wrote thirty-nine years later.[12]

Smith may have had even stronger reasons to promote judicial reform—depending on when he realized he wanted to be a high-court judge. Despite not liking the practice of law, he was an ardent student of jurisprudence and was intrigued by the potential good that a well-trained, high-minded judiciary could do for society and the country. He enjoyed every aspect of court work except trial advocacy. "A certain Mr. Marshall of Virginia is on the ground to argue an important question on a Writ of error," Smith wrote from Philadelphia while still a congressman. "I expect much entertainment & instruction." He did not admire Justice William Cushing of the United States Supreme Court. When Cushing refused appointment to the chief justiceship, and Oliver Ellsworth was named in his place, Smith wrote Plumer the good news. "[H]e is every thing one would desire," he said of Ellsworth. "I know this will give you much pleasure as you are as sincere [unclear one or two words] wishes to good Government & especially to a good judiciary; a thing which *we* know the value of by the want of it."[13]

New Hampshire had the *want*—and the need. It had a judiciary, of course, but not one a competent, educated lawyer could respect. It was deficient in both personnel and structure. Most of the judges were laymen. Very few had legal training. What law they administered was a folk law, a theory of adjudication that has been labeled "the jurisprudence of common sense," expounded by traverse juries, generally following their passions and prejudices, often without any guidance from the court.[14]

New Hampshire's court structure and trial process were just as deficient as its juridical science. The Inferior Courts of Common Pleas, which met in each county, had original jurisdiction over all cases involving real estate, except probate, and all other civil causes not triable by the justices of the peace.[15] They should have been the chief trial courts of New Hampshire, but, in fact, they tried few cases. Their process was shaped by quite technical rules. Any dispute litigated and brought to judgment in a Common Pleas court could be "appealed" to the Superior Court of Judicature, where the judges did not resolve questions of law, as in a twenty-first century appeal, but submitted the cause to a second jury; that is, parties losing their action in Common Pleas still had a right to appeal to a jury trial *de novo*.[16] Oddly, in some situations, there was a right to as many as four jury trials before litigation was terminated.[17] Writing a report on the judiciary for the Constitutional Convention in 1792, William Plumer summed up the problem: "The Courts of common pleas doth not appear to us a court of trials but of defaults a court calculated to delay Justice and put the parties to great and unnecessary expence, for no one can have a trial without the consent of the other party in actions originating there."[18]

The "default" process commenced when defense lawyers, to avoid multiple trials, bypassed suit in the Common Pleas by a practice known as "taking a case up on demurrer," but which might better be termed "default by demurrer." A demurrer was a plea to dismiss the plaintiff's case on grounds that it was deficient as a matter of law. After a plaintiff filed a cause of action, if the opposing attorney thought it deficient, he answered by demurring and, to support the demurrer, pleaded facts stating a defense good at law. To avoid a trial in Common Pleas, however, a New Hampshire defense attorney pleaded facts that *did not state a defense good at law*. To a claim of not paying money lawfully owed and due, for example, the defendant might answer "can't pay," "unable to pay," or, as the leading lawyer of the day, John Pickering, did in 1785, "never meant to pay the demand but if they must they were determined to keep the plaintiff out as long as the law would let them." In truth, it did not matter what the defense answered, as long as it made no sense as a demurrer. The court was obliged to rule the demurrer bad and enter judgment for the plaintiff. The defendant's attorney then exercised the right to "appeal" to the Superior Court for a jury trial *de novo*.[19]

Trial in the Common Pleas was a "defect" in New Hampshire's judicial system, one critic complained.[20] "Why," William Plumer would ask many years later, "subject suitors to the unnecessary expense of commencing such suits in the common pleas, when it is not in the power of that court, or either of the parties, to compel the other to have a trial there, or disclose the facts on which he relies?"[21] He knew the answers. Defense lawyers found the "farce" useful trial tactics, allowing them to delay their clients' day of judgment, a delay obtained without the expense of a single hearing on the merits.[22] Besides, the main income of most attorneys came from fees paid for each judicial filing, and both the action entered at Common Pleas and the answer were filings. Few lawyers defended the system, but even fewer worked for reform. Plumer and Smith were almost the only members of the bar urging the abolition of the Common Pleas.

Where most lawyers actively supported Plumer and Smith was on the most difficult task they undertook: to establish the independence of the judiciary. Too much legislative control was exercised over the judiciary, they believed, and had been from the very beginning of state government. Because New Hampshire was the first American jurisdiction to draft and adopt a constitution, the drafters, without any other model to guide them, reacted against the government they had known in colonial times, which had been controlled by a strong royal governor. Eschewing the executive, they concentrated all power in the legislature.[23] This is the constitution that was, as previously noted, inspired by the constitutional theory of John Sullivan. The judiciary did not exist as an independent entity.

Sullivan's theory—the theory of the Constitution of 1776—can be demonstrated by the offices it allowed Meshech Weare to hold. At one and the same time he was president of the Council, which was the upper house of the legislature, chairman of the committee of safety, the highest executive positive in the government, and chief justice of the Superior Court. He held these posts for the entire period of the Revolution, combining in one person the legislative, executive, and judicial powers of New Hampshire.[24] In fact, he can truly be said to have held two judicial functions, for the committee of safety did more than administer what little executive authority actually existed, such as collecting taxes and overseeing New Hampshire's war effort. It also had a juridical capacity, charging persons with crimes, trying them, and, if guilty, passing sentence—prosecutor, judge, and executioner all in one. Moreover, it served as an appellate court for the local committees of safety, which rendered judgment in a wide variety of legal matters, civil as well as criminal, hearing complaints without juries and granting the accused few of the rights that traditionally governed the trials of English defendants.[25] The constitutional theory was, in fact, a complete departure from the doctrines of the repudiated British constitution and the constitutional principles for which American whigs then were fighting.

Long before the Revolution was won, the constitution of legislative sovereignty came under attack. "Some men who would fain have been deemed wise, have imagined that the safety of a State consisted in its being governed by Laws and not by men," PHILOTEKNON reminded New Hampshire newspaper readers in 1779. "But your Constitution-Mongers have with superior Wisdom, vested the supreme Power of the State in a set of Men, who are to give Law to Law itself, who are to controul, alter and repeal the Common and Statute Laws of England, and the ancient Laws of this State, and even to propose Alterations in the Constitution itself." He meant that whatever the legislature said or did was constitutionally legal. It followed, therefore, that in republican New Hampshire passage of an ordinary statute could alter constitutional fundamentals, something that was not supposed to have happened under the royal government, although it sometimes did.[26]

The state's leadership attempted to write a more balanced constitution that year. Had they succeeded, it would have been the world's first popular constituent constitution, that is, a constitution drafted not by a legislature but by a convention of delegates elected for that purpose and then submitted to the people for ratification.[27] The voters rejected the work of the convention, but an *Address* to the people from the delegates contained the first official defense of the doctrine of separation of powers printed in New Hampshire, introducing some of the population to the theory of separation for the first time, including the notion that there was a separate judicial power. [28]

Although it was never adopted, the draft constitution is of interest to this study because it made no attempt to change the status of the judiciary. Judges were not mentioned, except that they were to be appointed by the legislature, could not be members of either house, and were to count the votes in certain elections. Constitutionally they were not independent. The assembly not only would have continued to define their jurisdiction but would have continued to exercise judicial powers, even trying prisoners who were under indictment in the Superior Court.[29]

No one was satisfied, and a second constitutional convention was elected. It met under the leadership of John Pickering, a Portsmouth lawyer destined to loom large in American judicial history. He was determined both to restore and improve the constitutional separation and balance that New Hampshire had previously known under British rule. In an *Address* to the people, the convention argued for dividing government into three powers: "The legislative, or power of making laws—The judicial, or power of expounding and applying them to each particular case—And the executive, to carry them into effect, and give the political machine life and motion."[30]

Pickering's first proposed constitution was also rejected by the voters. The convention redrafted some sections and circulated a *Second Address,* once more explaining why the judiciary should be separated from the other two branches. The reasons were simplistic and somewhat strange, apparently intended to win the support of anyone who thought the government too strong or too arbitrary under the Constitution of 1776. "If the legislative and judicial powers should be united, the maker of the law would be the interpreter thereof, and might make it speak what language best pleased him, to the total abolition of justice," the *Second Address* contended. And "should the executive and judicial powers be combined, the great barrier against oppression would be at once destroyed: The laws would be made to bend to the will of that power which sought to execute them with the most unbridled rapacity." This time the voters accepted what became known as the Constitution of 1784.[31]

A historian has said that the Constitution of 1784 reflected "solicitude for judicial independence." It did no such thing. It introduced the doctrine of separation of powers into New Hampshire constitutional law for the first time since the adoption of the Constitution of 1776, and it granted a bit more judicial independence than the first constitution had allowed—but not much. "The Judges all hold their offices during good behaviour; the only proper tenure, especially for the Judges of the Supreme Court of Judicature, as they ought, in a peculiar manner, to feel themselves independent and free," the convention argued in its *Address.*[32] The objective was to lessen legislative control of the courts, but there were no provisions preventing the legislature from exercising judicial authority or interfering with private litigation. In fact, the General Court was empowered "to impose fines, mulcts, imprisonments, and other punishments," which seemed to some observers in the twentieth century to be judicial rather than legislative functions. The new constitution might proclaim separation of powers, William Plumer later pointed out, but the legislature not only adjourned courts, it also voided judgments rendered even by the tribunals of last resort.[33]

Twentieth-century political scientist Edward S. Corwin agreed with Plumer. Many years later Corwin was amused to discover that the Constitution of 1784 not only declared that the legislature was separate from the judiciary but also stipulated that the two branches "ought to be kept as separate and independent of each other as the nature of a free government will admit."[34] The intention could not be clearer to Corwin, yet, he concluded, the New Hampshire legislature read the words "separate" and "independent" in a *sui generis* way, leaving the state judiciary neither separate nor independent. "[T]he laws of New Hampshire for the years 1784–1792," he summarized, "are replete with entries showing that throughout the period the state legislature freely vacated judicial proceedings, suspended judicial actions, annulled or modified judgments, cancelled executions, reopened controversies, authorized appeals, granted exemptions from the standing law, expounded the law for pending cases, and even determined the merits of disputes."[35]

The constitutional name for New Hampshire's legislature is "General Court." The word "court," Leon W. Anderson has observed, "was most apt for the nine-year period that the compromises of the 1784 Constitution existed, for the Legislature then was the court of last resort, both public and private, including divorces. In this brief period the Legislature often overruled decisions of the court system." Only a distinct minority of the state's population thought anything was amiss. One of the few was SOLON. That the three governmental powers be kept separate was supposed to be a fundamental constitutional principle, he complained in 1790. "But may it not be asked, have our legislative bodies strictly adhered to this part of the Constitution?" The answer was obvious. "If this is not the case," he asked, "how comes it to pass that the determinations of our judicial Courts in this State, are frequently set aside; inasmuch that a suitor has no certainty, that after obtaining a *final* judgment in his cause will not undergo a revision in the General-Court. Can this be anything less than the General-Court erecting themselves into a Court superior to the Superior Court?"[36]

SOLON was ahead of his time. His constitutional theory would eventually prevail, but during the decade when he wrote, the 1790s, the law courts were clearly subordinate under the legislative constitutions, which vested final judicial power in the General Court. The prime theoretical premise of the legislative constitutions was the opposite of that for a constitution of separate branches. The judges should not be independent. By giving the elected representatives the last word, judges were made amenable to the people, as should be all officials in a republican government.[37] Following that more democratic theory, the New Hampshire General Court that year created special tribunals, each to try one issue, sometimes with justices appointed for that one litigation alone.[38] Two other laws passed in 1790 permitted a defeated litigant to enter an appeal in the Superior Court that otherwise would not have been permitted, and the court was ordered "to take cognizance of and give judgment" in a particular complaint.[39] It was not unknown for a lawsuit, "commenced before a Justice of the Peace, [to] be carried to the General Sessions [of the Peace], thence to Common Pleas, thence to the Superior Court, and thence to the Legislature; to be by that body sent back to the Superior Court for final decision, and with the further chance of a new trial on a writ of review."[40]

It is not an exaggeration to say that, for some lawmakers, the legislative supremacy they read into the doctrine of separate powers meant that the judiciary should never question the constitutionality, legality, or wisdom of legislation that had been enacted. Shortly after the Constitution of 1784 was adopted, the General Court promulgated the "Ten Pound Act," providing for trial before justices' courts, without juries, of writs of debt and trespass when damages claimed did not exceed ten pounds, a substantial amount of money in New Hampshire at that time. Pointing out that in these cases the constitution guaranteed jury trial, Plumer, a member of the lower house, insisted that the bill was unconstitutional. He had, he said, protested "singly and alone," the only legislator to recognize, or at least to acknowledge, the problem of constitutionality.[41] Later, when the issue was adjudicated and the bill's constitutionality was challenged by a litigant, the Superior Court agreed with Plumer. The "Ten Pound Act" was ruled unconstitutional and not binding on the court.[42] It was a judicial affront to the legislature, unprecedented in New Hampshire history. At the next session of the House of Representatives the question was directly put—"whether the said act is a constitutional act." The house voted 44 to 14 that the act was constitutional, a resolution that today would be thought more judicial than legislative, for it was intended to overrule the judgment of the Superior Court. It annulled the decision of the *judicial* tribunal and gave the party who had lost the action leave to carry his case back to the Superior Court for retrial, on the same procedure as a regular appeal—that is, a jury trial *de novo*.[43]

When the "Ten-Pound Act" was again litigated, this time at the Rockingham County term of Commons Pleas, the court apparently chose to follow the precedent set by the Superior Court and, again, the act was not enforced, on grounds of unconstitutionality.[44] Plumer was delighted to discover New Hampshire judges asserting some independence from legislative control. "I am glad the Court have had firmness to act their own opinion," he wrote to a friend. His fellow legislators were much less pleased. At the next session of the General Court it was moved to impeach the Rockingham judges. The lower house voted 31 to 25 to take up the motion, but when the question was put, the members voted 35 to 21 not to impeach.[45] "[T]here were 21 out of 56 votes, against approval," William Crosskey pointed out. "So, it is apparent there was considerable sentiment in favor of impeachment." Had the vote gone the other way, it would have created a stunning precedent, at least in New Hampshire, even if the Senate had failed to convict.[46]

The point to keep in mind is that during the 1780s through the early 1800s a judicial decision holding a statute unconstitutional had different implications than it does today. It was legal precedent only for the judiciary. When the House of Representatives voted that the "Ten Pound Act" was constitutional, it was stating a judgment as valid in law as were judgments by the Superior Court and the Common Pleas. In all American jurisdictions, including the federal, the executive and legislative branches were equally competent with the judicial branch to decide questions of constitutionality and to pronounce legislation or executive edicts to be constitutional or unconstitutional.[47] In New Hampshire, it had been convincingly maintained that the legislature may have been more competent than the judiciary to decide constitutionality; at least the 21 members of the lower house who would have impeached the Rockingham judges believed it more competent. They understood that the constitution authorized them to impeach state officials only "for misconduct or mal-administration in their offices," yet voted it an impeachable offense for judges to refuse to enforce a duly enacted statute and told the General Court that its authority to write law was limited by the constitution.[48] The 21 representatives claimed legislative supremacy, as if the Constitution of 1776 had not been replaced in 1784. It is quite likely that, had they been asked, New Hampshire legislators during the 1790s would have said that they were just as supreme over the judiciary as the Revolutionary legislature had been under the Constitution of 1776. They certainly claimed supremacy and exercised its authority often enough to show that a clear majority of the members of both houses had no reservations about their supremacy over the Superior Court in matters of legislative and constitutional interpretation.

New Hampshire lawmakers had reason to think that the Constitution of 1784 granted them general supervision over the judiciary. It contained a provision that, in most other state constitutions, would be interpreted to make judges more independent of the legislature. Already quoted, it mandated that they be paid "honorable" and "permanent" salaries. After all, if the legislature was permitted to lower the amount or change the method of compensation at will, the judges could be intimidated.[49] Judicial independence, however, may not have been the intention of the delegates to the Constitutional Convention of 1781. Their *Address* to the public had explained that the purpose of fixed salaries was to insure honest and good judges. It had not claimed that honorable and permanent salaries were to strengthen judicial independence. Permanent salaries, rather, were an "inducement for persons to qualify themselves [to be judges], . . . an encouragement to vigilance, and an antidote to bribery and corruption."[50]

The mandate was also clear. In fact the delegates may have tried to insure its clarity by stating the principle not once but twice in the Constitution of 1784—two provisions that, in the twenty-first century, are still in New Hampshire's constitution. "Part I—The Bill of Rights" directed that the judiciary be paid "Honorable salaries, ascertained and established by laws," and "Part II—The Form of Government," provided that "Permanent and honorable salaries shall be established by law for the justices of the superior court."[51] But words perfectly clear elsewhere were not always clear in New Hampshire. There the words "honorable salaries, ascertained and established" and "permanent and honorable salaries" were read to mean "changeable year by year." At just about every session of the General Assembly during the 1790s, the two houses appointed a joint committee "to prepare and present a Bill for the establishment of permanent Salaries of the justices" or a committee "for establishing permanent and honorable Salaries for the Justices."[52] Some of these bills were even entitled "An Act establishing Permanent Salaries for the Justices," and the preamble of the one passed in 1797 actually said, "Whereas it is required by the Constitution of this State, that permanent and honorable salaries shall be established by standing laws for the justices of the superior court."[53] Yet the next year the amounts of judicial compensation would be debated as if nothing had been settled. In 1791, Jeremiah Smith was appointed to a joint committee "to devise a mode for giving efficacy to that part of the constitution which provides that permanent and Honbl Salaries be established by Law for the Justices of the Superior Court." On the first of February the lower house passed "An Act for establishing a fixed and permanent value for the justices of the Superior Court." On the 10th the same house voted the chief justice £180 and the associates £140, "each as an Annual Salary." Although these sums were substantially less than current Massachusetts judicial salaries, New Hampshire legislators reduced the pay. One house almost always found the amounts first proposed by the other house too high. This time it was the Senate that objected. On 16 February the figures were reduced to £150 and £130. What should be marked, however, is that the statute provided that the duration of the pay was "annual," surely not what the Constitution of 1784 had meant by "permanent."[54]

In eighteenth-century New Hampshire, "permanent" judicial salaries never meant inviolate judicial salaries. On the 19th of the same month, the *New-Hampshire Gazette* reported that a bill had been passed "granting permanent salaries to the Judges of the Superior Court." Yet in December, at the next session of the General Court, the House of Representatives appointed a committee to report what salaries the justices "shall receive." Even less permanent, the Senate, on 30 December, passed a judicial pay bill to apply from June 1791 to June 1792, not just for one year only, but retroactively changing the rate of pay from June to December.[55]

The General Court also arrogated to itself authority to rule when a judge had forfeited his judicial office. In 1789, the two houses elected Chief Justice Samuel Livermore to the United States Senate, and Livermore did not resign from the Superior Court. When approached by a committee of the state Senate, he gave no indication that he would step down, and the committee reported that as the federal legislative position was "incompatible with the Office of Chief Justice of this State, we are of opinion, that the legislature should address the Executive to remove him from that office." The full Senate concurred, and Livermore would probably have been the first New Hampshire judge addressed out of office had he not resigned before President John Sullivan and the Council could meet.[56]

A year later President Sullivan was appointed New Hampshire's first federal judge. Knowing that the United States District Court had little judicial business, except for some admiralty work, he decided to occupy both offices. A resolution was introduced in the January session of the General Court that "his Excellency President SULLIVAN cannot constitutionally act as President of this state while he holds the office of District Judge under the authority of the United States." After some debate, the House of Representatives voted to postpone the question until the June session. Jeremiah Smith, although a political ally of Sullivan's, was so upset that he filed a dissent, the only dissent he ever wrote as a member of the lower house. Four other members joined him. Interestingly, Smith was less disturbed by Sullivan's multiple office holding than by the blending of judicial and executive functions. In fact, Sullivan also blended legislative powers with the other two. As the elected chief executive of the state he was, by the Constitution of 1784, a voting member of the state Senate. That is what Smith meant when, in his protest, he complained that Sullivan, as a judge, might have to interpret laws that, as a "Legislator," he had helped make.

> [W]e consider the two offices . . . to be incompatible, inconsistent with, and subversive of our happy constitution, which we wish to transmit from our hands pure and unsullied. To exculpate ourselves from being accessaries to measures which might have been prevented, we think it our duty solemnly to protest against them, especially against the dangerous precedent of one person holding the aforesaid offices, being at the same time a Legislator in New-Hampshire, and Judge of the Federal Court under the authority of the United States, where as Judge he may explain and interpret laws which as Legislator he assisted to make, and as an executive officer was to carry into effect; which mixed authority we conceive tends directly to a consolidation of both governments—to blend powers that should be separate, to create diffidence and distrust in the minds of the people, when unanimity and confidence in the government are absolutely necessary.[57]

Sullivan did not understand what Smith meant because he still did not appreciate the doctrine of separation of constitutional powers. "I confess that I have never been able to discover any incompatibility in the two offices," he told the General Court. He had been elected president by the people, he said, and had a duty to remain in office until new elections. Besides, he had recently been "in company with the President of the United States, who knew that I was President of this State, and treated me as such, although he at the same time knew that I had long before accepted the office of Federal Judge." If George Washington was not upset by dual office holding, why should New Hampshire be? By the time the General Court met in June, Sullivan had become wiser. He exercised his last function as president, swearing in the legislators, and then resigned.[58]

The most public and extreme seizure of legislative control over the judiciary before the Constitutional Convention of 1791–1792 occurred when the House of Representatives impeached Woodbury Langdon, a Superior Court justice. He was accused of failing to go on some of the scheduled judicial circuits, causing at least five court terms to be cancelled, two of them in the most inland counties, Grafton and Cheshire. Langdon was the brother of John Langdon, the man who, in the next decade, would revolutionize New Hampshire politics, turning the state from a strong Federalist bastion into what would, by 1820, be one of the most Republican states in the union. Both brothers were successful Portsmouth merchants. The judge had accumulated much property as a businessman. He had never studied law, however. His one experience with the law had occurred when he served as a Superior Court judge in 1782, but he resigned in less than a year. The General Court then passed resolutions urging him to continue on the bench, but he insisted that the salary was too low. Yet when asked to serve again a few years later, he accepted reappointment.[59]

William Plumer may have been the only man of political influence in New Hampshire who had good things to say of Justice Langdon. "Woodbury Langdon's abilities and integrity are certainly far superior to John's," he told Smith of the two brothers. "In point of talents few men in the state are superior to the former; but very many are to the latter."[60] Although strongly opposed to nonlawyers serving as judges on the high court, Plumer praised Langdon for being a competent jurist. At least, he had more praise for him than for most of the other lay judges. Without any legal training, he explained, Woodbury Langdon "had acquired much knowledge of the laws. He had a strong, discriminating mind, and great promptness and decision of character. He readily discovered the prominent features of a cause, and dispatched business with great facility." Plumer believed Langdon "a man of great independence and decision. . . . He maintained his opinion with firmness and constancy, and looked with contempt on the mean and base acts that were usually practiced to obtain popularity."[61]

Although Plumer considered Langdon a friend, he readily admitted that the judge "was naturally inclined to be arbitrary and haughty." Those traits were one reason he had many critics and why his work on the court sometimes got him into trouble with legislators. A twentieth-century Supreme Court justice who was also a legal historian said Langdon was "outspoken and sarcastic," and his "vices were avarice and truculence." Jeremiah Smith did not like Langdon much, calling him "a man altogether unprincipled & ready for every evil word & work." During his four years on the Superior Court, Langdon constantly and publicly complained of the low pay and extensive travel and, loudest of all, of how the legislature indiscriminately overturned jury verdicts and granted litigants new trials.[62]

Langdon was especially unpopular in the counties furthest inland. All judges on the Superior Court were needed to make a quorum, and the farther a shire town was from Portsmouth, where he remained active in trade, the more often Langdon missed attending and the court was unable to sit. Representatives of the western counties complained, and, in 1790, the General Court assuming (without discussion) that it possessed authority, appointed a committee to investigate why judicial terms had been cancelled. The judges were ordered to explain, and they did, for no one—apparently not even the judges of the state's highest court—thought the judiciary was independent of legislative supervision. Judges Josiah Bartlett and John Dudley answered together, reminding the lawmakers that it was due to legislation that the lawmakers or their predecessors had enacted that prevented the court from holding a session in Grafton County, for the requirement that four judges preside at every jury trial was not a rule of court, it was statutory. "That the Hon[or]able Judge Langdon informed us that he could not attend at Plymouth last term & that in consequence of that information we thought it our duty to adjourn that court to prevent the suits & actions in the County from falling through." They were not trying to shift the blame unfairly onto Langdon. Everyone in the government knew it was his fault, and they understood why. "To Woodbury his own convenience was apt to be the first consideration in all matters," his brother's biographer has pointed out. In May 1789 he missed the scheduled session of the court in Grafton County, and the next spring he was absent from Cheshire and Hillsborough circuits as well as Grafton. "Apparently the reason for the Judge's absence was that his private affairs—a ship coming in or going out—made it advisable for him to be at Portsmouth."[63]

Langdon filed a separate answer. He surely intended that members of both houses would find it insulting, and most did. He started by asserting that only judges had the authority "of adjourning, postponing or putting off the business," meaning sessions of a county court, and that such authority "does by law exclusively belong to [th]em." Then he directly challenged the supremacy of the legislature and accused members of the General Court of not performing the constitutional duties that they owed to the judiciary. "I conceive *ergo* that the Legislature have no more right to make enquiry why the judges of the Superior Court adjourn than to know the reasons for their decisions in any matters that legally come before them as then said Judges have to enquire the reasons why the Legislature adjourn and decide in any matters within their province." As if that argument was not insulting enough, the judge raised another surely intended to irritate more. "It is true the Legislature are constitutionally bound to grant permanent & honorable salaries to the judges of the Superior Court & to see that the same be seasonably paid, how far this article has been complied with must be submitted to the legislature to determine, in every other respect I conceive the general Court & law Courts are & ever ought to be intirely independent of each other." In that one sentence he raised—for the first time in New Hampshire—both the issue of judicial independence and the issue of judicial equality. The judges, he claimed, had had no problem making quorums until recently, but after Chief Justice Samuel Livermore left the court on his election to the United States Senate, "a bare quorum had been attended with very great inconveniences especially to me as I had arranged my business in such a manner as not to go to the County of Grafton that circuit." Put more bluntly, the General Court had created the difficulty by electing one of the four judges to the national Senate, and the governor and Council were at fault for not appointing a new justice in Livermore's place.[64]

A motion was offered in the House of Representatives to address Woodbury Langdon out of office—that is, for the two houses to "address" the governor and Council to remove him from the bench. The motion was rejected by a vote of 18 yeas to 45 nays. It was not a victory for Langdon, however. Most delegates felt addressing out was not a strong enough sanction. They preferred the more accusatory action of impeachment. The next day articles of impeachment were passed, 35 to 29.[65] The articles did not assert legislative supremacy but made clear that the House of Representatives claimed authority to enforce all rules regarding the scheduling of court terms and also to determine standards of judicial behavior.

> [W]hereas it is essential to the preservation of the rights of every citizen of the State his life, liberty, property & character that the Superior Court of Judicature should be holden at the times and places by Law prescribed by all the Justices of said Court in order that Justice may be administered to the good citizens of the State impartially, promptly and without delay, And whereas the public are at all times intitled to the Services of their Officers receiving Salaries—And whereas the said Woodbury Langdon Esqr hath wilfully and corruptly in various instances misbehaved in his said office and hath neglected to attend the duties thereof by means whereof the said Courts have not been holden at the times and places by Law established and the administration of Justice delayed to the great injury of the good citizens of said State.

"And they do thereupon as the grand inquest of the State aforesaid impeach the said Woodbury Langdon of all and Singular the misconduct and Maladministration in his said Office of Justice of the Superior Court."[66]

Plumer and Smith both opposed impeachment and voted against the articles. Plumer told Smith that the prosecution was "instituted more to gratify personal pique and private resentment than to promote the public interest."[67] He was probably referring to the pique of Doctor William Page, whom he thought "a wild enthusiastic projector, fond of shew & parade." Representing Charlestown in the lower house, and a leader among the western members, he conducted a vendetta against Langdon. Although not a lawyer, he was appointed one of the managers of the impeachment—that is, one of the representatives who, on behalf of the House, conducted the prosecution in the Senate. The other managers were Smith and a young Portsmouth lawyer, Edward St. Loe Livermore. Plumer refused to serve and scolded Smith for accepting the office.[68] "Some of the enemies of the Bar say you have in this acted in character as a Lawyer," he lamented. "That as a member of the House you declared the Impeachment wrong, entered your vote on the record ag[ains]t it; but now as a manager before the Court you are to advocate it as a just & necessary measure." Smith accepted the appointment reluctantly; most likely he saw it as an opportunity to publicize some of the judicial reforms he was anxious to promote.[69]

The Senate decided to try Langdon out of term at a special session held at Exeter in the summer. When the time came, the managers announced that they were ready to proceed, and so did Langdon. But the presiding officer surprised both sides by proroguing the session, ruling that the Senate was not authorized to convene while the House of Representatives was in recess. The constitution required that they meet only when the lower house also was in session. Langdon wanted to be tried, still intending to challenge the authority of the legislature to control the judiciary. He demanded that the court of impeachment proceed. When the senior senator claimed too many members were absent, Langdon replied that they had a quorum, and, anyway, "he was even willing to dispense with the attendance of some who were present." It is evident that he had plans to use the trial for his own purposes, but the Senate voted to adjourn until the next session of the General Court.[70]

It is a guess, but there is good reason to conclude that Langdon was disappointed. He had planned to turn the proceedings around and to put on trial the doctrine of legislative supremacy by accusing the legislature of violating judicial independence and, also, of not giving the judges the support required by the new constitution. Although the evidence is spotty, from what is known, it seems certain that Langdon intended to ignore the main issue, readily admitting he had been absent from court terms in Grafton and Cheshire counties. Instead he would have challenged the constitutionality of certain aspects of the legislature's supervision of the judiciary, especially the practice of setting aside adjudicated jury verdicts—of ordering judges to grant new trials even though judgments had been entered in cases—and failing to pay honorable and permanent judicial salaries.[71]

Just as surely, Smith was disappointed. Although opposed to the impeachment, he had hoped to use the trial to make public arguments criticizing New Hampshire's practice of appointing businessmen to the court. We can measure how much the matter meant to him by the address he planned to make to the impeachment court. He wrote it out—something he did not usually do. It is his only forensic argument now extant. The knowledge of law that judges needed was not acquired at birth, he planned to argue, but with "the labor of close thought and reflection." Applying the law, a judge "must especially disengage himself from all other business and employment, and devote himself to the duties of the office." This "a judge never will do, if he is entangled with private affairs. The parties think, and have been heard to say, that when the honorable judge's brig goes to sea, he will be more at leisure. If the brig sails or arrives in term-time, the inhabitants of Cheshire and Grafton need not expect to see the honorable judge." The remarks were harsh, but Smith was outlining Langdon's reputation. The public of Cheshire and Grafton counties believed that his shipping business kept him in Portsmouth when he should have been on circuit. Smith took advantage of the discontent to try and persuade current legislators that nonlawyers should not be on the bench. He was adding the demands of business to his list of other reasons.[72]

The next session of the General Court was a January term. The court of impeachment was reconvened, but Woodbury Langdon did not appear. President George Washington had appointed him one of the three commissioners to settle the Revolutionary accounts between the nation and the states, and he was living in Pennsylvania. It would be reasonable to suppose that either he or his brother, who then was serving in the United States Senate, solicited a federal position allowing him to escape the impeachment trial. That may not be true. The president had appointed him to another office just after the Exeter postponement, and he had declined.[73] He did not want to give up the fight and, in fact, he extended it. His letter to the president of New Hampshire regarding resigning from the Superior Court was a philippic against the legislators for both controlling and neglecting the judiciary.

First he demonstrated to the General Court how well he could argue law by questioning the Senate's jurisdiction over mere judicial absence. "This honorable Court has I conceive in such case, no jurisdiction whatsoever," he contended. "It is only an impeachable offense (which always includes within it a crime triable & punishable at common law) that can legally come before your honors." For surely "the Senate have no constitutional authority to displace a man from office from their mere *will* & *pleasure*." Therefore, "where no corrupt motives influence the conduct of the Judges mere non attendance can be no more impeachable in a Judge than in a member of the General Court."[74]

It is not clear if Langdon was personally driven to make statements like the last one, taking digs at the collective membership of the two houses of the legislature, or whether he was speaking for the entire court, raising complaints that the judges voiced among themselves, as, for example, that the lawmakers should first consider their own conduct before investigating the judiciary. "[I]t appears to me exceedingly surprizing that the honorable House of Representatives (unless individuals thereof have some private ends to answer) should be so very anxious about the neglect of duty in me or any other of the Judges when they are so often culpable in this respect themselves?" Without hesitation, he brought up the most contentious questions, low judicial pay and legislative supervision or lack of any semblance of independence, saying it was "unreasonable" for the two houses "to expect punctuality in the Judges when their small salaries . . . are so badly paid while the members of the general Court were so scrupulously attentive to their own pay. . . . When too the Judges are so liable to be harassed & persecuted for a reasonable absence; & much more especially when the members of the late legislature discovered such a disposition to nullify the most solemn decisions of the Courts of law! . . . In fine where is the Independence of the judicial department? And if this be destroyed where is the security of the subject?"[75] Had Langdon been a lawyer he might have made that last point—judicial independence—the substance of his defense. He did not stress it, but what he did say was the first significant public statement made in New Hampshire on why the courts should be independent.[76]

Summing up, Langdon compounded his insult of the legislature by suggesting the state's president might appoint an insipid successor: "Many are impatiently waiting to fill my place, yet I hope the Executive will be directed to make choice of such a gentleman as will be a credit to the appointment—not an ignoramus—no sluggard—no sycophant." As a final stroke of contempt, Langdon included the answer he had prepared to the articles of impeachment as part of his resignation letter. Then he asked the president to send the letter and other papers to the two legislative houses, which the president did.[77]

Members of the House of Representatives were furious at the insulting words and reacted by attempting to assert even tighter control over the judiciary. The lower house resolved that "Woodbury Langdon Esqr. being under impeachment of this House for misconduct & maladministration in office as a Justice of the Superior Court of Judicature ought not to be permitted to resign his said office, but that the said Impeachment should be prosecuted to final Judgment of the Honourable Senate. . . ."[78] That same day, the representatives voted Langdon "guilty of a Contempt of both Houses and especially the Honbl Senate in as much as the Same papers contain pleas and answers to matters that are and ought to be before the said Honbl Senate in a judicial way." It would certainly have put the seal on judicial dependence had the rule been promulgated that a judge could resign only at the sufferance of the General Court and had judicial criticism of the General Court been ruled legislative contempt, but the Senate did not concur with the lower house. The senators, not the representatives, would have had to conduct the trial and would have experienced the embarrassment of ordering Langdon to answer while he thumbed his nose from Philadelphia. They unanimously told the other house that its resolve to continue the impeachment "if carried into execution, can operate no further than to effect a removal from office—by a letter of 17 January last he reigned." That resignation had ended the matter.[79]

The House of Representatives was still angry. Continuing to assume that Landgon had not resigned, that he remained a judge, the house addressed the president and Council, asking them "to remove the said Woodbury Langdon Esqr from his office of Justice of the Superior Court of Judicature." Then the house ordered Smith and the other managers "to enter a noli prosequi," withdrawing the impeachment from before the Senate. Addressing a judge from office required a majority vote of both houses, however, and the Senate did not concur. It postponed consideration when the house resolution was first introduced, and then, by not reconsidering the motion, let the question lie.[80]

"Thus ended this mighty fuss, disgraceful to the State, & vexatious to you," Plumer wrote to Langdon. "It has subjected the State to considerable expence, divided the Legislature into parties & delayed & embarrassed the legislative business."[81] Even more striking, the impeachment showed how much the courts were inferior to the legislature. That was the lesson Woodbury Langdon had hoped to teach New Hampshire, had he gone to trial. He may not have studied the full implications of the constitutional principle of judicial independence, but he had experienced the shortcomings of judicial dependence.

The impeachment became one more piece of evidence proving to Smith, Plumer, and other lawyers who thought as they did that the judiciary had to be strengthened. There was to be a constitutional convention that year, and both Smith and Plumer were elected delegates. They planned to introduce many political changes: to make the executive more efficient and more powerful, to decrease the size of the lower house of the General Court, and to abolish the religious test for officeholding. But their greatest expectation—the one they most wanted to accomplish—was to reform and strengthen the judiciary, making it truly independent of the legislature.

Plumer's Constitution

Jeremiah Smith and William Plumer cut their political teeth in the House of Representatives of the New Hampshire General Court. They served at least three years as members before Smith was elected to Congress. Service in the legislature taught them the apparatus of statewide politics and provided some of the foundations for their later advance to leadership in state government.

They may have been in the legislature, but legislation was not the main concern of New Hampshire legislators during the 1790s. "Very little business of a public nature has been done this session, . . . the time was chiefly taken up in hearing petitions, &c.," the *New-Hampshire Gazette* noted of the June 1790 session, the last held in Portsmouth when that town was still the state's capitol, as it had been all though colonial times. Nine years later, the work of the General Court was summed up in much the same terms. "[T]he business of the General Court has been principally of a private nature as usual," the *Gazette* reported; "the time has been principally taken up in hearing of petitions, appointing committees, filling up vacancies in the [state] Senate, passing accounts, etc."[1] In fact, the passage of personal acts had become increasingly common during the decade. When Smith was in his first year as a congressman, Plumer wrote to him complaining that the legislature was consumed by private bills to the extent that "public [business] is put off to near the end of the session, when the members become impatient." That situation prevailed to a diminishing extent throughout their years in government.[2]

Smith and Plumer rendered quite different services to the legislature. Smith was a workhorse, while Plumer was a political leader. Smith was on several important committees, some of which demanded much time. In his second term, for example, he was appointed to a committee of three "to draught all such public bills and resolves as may be thought to be passed the present session." In other words, he was to rewrite all the bills that had been enacted into law during the term, taking them as written by the untrained and, in some cases, semi-literate members of the General Court, giving them clarity and technical language that lawyers and nonlawyers could understand but, hopefully, could not manipulate. It was a strenuously intellectual challenge, for which he was well paid. The house voted him "six pounds, for draughting bills &c," quite a sizeable sum of money for a task started and completed in a single legislative term.[3]

The committee that demanded most of Smith's time was "appointed to select, revise and arrange all the laws and public resolves of this state now in force, in one volume, with a proper index." Smith had to do most of the work himself, taking over two years, but he produced the first reliable codification of New Hampshire statutes.[4] His duties included writing an index and serving with two other legislators "to inspect the press while the revised laws are printing . . . & Superintend and direct the business of printing and binding the said Laws."[5] Again he was quite well paid, receiving "Eighty five pounds nineteen shillings" for what was called the "revision of laws."[6]

Plumer served on as many committees as Smith, but not on those requiring work out of session. The committee he probably found most useful was appointed in January 1791 "to take into consideration the present judiciary System and report such alterations therein as they may think necessary or propose such new mode to the administration of Justice as may to them appear expedient." He expected to be a delegate to the constitutional convention meeting in a few months at which he was planning to restructure New Hampshire's courts. Plumer already knew what he wanted to accomplish, so he probably did not use the committee to uncover judicial problems. It is more likely, as most of the delegates to the convention would be fellow members of the General Court, that he made the committee a platform for propagating some of his ideas.[7]

At the June 1790 term, when the clerk of the House of Representatives got sick, Plumer agreed to serve until the man recovered, and a few days later Plumer became the permanent clerk for the remainder of the session. The next year he was elected speaker of the house. It was only his fourth year as a member of the General Court, and already he was the highest ranking representative in the state. In three months the constitutional convention would convene, where he would be the undisputed leader. He was just thirty-one years of age.[8]

A majority of town meetings in the state had instructed the General Court to call the constitutional convention. There was widespread dissatisfaction with the Constitution of 1784, mostly concerning "the want of an executive distinct and independent of the legislature," unhappiness with the costs and delays of litigation, and belief that Portsmouth and Exeter on the seacoast exercised too much weight in government.[9] The legislature responded by voting funds for a convention. Elections were held in August, and the convention met in September. Smith was chosen the delegate for Peterborough in Hillsborough County, and Plumer represented Epping in Rockingham County.

We know little of the preparations for the convention. It is a good guess that Plumer spent time recruiting young lawyers who thought as he did because, when the convention met, he was surrounded by a clique of supporters who immediately thrust him into the leadership. What we do know are the objectives that he and Smith hoped to accomplish. One that they felt strongly about, but for which they lacked sufficient support, was to eliminate the provisions in the Constitution of 1784 making only Protestants eligible for certain offices. Plumer was then one of the very few political leaders in New Hampshire who publicly advocated dividing church and state, espousing principles of separation much like those that would come into vogue in American constitutional law around the middle of the twentieth century. His first publication had been a newspaper article urging voters to reject the Protestant requirement when it was originally proposed. "Why then have not those who profess a religion different from that of Christianity, an equal right to be protected by those laws, to whose support they contribute?" he asked. As soon as he had become an attorney he had sought to answer the question by adopting a rule he would adhere to during all his years at the bar. "I had scrupulously declined, as a lawyer, being of council for any town or society in cases where they attempted to compel men to pay taxes for religious purposes," he noted some years later in his autobiography. "But I promptly afforded my aid to those who claimed an exemption from those taxes; & was employed in all cases of that kind which were brot in the counties of Rockingham & Strafford. . . . It was my opinion that no man ought to be *compelled* to contribute anything to the support of religion, but every man left to the perfect freedom of his own will to join or not join any society, & to contribute or not to its support."[10]

Smith's theory of the relationship between church and state was much nearer to the mainstream than Plumer's. He attributed the strength of the social morals of the population and their obedience of law to religious teachings, and, to preserve morality, he believed that government had to support religion with taxation. But like Plumer, he was ardently opposed to the Protestant test, though his reasoning was sometimes peculiar. "It is a shame to us Protestants that a Papist set the example, in America, of equality of rights in religious matters," he later observed of Lord Baltimore and the early colony of Maryland. "It seems a very unkind return for this excellent example, set by a Roman Catholic, to exclude this sect of Christians from any participation in our government."[11]

Plumer also went to the convention intent on strengthening the executive and diminishing the size of the legislature. He wanted to make the executive independent of and in political strength the equal to the General Court and especially vest in the president of the state the power to veto bills. The House of Representatives was too large, he believed: "The evils which result from a numerous legislative body are many—they proceed from the want of deliberate, despatch, and responsibility."[12]

Plumer's overriding objective—the main purpose that brought him to the constitutional convention at Concord in September 1790—was judicial reform, and he had Smith's complete and enthusiastic support. It was also the issue on which they faced the strongest opposition. The first step they hoped to take was persuading the convention to abolish the Court of Common Pleas. "What an absurdity in jurisprudence," Plumer said of Common Pleas, "so feeble" it could not bring any case to trial without consent of both parties. Smith would have abolished the court because all the judges were nonlawyers, and, if that could not be done, he hoped to change its rules of procedure so that civil causes actually went to trial and its "judgments" on facts were "conclusive," by which he meant final.[13]

General Sessions was another court they planned to abolish. It consisted of all the justices of the peace in a county and, of course, in every county was almost always staffed by nonlawyers. From colonial times, it had been the court that most directly effected the lives of New Hampshire people. Although it had large criminal and civil judicial powers, its most significant functions were administrative. General Sessions supervised roads, licensed ferries, determined where and when public works were built, and, most importantly, set all local taxes not voted in town meetings. It was, however, General Sessions' jurisdiction over civil causes that lawyers like Plumer and Smith believed harmed New Hampshire jurisprudence. A lay tribunal, whose judges lacked legal training, it had few manuals explaining rules or encouraging uniform procedures and, therefore, tended to stint the development of statewide law, keeping it splintered and making unification of doctrine difficult. "The criminal business now done in the sessions should be transferred to the Supreme Court sitting in each county," Smith advised Plumer, and "the business of raising money" should be transferred to the General Court.[14]

At the very top of Plumer and Smith's wish list were two amendments, which, had they been put into the constitution, would have substantively changed New Hampshire's judiciary. One was creation of an equity jurisdiction, either as a new, separate court, or vested in one of the existing common-law courts, most surely the Superior Court. The second was to entrench into the constitution the Superior Court of Judicature. The Superior Court was not a constitutionally entrenched court; that is, it was not created by constitutional provision. Its existence and authority sounded in legislation. It had been created by the legislature, and, consequently, the legislature could abolish it by repealing the statute of creation. Lawyers contrasted it to the United States Supreme Court, which was entrenched in the national constitution. "The judicial Power of the United States, shall be vested in one supreme Court, and in such inferior Courts as Congress may from time to time ordain and establish," article III provides. That article lists courts of different constitutional status. One was the Supreme Court, entrenched by constitutional creation. The other status came from the discretion of Congress to ordain and establish, from time to time, inferior courts that, by the same discretion, Congress could, from time to time, abolish and then ordain and establish others in their place. All New Hampshire courts, including the highest judicial court, stood on the same constitutional basis as the federal "inferior" courts—lacking constitutional permanence.[15]

The convention met in Concord on 7 September 1791 with "upwards of eighty members" present. The state's most important men were in attendance, including many who had been active in the Revolution. Samuel Livermore, formerly chief justice and currently United States senator, was elected president. Chief Justice John Pickering, the framer of the Constitution of 1784, also was active. But it was Plumer who quickly set the direction of business, partly because he knew what he wanted to accomplish, was thoroughly prepared, and was willing to do most of the work serving on all the drafting committees. There were few entries in the manuscript journal "which is not either in his handwriting, or that of Jeremiah Smith—about three times as much of the former as of the latter." Smith was in Congress. In fact, during the convention he was reelected to a second term, receiving the highest vote among ten candidates. Although he had to be in Philadelphia and missed many sessions, the historian who edited the official journal claimed that Smith "was one of the most active and influential members of the convention."[16]

At the start of the convention the text of the Constitution of 1784 was read section by section. Delegates dissatisfied with any provision stated their objections, debate was allowed, and those wanting changes offered amendments.[17] The voting began with a defeat for Plumer and Smith. Someone on their side of the debates moved to strike the constitutional provision that a representative, "Shall be of the Protestant religion." The motion lost by a vote of 35 to 51. Plumer was so determined to expunge the Protestant test that he later persuaded the drafting committee to omit it from the clauses of the 1784 constitution that contained it. The convention accepted the draft, but these omissions were rejected by the people when the proposed amendments were submitted to a popular vote. Protestantism remained a requirement for office until 1876.[18] Plumer also failed to lessen the number of representatives, losing 22 yeas to 73 nays. But he was more successful in strengthening the principle of separation of powers by removing the president from the state Senate, also providing him with a qualified veto over legislation enacted by the General Court.[19]

"When the convention reached that part of the constitution dealing with the judicial branch of government, it embarked upon a stormy sea indeed," Lynn Turner has observed. The judiciary took up much of the convention's time and provided the substance of most of what was debated in public by polemical writers. "[S]ome were for laying the ax to the root of the tree and at one stroke to level the whole System to the ground," a convention delegate explained; "others were for authorising the General Assembly to arrange the Judiciary System as experience might be found beneficial, then as they had power to annihilate any Court, they would have power to place the business of that Court in some eligible train." To have done so, of course, would have left the judicial branch right where it was under the Constitution of 1784, exactly what Smith and Plumer did not want. Smith was present only for the first and last series of debates. When the second round took place he was attending Congress. "Provide for a good judiciary and you have my free Consent to manage the rest of the petty things in the bill of Rights," he wrote Plumer from Philadelphia. Most likely Plumer read these words as saying that, compared to the importance of reforming the courts, everything else was relatively minor.[20]

Plumer suffered a major defeat at the start of the judiciary debate. He lost a reform he quite likely had expected to win. "Resolved," his motion would have provided, "That it is the duty of the Legislature to abolish the Courts of General Sessions of the Peace." The vote was 37 yeas, 50 nays. Too many justices of the peace were delegates to the convention for the reformers to prevail. The justices wanted to retain the right and, especially, the prestige of joining together in court sessions. They were not concerned with remaining as justices. They knew that lawyers did not want to abolish their institution. Sitting alone, without juries, usually in their own houses, exercising civil jurisdiction over small claims, the justices of the peace served a useful judicial purpose, more or less indispensable in the isolated communities of New Hampshire's interior counties. The office had too many duties attached to it that no one else in small rural towns performed: supporting the poor, performing marriages, and administering some oaths, as well as jurisdiction over minor criminal prosecutions and civil disputes. Plumer did persuade the convention to set four pounds as the highest amount of damages justices could award. The purpose may have been to deprive the legislature of discretion to raise the sum even higher for the justices were one of the very few influential lobbies in New Hampshire, and there had been efforts to extend their competency to as much as ten pounds.[21]

Plumer also failed to have the convention abolish the Court of Common Pleas. But by a vote of 55 yeas to 31 nays, he got a relatively strong recommendation that the General Court do so. Resolved, it was voted "That it shall be the duty of the Legislature to abolish the Inferior Courts of Common Pleas." The wording was a compromise. Unable to muster sufficient votes to abolish Common Pleas by giving to the Superior Court all original jurisdiction over civil litigation for damages above four pounds, Plumer persuaded the delegates to tell the legislators that the General Court should abolish it. It was not a constitutional mandate, however, but a statement by the convention of what the General Court had a "duty" to do but was not required to do. Perhaps Plumer's most important coup was getting the convention to authorize a committee, consisting of ten delegates who also were members of the General Court, to construct a new judicial system. During the November session of the legislature, when the convention was in recess, the committeemen met every evening in Plumer's lodgings to do the work, and the legislature granted permission for them to examine dockets of the courts without paying the usual fees to the clerks. Plumer did the investigation, finding that in the three counties he studied, out of 2,388 actions entered in Common Pleas, only 110 had gone to jury trial. Of those 110 that were tried, 81 had been "appealed" to the Superior Court for a second jury trial. "The Courts of common pleas doth not appear to us a court of trial but of defaults," he wrote in the explanatory report of the committee.[22]

"I would ask, might not the actions defaulted at the inferior court be as well commenced at the superior court, and then defaulted," a critic of Common Pleas procedure wondered, his tongue in cheek. "May not the cause usually demurred be as well tried at the superior court by being brought there as well as when they are carried there by demurrer?" As all of the men then gathered in Concord had experience with Common Pleas, it surely was obvious to everyone—except, of course, to the judges of that court—that changes should be made.[23]

The problem of introducing an equity jurisdiction was as difficult to resolve as reform of the Court of Common Pleas. It is very unlikely that Plumer and Smith asked the convention to promulgate a court of equity separate from the common-law courts. A distinct court, with its own chancellor, would have been extravagant for so small a state and certainly too expensive for the niggardliness of New Hampshire. It is even doubtful if they gave serious thought to conferring equitable jurisdiction on an existing court. What they did succeed in obtaining from the convention must have given them great satisfaction. By a vote of 72 to 26 the delegates adopted an amendment authorizing the legislature either to create an independent equity jurisdiction or to vest an existing "Judicial Court or Courts" with "the power of hearing and deciding in causes of equity." It may not have been what Plumer would have liked but was probably more than he had expected to obtain. It encouraged the General Court to confer a complete equity jurisdiction on some judicial tribunal, which it well might have done once the voters of New Hampshire got over their dislike or distrust of equity.[24]

All that occurred at the convention was not defeat for Plumer and Smith. They did win a few major issues. They got everything they worked for on the two most important judicial matters raised in the convention. First, they stopped all efforts to change the tenure of Superior Court justices from good behavior to election for a term of seven years. That proposition had so little support that it did not even come to a vote; at least no vote was recorded. And they persuaded the convention to entrench the state's high court into the constitution. "Resolved," the delegates voted, 61 yeas to 34 nays, "That there shall be one Supreme Judicial Court of Law who shall have original jurisdiction of all causes where the sum exceeds four pounds, and appellate jurisdiction in all cases to be provided by law."[25] The new court would have six judges, Plumer wrote Smith, who was still attending Congress, "to hold three terms a year in each County. At the two first, two justices to make quorum, & at the third, which is the *Law term,* four judges to be a quorum. This Court to have original jurisdiction in all causes of the value of £4. & upwards, with appellate jurisdiction."[26] If the people accepted this amendment, the high court would be entrenched in the constitution, for both its original jurisdiction and its judicial personnel.

Before the work of the convention could be submitted to the voters, the resolutions had to be reworded into language suitable for amendments to the constitution. Again Plumer took the lead, serving on every drafting committee. For example, he and Smith were on a committee of three "to reduce to form the proposed amendments," and he was on a committee of ten to "prepare and report to the Convention at adjournment, alterations and amendments to be submitted to the people."[27]

The addresses published for the general public summarizing the work of the convention and explaining the scope and purpose of the proposed constitutional amendments on which the people would vote were almost all drafted by Plumer. Some of his sentencing shows too much haste. His rewording of the amendment entrenching the high court into the constitution, reads: "The Judicial Power of the State shall be vested in a Supreme Court of Judicature, except as hereafter provided: —This Court shall consist of one Chief Justice & not more than nine nor less than six associate Justices. The Supreme Judicial Court shall be, and they hereby are fully authorized & empowered to grant new trials and restorations to law in all cases where it shall to them appear reasonable." Plumer undoubtedly felt his wording improved the article, as the entrenching purpose was more strongly implied, the personnel of the court would have to be maintained at seven judges or more, and, if the restorations-to-law clause was interpreted as conferring exclusive jurisdiction on the court, the legislature could no longer claim a power that was its most blatant interference with the judicial process. But he named the high court inconsistently, calling it both "Supreme Court of Judicature" and "Supreme Judicial Court," when it was most commonly then called the Superior Court of Judicature. The wording has the appearance of being sloppy, but Plumer was following an unusual precedent. In both the Massachusetts Constitution of 1780 and the New Hampshire Constitution of 1784, the high court was given two names. It was an odd feature of the early constitutions that apparently did no harm.[28]

Because the convention had refused to create an equity jurisdiction, Plumer was unable to persuade the delegates to entrench the high court as firmly in the constitution as he might have liked. "The power of hearing & determining causes in Equity," he said in the same article, "shall, by the Legislature, be vested in the Supreme Judicial Court; —which power shall be limited & defined by law." The words were carefully selected in the hope of overcoming some of the opposition to equity. Quite likely a few of the more moderate opponents to equity who might have been persuaded to change their minds would never have voted for a chancery that was entrenched. What Plumer proposed was that, although the court and its original jurisdiction would have been entrenched in the constitution, its equity powers would not have been. They were to be created by legislative discretion and were subject to legislative alteration or abolition.[29]

When word seeped out to the public concerning what topics the convention planned to submit to the voters, most controversy centered on the judiciary. Surprisingly, more was written by critics of the convention against changing the court system than was directed against proposals to clarify the rights of non-Congregationalists to avoid taxation supporting Congregationalist ministers. No one seems to have found fault with entrenching the Superior Court in the constitution, though that may be because the amendment was never submitted to the voters. But even had it been, it is likely only a few in the general population would have understood what entrenching was all about, and even fewer people would have cared whether the Superior Court was entrenched or not. Of more importance to most people writing political correspondence to newspapers was the right to trial by jury, threatened, they claimed, by reports that the convention would ask voters to approve greater appellate powers for the Superior Court and to end the multiplicity of jury trials in a single cause of action. "Though one jury may materially mistake in a matter of fact, yet the sufferer must rest contented—Why?" a critic asked. Because should another jury try the issue it would render the first trial a "farce or mockery." "Why . . . [not] say, after I have applied to one LAWYER for his sage advice, with which I am dissatisfied, I must not apply to another, for fear his opinion might be different (though right) because it would make the opinion of the *first* a 'farce or mockery.'"[30]

Aside from defense of the right to trial by jury, almost all opposition to judicial reform was directed against creating an equity jurisdiction and abolishing the Court of Common Pleas. There was no difficulty in making a strong argument. The words "equity" and "chancery" were used by opponents to conjure up memories of arbitrary British rule in New Hampshire, carrying suggestions of unrestrained executive power and unchecked discretionary justice. One pamphleteer cleverly complicated the issue by admitting some equity powers might safely be vested in a common-law tribunal but never in a separate court presided over by a single chancellor. "In the hands of one man," he warned, "it might become the greatest engine of oppression, as has often been severely experienced in England, where it has become proverbial (from the tedious delays, in that Court) upon the recital of a lengthily story, to say, '*It is as tedious as a Chancery suit.*'" Writers for the other side, those supporting equity either as a separate jurisdiction or as a power added to common law, may have been drowned out by their opponents. "The disadvantages we labour under for want of a court of equity have been seen with regret by men the most enlightened among us," one wrote. "And for want of this court, people have been driven to apply to the legislature. This is not only an expensive mode, but really in most cases an unconstitutional redress." Few in New Hampshire could have been convinced by the last point. They were too conditioned to legislative supervision of the judiciary to be persuaded that legislative correction of judicial error was unconstitutional. More persuasive was the contention that equity itself was manifestly unconstitutional because trials were held by a judge without juries. "It is the peculiar priviledge of an American to be tryed by his COUNTRY [i.e., a jury] and the LAWS OF THE LAND," FREEMAN contended, "whereas this method deprives him of both, by putting his estate in the disposal of a single person, who is to make discretion alone, his Judgment." The last assertion was not true, but it was surprisingly effective in New Hampshire. As much as fifty years later one of the very best trial lawyers in the state so misunderstood equity, he believed discretion was the chancellor's only guide.[31]

Considering in whom political power was vested in New Hampshire, it is not surprising that abolition of Common Pleas jurisdiction aroused even more opposition than did creation of equity. The judges of that court, all local politicians and nonlawyers and resident in every part of the state, fought for their court, and they were an effective and persuasive voice among the voters. "The annihilation of the court of common pleas has been a favorite subject with some who have not as I can learn substituted any thing better in its room," one supporter of the court told the *Political Repository*. "[W]hoever does this without shewing us the evil . . . creates a suspicion that the evil is only imaginary." Of course, there was really an evil, an anonymous writer pointed out: the multiplicity of jury trials. To make his case, he did not need to see the evidence that Plumer had gathered from the court records that the legislature had opened free of charge to his committee. "There seldom are more than three or four actions tried at the inferior court at any one term," the pamphleteer pointed out, "and the judgments [are] commonly appealed from. What then becomes of the one, two, or three hundred actions brought to the court? Some are defaulted, some are demurred, making use of the inferior court as a sieve." In reply A FREEMAN, meeting the issue head-on, claimed that multiplicity of suits served practical, even useful, purposes. "[T]he policy of this institution is that the litigants may have an opportunity of examining their strength & discovering what evidence is or may be necessary at the higher Courts, to entitle them to a Verdict or to be able to obtain the public opinion of the justice or injustice of their causes," he explained. "[W]ill our liberty and property be more secure from the loss of one trial by jury?" he wondered, answering the question by asking it.[32]

Thomas Cogswell was the most vocal opponent of abolishing the Court of Common Pleas. He had substantial motivation. He had been a judge of the court since 1784 and remained in that office until 1810, for some of those final years serving as presiding judge. He had been a colonel in the Revolution and was influential in the towns around Gilmanton, where he lived. In a pamphlet he became rather personal in his criticism of Plumer and Edward St. Loe Livermore, one of Plumer's young lawyer allies. "[H]ow came it about," Cogswell asked, "that these gentlemen should be so anxious to alter our laws and judiciary system? Is it out of pure regard to the love of liberty, and the citizens of this State? Or is it because they once had an antipathy to our government, and still retain it?"[33]

When Cogswell's pamphlet was published, Smith was in Philadelphia. Plumer sent him a copy with the comment, "If you have an unusual stock of patience you will read it." "I should," Smith replied, "were I in your case say as Parsons Adams did when a gentleman made him the subject of some vile poetry, 'I had rather be the subject than the author of such stuff.' These attacks are the price you pay for being a great man for being inflexibly honest."[34]

When the convention reconvened the third week in February, it was immediately evident that sentiment had shifted against judicial reform. To protect their jurisdiction, the justices of the peace and the judges of Common Pleas had lobbied the delegates and rallied public opinion in their localities. A minor but revealing instance is the resolution to set at four pounds the amount of damages that could be awarded by a justice's court. As rewritten into a constitutional amendment by Plumer's committee of ten, it gave "to Justices of the Peace (who shall by the Executive be specially commissioned for that purpose) jurisdiction in civil cases when the damages demanded shall not exceed four pounds." Plumer had slipped in the words, "who shall by the Executive be specially commissioned," hoping to introduce a process allowing the president of the state to restrict trials to the more competent justices. The justices of the peace realized what could happen and did not want their jurisdiction splintered. At the reconvened session it was moved to strike the words. The motion carried 64 to 34, and the clause was struck.[35]

No other part of Plumer's drafted amendments "caused such stormy debate," Lynn Turner has observed, than the clauses dealing with the judiciary. The dissenting minority of Plumer's committee carried its fight to the floor of the convention. Unfortunately for Plumer—who did not have help from Smith, who was away at Congress—the opposition was strongly supported by Chief Justice John Pickering, a formidable foe. His chief support came from Edward St. Loe Livermore, one of the better lawyers in the state but, Turner concluded, "so tactless and violent as to stir up needless opposition."[36]

Plumer and Livermore became so anxious to save whatever they could, they introduced some amendments that were watered down substitutes of what they originally had hoped to accomplish. "It shall be the duty of the General Court," it was moved on behalf of the committee of ten, "to make a reform in the Judiciary System, that Justice may be administered in a more cheap and expeditious manner than is now practised; and that no party shall have a review after the cause has been determined twice against

him by jury." This amendment would not have saved much of what the reformers wanted, but it would have encouraged the legislators to abolish
Common Pleas and General Sessions and would have limited multiplicity
of jury trials to two. The motion was extensively debated, and at least three
substitutes were offered, each omitting the commands that it was "the
duty" of the General Court "to make a reform" and that multiple jury trials
be restricted to two. The version that was accepted provided: "The General
Court are hereby impowered to make alterations in the power and jurisdiction of the Courts of Common pleas and the Court of General Sessions respectively, or if they shall judge it necessary for the public good, to abolish
those Courts or either of them, and invest such other Courts as they may
establish, with the jurisdiction and powers now vested in said Courts of
Common pleas and Courts of General Sessions of the Peace, as the General
court shall from time to time judge expedient for the due administration of
Law and Justice." This resolution added nothing to Plumer's judicial program, because it granted no authority to the legislature that it did not already possess. It did not tell the General Court what the convention hoped
would be done, not even that the courts should be abolished, only that
abolition was within the legislature's discretion. About the only feature that
could have given Plumer any satisfaction is that the General Court was not
reminded that it also had authority to abolish the Superior Court.[37]

The convention retained the equity clause as had previously been voted but
struck the words "ought to," making the General Court's authority to create
the jurisdiction discretionary rather than semi-mandatory. But Plumer's main
reform, the clause entrenching the Superior Court into the constitution,
dropped from sight. Few people probably noticed. There was no debate, and
the records indicate no vote. Perhaps there was none. It was a matter that only
Plumer, Smith, and a handful of others may have cared about. Yet it was unquestionably the most important decision made by the convention. The judicial history of New Hampshire for the next 106 years would be drastically different from that of other nineteenth-century American states because of it.[38]

The amendments on the judiciary that the convention submitted to the
people contained so little of what Plumer had hoped to accomplish that he
might easily have lost interest and withdrawn from the debates. Instead he
fought for the adoption of all the amendments among the electorate,
which, considering the limits on travel and communications in those days,
meant primarily speaking at the Epping town meeting. The opposition was
more effective. When the popular vote was counted in May 1792, Plumer
announced that 46 of the 72 proposed amendments had been accepted by
the necessary two-thirds vote. The only major victory for Plumer and his
supporters was the executive branch. The chief magistrate, renamed "governor" in place of "president," was given sufficient strength to make the office independent of the General Court. There were a few other accomplishments, but the most important judiciary reform remaining on the ballot,
creation of an equity jurisdiction, was rejected.[39]

After the smoke of battle cleared and the final votes were tallied, the judiciary was hardly changed. The most significant court reform was a clause in the constitution prohibiting judges, registers, and clerks from acting as counsel in litigation. Some registers of deeds apparently had been doing so, and the amendment ended the practice. Another amendment provided that lawyer-members of the legislature no longer could represent parties whose petitions or memorials were under consideration by the General Court. Although he himself had undertaken such representation many times, Plumer called the practice "a dereliction of principle, equally degrading & improper," for it combined the incompatible functions of advocate and judge. Neither amendment could be called a reformist triumph, however, because in 1792, New Hampshire voters would support any measure placing restrictions on lawyers. Plumer probably took some comfort in the fact that the convention had rejected a serious effort to forbid lawyers "from holding a seat in the Legislature." It was defeated, 15 yeas to 79 nays. Had it passed, it quite likely would have been adopted by the people.[40]

It may well be that William Plumer did not feel the satisfaction that he surely was entitled to feel. After all, at only thirty-three years old, he had dominated the deliberations and the work of the entire convention. Credited with sponsoring most of the proposed reforms, he was clearly a leader in state government, a man who would leave his mark on events in the coming decades. Historians have praised his role in the convention, taking special note of the fact that the Constitution of 1792 was soon being called "Plumer's constitution."[41] But the name was not the compliment that one might think today. "He was," one of the Livermores said of Plumer, "by all odds, the most influential man in the convention; so much so that those who disliked the result, called it Plumer's constitution, by way of insinuating that it was the work of one man, and not the collective wisdom of the whole assembly."[42]

Although not "the work of one man," the Constitution of 1792, when viewed from the historical perspective in the twenty-first century, must be given credit for one remarkable result. The people of New Hampshire had called this convention just seven years after adopting the Constitution of 1784. They would not call another until 1852, sixty years later, a longer time than any other state would go without changing its constitution. It was not until 1877 that extensive amendments were added to Plumer's constitution.[43]

Looking back many years later, Plumer concluded that he had received an important personal benefit for his labors at the constitutional convention. "In the course of the year my acquaintance with Jeremiah Smith became more intimate," he explained. Smith, too, felt some satisfaction. "I am glad the Constitution has fared no worse," he wrote from Philadelphia. "I had apprehensions that your divisions would produce the most mischievous consequences. I am glad to find it is as it is." Had Smith been able to look into the future, he surely would have changed his mind and said that, by failing to entrench the Superior Court into the constitution, they had produced "the most mischievous consequences."[44]

Three

Restoring to Law

Plumer's constitution did not raise the status of the judiciary. "It appears that Judicial officers may be removed by impeachment, or in consequence of an address from both Houses of the Legislature to the Executive," New Hampshire's governor pointed out in a 1799 gubernatorial address to the General Court, "but Sheriffs and others only by impeachment." He found the difference hard to believe. "It is scarcely presumable the Constitution intended these should hold their offices by a tenure less liable to removal from office than do the justices of our highest court of Judicature."[1]

That condition of tenure was almost a caricature of the status of New Hampshire judges in the decade following the constitutional convention of 1791–1792. They had a semblance of security in their offices, but it was a tenure less secure than that of "Sheriffs and others." Just about the only satisfaction that William Plumer would get from judicial events during that decade—the decade before Jeremiah Smith would become chief justice of the Superior Court of Judicature—was when the legislature accomplished something he had not been able to do at the convention. It abolished the Court of General Sessions. The judicial business of General Sessions was transferred to the Common Pleas, and the court's taxing authority for each county was vested in a convention of that county's representatives in the General Court. "It gives me much pleasure to learn that the Legislature of N H have abolished the Court of General Sessions," Smith told Plumer. "The next step (and I do not disdain to see it speedily taken) will be to abolish the Court of Common pleas. This is a confirmation devoutly to be wished."[2]

Judicial dependence did not change. The legislature continued to super-vise the courts, sometimes defining, at other times increasing the jurisdic-tion of the Superior Court.[3] For example, of the six statutes published in the *Sessions Laws* for June 1797, five had to do with regulating the courts.[4] Although there were enough favorable votes in both houses to have joint committees appointed "to form a bill for erecting and organizing a court of equity in this State," their numbers were not sufficient to create either a new court or to vest equity powers in an existing court of common law.[5] The most they could effect was piecemeal legislation, obtaining for the Su-perior Court certain chancery powers previously exercised by the legisla-ture. An early instance, described by Plumer, vested the court with jurisdic-tion over "obligations containing a *condition,* and . . . deeds of mortgage, where the forfeiture or penalty should be found by the verdict of a jury, by default, or confession of the obligator, to render judgment for such a sum as should be due, according to equity and good conscience." That is, the court was empowered to "give judgment therein, that such forfeiture is or is not incurred, and to judge and decree as a Court of Chancery."[6]

It is an instance of how much Plumer failed to correct what he knew were shortcomings of the judicial system that, in 1792, he did not clarify what the Constitution of 1784 had intended when it mandated that judges be paid honorable and permanent salaries. It was a matter immediately noted at that time. "The article of the constitution," a Portsmouth newspa-per complained, "making it the duty of the general court to fix by standing laws, the permanent and honorable salaries for the judges of the superior court, is not altered though it has been so grossly violated by every legisla-ture since the constitution took place."[7] It would continue to be violated. For several years after Plumer's Constitution of 1792 went into operation, the two houses of the General Court established judicial salaries that were neither honorable nor permanent. During the decade following the consti-tutional convention, the General Court at just about every session passed legislation, usually entitled "[a]n act establishing permanent salaries for the justices of the superior court of judicature." But, as before Plumer's consti-tution was adopted, the salaries were regularly being altered; they were not permanent. "If any deficiency of compensation to Judges, . . . now exists from any cause," the two houses assured the governor in 1795, "we shall esteem it our duty to make equitable and ample provision for them," but most of the judges said the pay was less than honorable.[8] For some judges the legislature voted no fixed salaries at all. In 1793, when pro-bate judges were compensated only by the fees paid into court by parties, a question was put to the members of the lower house: "Shall the several Judges of Probate within and for this State, either in whole or in part, have compensation for their services by way of salaries." The motion passed in the affirmative, 58 to 42, but never went beyond good inten-tions. Thirty-two years later, Plumer would lament that probate judges still were paid only in fees.[9]

Sometimes the General Court may have legislated judicial salaries designed to do more than compensate judges. In 1796, for instance, the Senate decided to make "an addition to the compensation of the Justices of the Superior Court." It voted $400 "to be paid out of fees, and equally divided among those justices who attend." It is not certain, but this legislation appears to be a scheme for encouraging better attendance at court terms by the judges.[10]

The General Court certainly had reason to be concerned about judicial attendance. Woodbury Langdon's impeachment had not been an isolated aberration. New Hampshire legislators continued to assume that it was their right to investigate why judges missed a circuit. In 1797 they had made a statutory exception to the rule that all four justices had to be present for a quorum of the Superior Court. When there was "any legal disqualification of one or more of the justices," those judges not disqualified were now a quorum, even if there was only one. But the legislature made no further exceptions. All judges not disqualified had to attend every trial during every term of court. They did not always do so. At the turn of the nineteenth century, New Hampshire's high-court bench had a marked propensity for missing circuits. "The repeated delays of the due administration of justice in the Supreme Judicial Court of this State, consequent upon the non-attendance of some of the judges," Governor John Taylor Gilman warned the two houses, "is a subject of great complaint . . . ; painful as the subject is, I have thought it my duty to lay it before you." In their reply, the two branches of the legislature assured him that he had acted properly. It was their constitutional prerogative to discipline judicial absences. "[O]ppression in one part, or delay in the other," they told Gilman, "though not equally grievous, ought to be remedied by every constitutional means in their [the two houses'] power."[11]

By "constitutional means," the General Court meant legislative supervision of the judiciary. One way, as the impeachment of Woodbury Langdon showed, was enquiring why justices missed scheduled terms of court. At its June 1789 session, for example, the Senate's judiciary committee reported that the "Justices of the Superior Court have neglected to perform their Circuits agreeable to the Laws of the State." Committees of both houses were appointed to ask the judges why. Only one member of the court, Chief Justice John Pickering, explained why he had missed his circuits. The legislators found his reasons to be "fully satisfactory."[12]

Four years later Pickering's explanations were less satisfactory. Court sessions had been canceled in three counties: Hillsborough, Grafton, and Cheshire. Complaints grew frequent enough that Governor Gilman urged the General Court to investigate. The two houses appointed a joint committee "to enquire into the causes of the non-attendance of the Judges of the Supreme Judicial Court [i.e., Superior Court] in the several counties in this State, and report what measures are necessary to be taken to remove the inconveniences complained of." Again claiming it was the legislature's constitutional prerogative to promulgate corrective measures, the House of Representatives voted it had responsibility "to inquire into the causes of such failures of justice, and endeavor in a constitutional manner to remove them; and that a message be sent immediately to the Justices of the Superior Court of Judicature, requesting each of them to inform the House why the said Court had not been duly holden, and the business thereof compleated."[13]

Fifteen days later all of the judges had replied. A second committee was appointed to study the answers "and report what measures they may judge necessary to be taken respecting the said Court." The committee recommended that the General Court again alter the judiciary system by authorizing "two of the Judges of the Superior Court to be a quorum for business, until the end of the next session of the General Court." It was an eminently sensible suggestion. Current statutory law required all four judges to be present, not just to hear motions and legal arguments, but to hold jury trials. Unfortunately the proposal meant that trials might be conducted by two judges who had no legal training, something many lawyers opposed. The motion was defeated in a tie vote, 58 to 58.[14]

Attention was then turned on Pickering, who again was the culprit. From the perspective of New Hampshire jurisprudence it was a most unfortunate situation. Governor Charles H. Bell later observed that Pickering had "brought to the position [of chief justice] more law learning than any judge who had sat there before him." He seems to have been the first New Hampshire judge who made rulings according to common-law methodology. Chief Justice Samuel Livermore, who had served earlier, had been a well-trained and successful lawyer and was more brilliant than Pickering, but on the bench he had been an extreme exponent of common-sense adjudication, not of the common law. He entrusted most decisions to the good sense of the jury. On the occasions when he made rulings, his judgments were based on nonlegal factors; that is, they were in the tradition of common-sense jurisprudence, which usually has been associated with lay judges, not with lawyers. Where Livermore had disdained legal authority, Pickering attempted both to create and follow authority. He may not, however, have appreciated the purpose of common-law forms of action, once referring to rules of procedure, such as a plea in demurrer, as "inventions of the bar to prevent justice."[15]

The reasons for Pickering's absences from court made the task of disciplining him especially difficult for New Hampshire's politicians. He had not missed the inland circuits because he had private business affairs to attend to in Portsmouth, as had Woodbury Langdon. He missed because the three counties of Hillsborough, Grafton, and Cheshire were far inside the state, and the further distance he traveled, the more rivers and streams had to be crossed, and he was fearful of passing over water. William Plumer, who, of course, was no alienist, attempted to diagnose Pickering's affliction. "Like many sedentary men," he explained, Pickering "was subject to *nervous complaints,* which induced him to think he was unable to travel, or perform much business; the consequence was, he partially neglected the court. In 1794 he was grievously afflicted with the *hypochondriac affection,* a disease which finds but few disposed to pity, or commiserate with the sufferer."[16]

Plumer was wrong. A large number of New Hampshirites commiserated with John Pickering. He aroused widespread sympathy, though perhaps not much from Hillsborough, Grafton, and Cheshire counties. Many who were sympathetic, however, appreciated that he could not remain on the bench. It was moved in the House of Representatives "that an address be made by both branches of the Legislature, to the Governor and Council to remove the Chief Justice of the Superior Court from office." Again the vote was tied, 60 to 60, and the motion to address the chief justice from office failed. Pickering was saved only because the speaker, John Prentice, was able to vote. He was a lawyer, and Plumer thought that he had had no choice except to support Pickering. Prentice was a candidate for the bench and would have damaged his reputation had he voted to address off the court the man holding the office he most coveted.[17]

Not every lawyer supported the chief justice. Just after the House of Representatives had voted to send messengers to the judges asking the reasons for the canceled sessions, it was moved to reconsider. The member who was perhaps the best young lawyer then serving in the house, Arthur Livermore, voted no. He wanted Pickering's absences confronted. Jeremiah Smith was also unhappy. "Why did you not remove him?" he scolded his brother, who was a representative. "Surely there has been time enough for experiment. Want of nerves, (or whatever his disorder may be,) as effectually disqualifies him for the office he holds, as want of integrity or capacity." Smith feared that if judges who neglected court sessions were removed, the vacancies would not "be *well* filled; but the main thing is, to have them filled with men who would do their duty in attending at the several terms; for be assured, it is of more importance that causes should be *tried,* than that they should be *well* tried."[18]

Fifteen days after the tie vote, John Sullivan, United States District Judge for the district of New Hampshire, died. Pickering badly wanted to succeed him, even writing Justice William Cushing of the Supreme Court for support. "May I ask a favor," he enquired. "Your recommendation of me to fill the Office of District Judge for New Hampshire. . . . The fatigue of the office of Chief Justice—the smallness of the Salary, my attachment to the Federal Government and the honor of occasionally sitting with you in the Circuit Court, inclines me to resign my present Office for that of District Judge."[19]

Of course, Pickering would resign the chief justiceship. The federal district judgeship was far less demanding than being chief justice, with much less travel and fewer rivers to cross. When he sat with Cushing, part of his duties as district judge would be either in Portsmouth, where he lived, or in Exeter, to which he could go by crossing only one river. Civic leaders, especially Federalists, saw a golden opportunity to rid New Hampshire of a serious problem and urged the president to appoint him. Plumer was particularly

eager, as he was anxious to get a competent, active, and learned chief justice at the head of the state's judiciary. Six years later, when he was the
leading candidate to become New Hampshire's next United States senator,
he was willing that the position go instead to Simeon Olcott. Olcott was
then chief justice of the Superior Court and had been so for only about five
years, but Plumer thought him incompetent and wanted him out of that
office, hoping that Jeremiah Smith would be appointed in his stead. To
Plumer, the post of chief justice was much more important than that of
senator or district judge, and he had no reservations about urging the president to appoint a mentally unbalanced man to the district court if it would
rid the state judiciary of a mentally unbalanced chief justice. For once,
Smith disagreed with his friend. He wanted the appointment to go to Edward St. Loe Livermore and told Plumer he could not support Pickering.
"P——gs conduct since he has been chief justice has lessened him in my esteem," he explained. "One who was not on the spot and concerned either
as a party or an advocate can form no true Judgement of the Injury the
Counties of Hillsborough Cheshire & Grafton have sustained. . . . I should
certainly have voted for his removal. I love the man but abhor the judge. . . .
I shall not oppose his appointment tho' most assuredly if the choice rested
with me I could not in conscience appoint him.[20]

The administration apparently did not ask Smith. Pickering was appointed district judge about three weeks after Sullivan's death. "I congratulate you on this event," Smith wrote Pickering's brother-in-law, "and assure
you that I participate in the pleasure it must afford him and his friends.
You will not call my sincerity in these professions in question, when I add
that I should have given my voice, if I had been consulted, in favor of another. . . . I am very happy to learn that Mr. P.'s health is restored; it is the
only circumstance which has prevented his talents from being eminently
useful to his fellow-citizens." Smith was right. Pickering had once rendered
valuable service to New Hampshire, and had he been mentally stable, he
would have been the state's first important chief justice. Smith was also
right that someone else should have been appointed to the federal court.
Had his advice been followed, New Hampshire and the nation would have
been spared a very painful experience.[21]

John Dudley was appointed to succeed Pickering as chief justice. He had
been on the Superior Court since 1784, before Plumer's Constitution of
1792 prohibited judges from serving after reaching the age of 70. By late
1796 Dudley had turned 70. He believed the provision was not retroactive
and, therefore, did not apply to him. Members of the General Court
thought differently. Confident of its own prerogative to interpret the constitution as it saw fit, the House of Representatives did not ask the other
justices of the Superior Court for their opinion. It appointed a special committee that ruled unanimously that, no matter when appointed, a judge
could not remain on the bench after turning seventy.[22] The house voted to
accept this ruling of law and, together with the Senate, addressed the gov-

ernor and Council, "requesting the removal of the honorable John Dudley, Esquire, from the office he now holds as Judge of the Superior Court," citing as reasons not the constitutional age limitation but "delays of nature and infirmities of age." "The gen Court in my opinion have done right in addressing the Governor to remove Dudley," Smith told Plumer. The governor and Council notified Dudley that, if he wished, they would hear him on why he should not be removed as chief justice. At the same time, the governor sent a friendly letter, advising him to resign. After thinking the matter over for two weeks, Dudley resigned.[23]

Dudley was "addressed" by the two houses, not impeached by the lower house. An opinion shared by some lawyers in New Hampshire held that although the constitutional grounds for impeachment were quite broad, to arrive at age 70 and not to resign was not impeachable. It was addressable. Addressing out of office was authorized by a number of the early state constitutions, although there was a good deal of dispute about the process and extent of its reach.[24] A few lawyers in New Hampshire contended that judges could not be addressed out unless specific charges were brought by the General Court. "Judges can be removed by address; but not without a cause: for this construction would leave them entirely dependent," Estwick Evans, of the Rockingham County bar, contended: *"Shall the declaration in two places in the constitution that the judges ought to be independent, and in one that they shall be so, which declarations cannot be construed contrary to their apparent meaning, yield to a provision, which seems to render the judiciary dependent, but which may be fairly and rationally construed so as to make sense of the whole instrument?"* Evans's argument is persuasive, but it was only the theory of a single lawyer; it was not law. By the time both Plumer and Smith retired from public life, the rule was well established that judicial removal by address of a judge could be made for any cause, or for no cause, and no reasons needed to be assigned.[25]

Governor Gilman and the Council had offered Chief Justice Dudley a hearing, but their gesture did not become a precedent. Although also not law, A FRIEND TO TRUTH may have been a little closer to stating an accepted legal principle when he suggested that Governor Gilman could not have given Dudley a hearing because he and the Council had no discretion to do so. "[W]henever the legislature should express their *pleasure* to the Executive *in any form* to have Judges removed from office," he contended, "the Executive must remove them." That position would have meant that, if there was a hearing, it should be before both houses of the General Court meeting in convention or before each house separately. It never became the rule. Even William Plumer, an advocate of due process, did not think judges being addressed out had a right to be heard. When he was governor in 1816, Plumer persuaded the legislature to address six judges from office, and none of them received a hearing.[26] Removal by address, then, was entirely at the discretion of the other two branches of government and could be exercised for any political reason, including addressing out the judges of one party to make judicial places available for members of the other party.[27]

It is important to the theme of this study to mention that most opposition to the addressing power was not over lack of procedural safeguards but rather on the ground that addressing out violated judicial independence. It is also significant that the connection between the power to address judges from office, without cause or trial, and judicial independence was made by lawyers who were not members of the New Hampshire bar. When at the federal constitutional convention it was proposed to give Congress authority to address judges out of office, Gouverneur Morris argued it would be "a contradiction in terms to say that the Judges should hold their offices during good behavior, and yet be removable without a trial," and James Wilson warned that the "judges would be in a bad situation if made to depend upon every gust of faction which might prevail in the two branches of our Govt." After he left Portsmouth and changed his residence to Boston, Daniel Webster sought to have the addressing clause removed from the Massachusetts constitution. "If the judges, in fact, hold their office only so long as the legislature sees fit," he told the constitutional convention of 1820, "then it is vain and illusory to say that the judges are independent men incapable of being influenced by hope or fear; but the tenure of their office is not independent." The man destined to become the country's greatest state judge was even more emphatic. "By the constitution as it stands," Lemuel Shaw said of the addressing clause, "the judges hold their offices at the will of the majority of the legislature." New Hampshire critics of judicial independence, therefore, had a valid argument when they contended that the doctrine of judicial independence was unimportant, if not meaningless, for as long as the legislature and executive could address out judges at pleasure, New Hampshire's judiciary was not independent.[28]

It may be that the New Hampshire legislature expressed respect for the separate and equal status of the judiciary only once during the decade before Jeremiah Smith became chief justice. When the General Court in 1799 was asked by the legislatures of Kentucky and Virginia to endorse their resolutions condemning as unconstitutional the Alien and Sedition Acts passed by Congress, New Hampshire representatives refused. "[T]he State Legislatures are not the proper tribunals to determine the Constitutionality of the laws of the General Government," they unanimously resolved, "the duty of such decision is properly and exclusively confined to the judicial department."[29]

It was a clear, emphatic vote for the principle of separate and independent judicial authority—the clearest and most empathetic support stated by New Hampshire lawmakers before the nineteenth century—but it was an isolated endorsement. At first sight it might be thought that the New Hampshire legislature was supposing that the federal judicial system enjoyed greater constitutional autonomy than did the state's. But that would not be true. Most New Hampshire legislators at that time thought the federal judiciary was as subject to congressional supervision as the state judiciary was to them. Six years earlier both the governor of New Hampshire and the

General Court had vigorously protested a ruling by the federal Circuit Court sitting at Exeter. "By this decision," the *New-Hampshire Gazette* charged, echoing the opinion of most people in the state, "the sovereignty of New-Hampshire is completely annihilated, its right of legislation controverted, and the liberties and properties of its subjects invaded . . . ; these are the blessed effects of our Federal Courts." The General Court petitioned Congress to take measures "to prevent and annihilate such illegal acts of power." In other words, the legislators told Congress to adopt New Hampshire constitutional theory and do what they would have done—reverse and set aside a judgment of a court of law.[30]

The dispute was old, originating in 1777 when the New Hampshire privateer *McClary* captured the brigantine *Lusanna* and brought her into Portsmouth as a prize. *Lusanna* was sailing under British papers, but the owner, a Massachusetts citizen, asserted that the papers were a disguise to protect the vessel from British capture and asked the New Hampshire Court Maritime to rule that she was not a prize of war. In New Hampshire a judge could not make the ruling; even though the proceedings were in admiralty, the decision was for the jury, and a Portsmouth jury found for the privateers. The judge, then free to rule, decreed the brigantine a lawful prize. New Hampshire law did not permit appeal outside its jurisdiction, and the court refused to allow the Massachusetts claimants to appeal to the committee of appeals of the Continental Congress. After losing a series of Superior Court trials in New Hampshire, the libelee obtained a congressional hearing via petition. The committee on appeals of the Continental Congress held that it had jurisdiction, but New Hampshire refused to recognize the committee's authority. The case continued through the era of the Articles of Confederation to the adoption of the United States Constitution. It was the newly created federal judiciary that had ruled at Exeter that the committee on appeals had possessed authority to overturn the original New Hampshire judgment. The federal court ruled for the libelee, assessing the enormous sum of $38,000, in part because the libelants had ignored the jurisdiction of the committee on appeals and its successor, the Court of Appeals in Cases of Capture, for which they should not have been blamed as New Hampshire legislation had directed them not to acknowledge the venue of those courts.

The people of New Hampshire were outraged. "[M]any reputable gentlemen in this town are become the subjects of ruin and distress, for supporting the law of their own State," Portsmouth's *Gazette* complained. The libelants had two routes of appeal: to Congress and the Supreme Court. Both houses of the New Hampshire legislature remonstrated Congress in 1783, 1794, and 1795, saying that "while they chearfully acknowledge the power of Congress in cases arising under this constitution, they equally resolve not to submit the [state] laws made before the existence of the present government, by this (then independent) State to the adjudication of any power on earth, while the freedom of the federal government shall afford any constitutional means of redress." They were asking Congress to overrule the judiciary and reverse the decision against the Portsmouth libelants.[31]

When New Hampshire's last remonstrance arrived in Philadelphia, Senator Samuel Livermore laid it before the Senate, where it was tabled. In the House of Representatives Jeremiah Smith did not want to present the petition. "[W]hat has the General Court of N.H. to do with the matter?" he asked Plumer. "The act of the State ought not and I presume will not, have any influence on Congress."[32] Congressman John Samuel Sherburne introduced the memorial, which was submitted to a select committee chaired by James Madison. He read New Hampshire a lesson in constitutional law, dismissing the remonstrance on grounds that still were not well understood in the state: separation of powers. "[T]he subject of the said memorial being of a nature wholly judicial," he pointed out, referring to the Supreme Court's ruling, "the Committee have conceived themselves precluded from all enquiry into the particular merits of the case: nor can perceive any ground, on which legislative interference could be proper."[33]

Madison stated the legal principles that had already begun to dominate federal, but not New Hampshire, constitutional theory. They certainly had no impact on New Hampshire legislation. All through the decade between the adoption of the Constitution of 1792 and the appointment of Jeremiah Smith as chief justice of the Superior Court, New Hampshire lawmakers passed special statutes that paid slight heed to separating the powers of government and treated the judiciary as an appendage of the General Court. The essence of judicial independence is the preservation of a separate branch of government that adjudicates actions at law and suits in equity with impartiality and finality. The New Hampshire judiciary, even after Plumer's constitution, did not enjoy this degree of independence. In *Federalist* 81, Alexander Hamilton scoffed at the suggestion that an American legislature would "reverse a determination once made, in a particular case." During the 1790s, the New Hampshire General Court did so at almost every session. It was only a minority of New Hampshirites who protested and spoke out for this aspect of judicial independence. "[H]ow comes it to pass, that the determinations of our Judicial Courts in this State, are frequently set aside: insomuch that a suitor has no certainty that after obtaining *a final* judgment his cause will not undergo a revision in the General Court," SOLON asked in 1790. "I lay it down as a proposition uncontrovertible—that reserving, setting aside, nullifying, or abrogating the judgment of a court of law, for any cause whatever, is an exercise of Judicial authority. That a new trial, originating otherwise than by Appeal, Writ of Review, or Writ of Error, according to the standing laws of the state, is an appendage of the Judicial authority."[34]

SOLON was wrong. That was not New Hampshire law. All through the last decade of the eighteenth century, the General Court of New Hampshire was more than the state's supreme legislature; it also was the state's highest judicial tribunal. It acted on the assumption that it was constitutionally authorized to enact special legislation to alter rules of procedure as, for example, in 1792, "An act to limit the time of prosecuting demands against the estate of Thomas Simpson," and the opposite in 1795, empowering a probate judge "to lengthen the time for receiving claims on the estate of Isaac Frye."[35] The two houses granted individual litigants the right "to enter an action,"[36] "to review a certain action,"[37] to commence "a new trial in review of a certain action,"[38] "a new trial or review in a certain action,"[39] and "to take an appeal from a certain decree of the Court of Probate;"[40] "to bring in a bill enabling him [the petitioner] to review his action before the court of Common-Pleas,"[41] and "to secure to the inhabitants of the County of Cheshire a trial by Jury in a certain case."[42]

The General Court also remitted penalties imposed by the Superior Court[43] but apparently did not pass legislation staying the collection of private debts in times of hardships.[44] Most frequently, it granted new trials to litigants who had lost a civil suit[45] or, as bills for new trials were commonly worded, "to restore" the petitioner "to his Law"[46] or "for restoring" a petitioner "to his law."[47]

"Restoring to law" was a term frequently employed in various contexts during the years before New Hampshire lawyers learned to use the word "appeal" as it is now understood. In one of the reports that he prepared for the constitutional convention of 1792, for example, Plumer mentioned "[t]he power given to the supreme court of granting . . . restorations to law."[48] Legislation restoring people to their law had not been common during colonial times. That there were so many instances by 1800 may have been a legacy of the "legislative" constitutions of 1776 and 1784. At the December 1791 session of the General Court, three petitioners were restored to their law. At the November 1797 session, the House of Representatives restored three people in one day.[49] Some lawyers objected strongly to the process, most memorably William Plumer. It is a telling fact that Plumer's first significant step toward reforming New Hampshire's judiciary occurred as a practicing attorney, not as a legislator or a constitutional framer.

In 1789 Plumer, on behalf of a client, Nathaniel Gilman, filed suit against Elizabeth McClary for a sum of money alleged to be due Gilman. Referees decided for Gilman, and the Superior Court entered judgment against McClary. Dissatisfied, McClary petitioned the legislature, praying to be restored to her law. The House of Representatives voted that Gilman "be served with a Copy of the Petition and order of the [General] Court thereon three weeks prior to the Sitting of said Court that he may appear and Shew cause why the prayer thereon may not be granted and that the Execution against the Petitioner be stayed until the decision of the General Court." Whether Gilman appeared is not clear, for, had he appeared, it would have been before a joint committee, not a conference of both houses, and, therefore, is not part of the printed record. At that time legislators could still represent clients before either house, and it is likely Plumer represented Gilman, even though he strongly criticized the practice. In any event, whatever objections he raised did not prevail. An act was passed "to restore Elizabeth McClarey [*sic*] to her law."[50]

Retrial was scheduled in the Superior Court for Rockingham County at the September 1791 term. Although that was the same month as the opening sessions of the constitutional convention, Plumer again represented Gilman. He challenged the validity of the restoring act, contending "that the law was unconstitutional, and therefore void, on the ground, that, if it reversed the former judgment, it was repugnant to the bill of rights, and the constitution of the state; and that, if it did not reverse it [the judgment], the court could not render another judgment in the same case, while the first remained in force."[51] It is striking that Plumer's argument was that legislative restoring to law deprived Gilman of his right to trial by jury. He did not contend that restoring to law was a violation of judicial independence or separation of powers, but then neither did Chief Justice John Pickering in his decision holding the McClary restoring statute unconstitutional. That Pickering did not is even more striking, for he was the man most responsible for writing into the Constitution of 1784 the clauses on judicial independence and the need to separate the legislature and the judiciary.

> Upon motion it was objected by counsel for the Original plaintiff that the Act of the General Court by virtue of which this action was reentered could not entitle the original defendant to a trial by jury by way of appeal because if it reversed the judgment of the Court rendered on the report of referees it was repugnant to the constitution of the state and if it did not reverse the judgment the same might be pleaded in bar on the appeal. Whereupon after a full hearing of the parties by their counsel learned in the law and fully deliberating upon the constitution of the state and the nature and operation of the Act, it appears to the Court that if the Act virtually or really reverses the judgment of this court it is repugnant to the bill of rights and constitution of this state and that if the Act does not reverse the said judgment the court cannot render another judgment in the case upon appeal while the first judgment remains in force. It is therefore considered by the Court that the said Act is ineffectual and inadmissible and that the said action is dismissed.[52]

Gilman v. *McClary* was the most significant pronouncement of judicial independence in New Hampshire since judges in Rockingham County refused to enforce the "Ten Pound Act." Yet the doctrine of separation of powers was most forcefully argued by critics of the decision, who attacked the judges for "putting themselves above the Legislature." The General Court, however, did not react this time. The judgment stood, and Elizabeth McClary had to pay Nathaniel Gilman. Legislators became more reluctant to grant petitions seeking restoration to law. The practice did not end, but its more extreme instances did, such as statutes that both restored a petitioner to her law and also "reverse[d] a determination of the same Court."[53]

Restoration acts were regular legislation and, therefore, after the adoption of the Constitution of 1792, subject to executive veto. Vetoes were quite rare. One of the very few occurred in 1797, when Governor Gilman vetoed a bill granting a new trial to Josiah Sanborn. It was a veto the two houses overrode. The statute granting Sanborn his law is worth attention for what it says. Its wording clearly demonstrates that restoration to law was far more a judicial determination than an instance of legislation. If the words can be taken at their face value, and were not used to hide personal or political decisions, they make clear that the General Court gave Sanborn a new jury trial not for politic or legislative policy reasons but on a determination of facts much like a court of law, facts that few of the representatives could have had time to evaluate.

> Whereas Josiah Sanborn, . . . hath petitioned the General Court, . . . that some time since an action was commenced against him, by Samuel Holland, to recover a certain tract of land . . . , which land the said Sanborn held by vendue title, that said . . . cause was put to a jury, who gave a verdict in favour of said Sanborn, who recovered judgment thereon for his costs; that afterwards on another trial on review, the jury gave a verdict in favour of the said Sanborn which was publicly read, recorded by the clerk and affirmed by the jury, and they dispersed, some time after which, some of the jurors said that the jury intended to have given the cause against the said Sanborn; whereupon the same being made known to the Court, upon motion of the plaintiffs counsel, without the jury's having been sent out again, or all present the record was altered and a verdict of said jury against him was recorded, which he conceived unjust. Wherefore the said Sanborn prayed to be restored to a new trial in said action; the principal facts in said petition appearing to be true, and the prayer thereof reasonable.
>
> Therefore, *Be it enacted* . . . That a new trial be granted to the said Josiah Sanborn.[54]

Even the most indifferent legislator could not miss how much more legal than legislative Sanborn's special act was. It was a statute enacted by the New Hampshire General Court that made both a determination of facts *and* a finding of law. That must have been the case for many, if not most restoring-to-law bills. How could restoring legislation help but do so? In Sanborn's case the majority of representatives ruled that, as a matter of law, the Superior Court had not acted properly when it altered the record, changed the jury verdict, and awarded judgment for Holland. Unlike a court of law, the legislators did not have to give or even think of reasons; that is, they did not have to rule whether it was beyond the competence of the Superior Court to alter the record, whether Sanborn should have been heard, whether the jury should have been recalled, whether jurors should have been put under oath, or whatever. Gilman made this point in his veto message: "The bill [to restore Sanborn] is predicated on the principle that the record of the verdict of the jury was altered," the governor pointed out: "if this was the case the Governor would presume, until he had evidence to the contrary, that the court had sufficient legal reasons therefor[e], but having no other view of the case, but what is contained in the petition and proposed bill, he cannot approve the bill."[55]

An odd but undoubtedly necessary aspect of the restoring procedure was that a bill to restore a person to law was not created by regular legislative process. It was drafted by the petitioner or his attorney. When the Senate granted Josiah Sanborn's petition, it voted him "liberty to enter a certain action at the next Superior Court, with leave to bring in a bill accordingly."[56] Of course, when the bill was brought in, both houses again had to consider and vote on the issues that had been raised. The process was time-consuming. First, a joint committee had to be appointed for each petition submitted.[57] Then the members had to report to their respective houses and floor debate could follow.

If it was decided that the petition had merit, the parties were assigned a date at which to be heard by a joint committee. It was at this stage that one of the few procedural safeguards was imposed on the petitioner: notice to the opposing party. When the committee on the petition of Jeremiah Eames "reported in favour of a day of hearing," Eames was instructed to "cause that Colonel Edwards Bucknam be served with a copy of the petition and Order of the [General] Court thereon, also cause that a like copy and order be posted in some public place in the town of Northumberland six weeks prior to said day of hearing, that any person or persons may then appear and shew cause (if any they have) why the prayer thereof may not be granted."[58] A variation on this procedure was to order that the documents "be published three weeks successively" in a specified newspaper or be posted in some public place and also printed in a nearby newspaper.[59]

Remedies voted for petitioners seeking restoration to law varied somewhat. A new jury trial was most usual, but in some situations the legislature gave the petitioner the right "to have a re-hearing in said action, either in the courts of law, or before the referees once appointed for that purpose."[60] At other times the legislature limited the procedure, such as when it ordered a petition "be so far granted as that he have a new trial and no further" or that a petitioner be given a hearing but "the said judicial proceedings be not stayed by order of this Court."[61]

A clue as to how much legislative time was absorbed in weighing petitions in which a citizen asked to be restored to law may be gleaned by following the prayer of William Gregg. On 19 December 1794, the House of Representatives appointed a committee of three members to consider, jointly with some senators, Gregg's request "to be restored to his law in a certain action." Four days later the committee and then the house voted to hear the petitioner on the first of January if he served his opponent with a copy of the petition six days before that date. On the first day of the new year the petition was heard, debated, and a motion was made to dismiss it. Someone asked for a roll call, and the petition was not dismissed, 49 yeas and 60 nays. The next day the house resumed consideration and voted 63 yeas, 54 nays, "to grant the prayer of the said petition." That was the first reading. On 8 January the Senate sent the House word that it concurred, but on the condition "that a proviso be made in the bill, that the said

Gregg, on his part, shall consent to submit all matters in dispute betwixt him and the petitionee to the determination of referees." The Senate even stipulated how the referees were to be appointed. That afternoon the bill was read again in the house "and at 10 o'clock tomorrow assigned for a second time of reading." The following day another committee of three was appointed "to consider of a bill for restoring William Gregg, Esquire, to his law." On the 12th the act finally passed the House of Representatives, 71 to 36. At the next session of the General Court the act restoring Gregg to his law was amended and given the title "an act in addition to an act to restore William Gregg, Esquire, to his law in a certain action."[62]

So much time was taken by special bills that at a few legislative sessions some of them had to be deferred. The year before the Gregg petition was heard, the two houses "Voted that it is not expedient for the Legislature to attend to any more private business, or petitions, until the public business be compleated."[63] During the last decade of the eighteenth century, special legislation changing, restoring, or rearranging private litigations that had been adjudicated in the courts of law were not thought of as we in the twenty-first century would think of them. They were regarded not so much as legislation that invaded the constitutional terrain of the judiciary but as a process both practical and necessary. After all, special judicial acts could be, and frequently were, used to remove default judgments. The process seems especially necessary in that epoch when defaults were not uncommon in New Hampshire with its harsh winters, faulty transportation, and underdeveloped communication. In 1795, Peter Grant prayed "for leave to review an action at the Court of Common Pleas in Grafton county, which was defaulted without his knowledge."[64] Other special acts removed procedural roadblocks or vested courts with authority to take procedural steps to correct mistakes. In 1794, for example, Nathaniel Adams, the clerk of the Superior Court, petitioned the legislature, "praying that he might be authorized to bring forward a certain action on the docket of said court, which by mistake had been discontinued."[65]

Perhaps the most important function of special legislative adjudication was to serve as substitute for an equity jurisdiction. When the voters rejected the proposed amendment in Plumer's constitution to authorize the legislature to create some form of chancery jurisdiction, they deprived losing parties in litigations of potential remedies to correct some mistakes of procedure, some errors of law, and other matters of mistrial not corrected by the writ of error. Without equitable relief, many distressed parties would have had no remedy if they could not petition the legislature to restore them to a new trial or grant them other special relief. An example was recorded in 1794 when three "joint partners in trade" petitioned the General Court, "praying that in order, that they may meet with no legal impediment in the recovery of their bonafide debts, they may be authorized to prosecute and support any actions necessary for the recovery of the same." Three years before, two men petitioned, "representing that they were bound for the appearance of one David Dodge at the Superior Court . . . and that the said David hath absconded so that they could not surrender his body into Court agre[e]ably to the tenor of their recognizance whereby they have become liable to pay the Sum of One hundred pounds each and praying that they may not be prosecuted therefor[e] but the Same be remitted unto them." The House of Representatives remitted the penalties, requiring the petitioners to pay all costs.[66]

It appears from the records that most of the petitions for "new Law" seeking to compensate for New Hampshire's lack of equity jurisdiction were more in the nature of appeals than restorations to law. A revealing example was "An act to establish a certain judgment of the Quarter Sessions of the Peace for the County of Hillsborough in favor of John Smith against the selectmen of Peterborough." The bill corrected a clerk of court's mistake.[67] William Plumer was counsel in the petition of Mary Tufton Mason, again more of an appeal than a restoration. She was executrix of her husband's estate. Without her knowledge or the knowledge of her agent, Nathaniel Appleton Haven had been granted administration by the probate court, a ruling of which she did not learn until the time for appealing the decree had elapsed. She prayed the two houses of the legislature for "liberty . . . to appeal from said Decree to the next Superior Court . . . the foregoing accidental lapse of time notwithstanding." We may safely assume that the decree had been an innocent mistake and that her plea was meritorious, for Haven joined her petition. The legislature ordered the probate court to vacate the decree.[68]

That the General Court had to enact so much special legislation had given Plumer one of his strongest arguments why the Constitution of 1792 should have created an equity jurisdiction. Two years before the constitution was adopted, the House of Representatives had appointed a committee to consider easier and less expensive ways of hearing and determining petitions. The committee suggested empowering the common-law courts to adjudicate "petitions for being restored to law" and to grant "new trials in all cases which have been tried before them." Neither recommendation was adopted. There was great opposition to giving the courts power to overturn jury verdicts, which was the process favored by lawyers, instead of granting new jury trials *de novo* by restoring litigants to their law.[69] The same committee recommended that a second committee "be appointed to bring in a bill for establishing a court of chancery." Nothing came of that proposal, or of any others to create an equity jurisdiction. But in 1794, two years after adoption of Plumer's constitution, the General Court decided to give something to the judiciary. "Whereas," the preamble of a statute provided, "petitions are often preferred to the General Court praying for restoration to a course of law, which mode of relief is not only burdensome to the Legislature and to the State, but also extremely expensive to individuals who often live at a great distance from the place of holding said [General] court, for remedy whereof," the common-law courts were given, concurrent with the legislature, limited authority to grant new jury trials. The Superior Court was "vested with the power of hearing and deciding, and granting one review or new trial after judgment that hereafter may be rendered" by any New Hampshire court in eight categories of trials. Nothing was said concerning whether litigants, to whom the judges denied a new trial, could then petition to be restored legislatively to their law.[70]

Theoretical arguments justifying special acts and restorations to law were more often stated in political rather than legal terms. After the Constitution of 1784 divided the government into three separate branches, it became difficult to justify legislative supremacy as a constitutional principle, but it could be, and often was, defended on republican grounds. As the *New-Hampshire Gazette* explained, the elected, republican legislature should not leave questions "to the discretion of any other court," but should act "as the supreme Court over all others." The theory was probably best stated by the *New-Hampshire Patriot* in 1811 when the Superior Court refused to retry the cause of *Clark* v. *Chickering*, even though the plaintiff had been restored to law. "It remains to be seen whether the People in their Legislature is to make laws that are binding, or whether the caprice of one man or set of men is above all responsibility of the People," the *Patriot* argued, urging the legislature to slap down the uppity judiciary and assert its supremacy over the Superior Court. "The extent of the power of the Justices of the Superior Court is not defined in the Constitution: but because no particular power is given, shall it be presumed that their authority is supreme—above all responsibility?" the *Patriot* asked. "[W]e no longer deserve the name of a *republican government* if the will of one man or two men is to govern us in all cases."[71]

In contrast to republican-oriented arguments in support of the legislative authority to restore private litigants to their law, arguments against restoring turned on definitions of the judicial process and theories of the constitutional independence of the judiciary from legislative supervision. "[W]henever the General Court of this state, by an act or resolve, interfere in such matters, they are acting directly counter to the letter and spirit of the Constitution," SOLON argued, almost in answer to the *Patriot,* although writing two decades earlier. "And the judges would be fully justified by the Constitution . . . to pay no regard to such legislative Acts, Orders or Resolutions."[72]

The judges of New Hampshire would not take SOLON's advice for another quarter century. Looking back from that time, William Plumer summed up the process of restoring to law. The legislature, he reminded newspaper readers, "adjourned the courts of law, received petitions, heard the parties, considered the merits of suits, and not only ordered new trials, but passed laws revoking and making void judgments rendered by the highest judicial tribunal in the State."[73] It was a matter of developing legislatively created "judicial" rules safeguarding the rights of litigants as much as setting aside the doctrine of separation of powers. "Our liberties, our rights & property have become the sport of ignorant State legislators," Plumer complained in 1787, meaning that legislation was subject to popular opinion, prejudice, and clamor. "Sound policy requires that a period should be fixed beyond which litigation should not be permitted," he told Smith, reflecting on how restoring to law could protract litigation well beyond the unreasonable delays of the ordinary judicial process. Moreover, special acts hampered the development of precedential law by creating uncertainty and perhaps causing lawyers to put less effort into planning trial strategy, knowing that no matter what they did, it could be arbitrarily overturned in the legislature by private interest and public passion.[74]

Four

A Midnight Judge

"I still continue to dislike Congressional life," Jeremiah Smith wrote after he had been in the House of Representatives but a few months. He never came to like it. "This is a disagreeable life my friend," he told William Plumer more than four years later. Were it not that being in Philadelphia gave him the opportunity "of seeing & conversing with such men" as Oliver Ellsworth, John Jay, and Alexander Hamilton, "there would be nothing to induce one to live in this perpetual fire." "In short," he concluded, "I am sick of this life."[1]

Actually, Smith was sick of political life. He had always been fascinated by politics, and politics would continue to form a large part of his career, but he never enjoyed participating in it. It was not electioneering that bothered him, as candidates for public office in New Hampshire did not have to campaign. It was the politics of the legislative bodies in which he served that he found tiresome.[2] In extant letters to his friends, he would discuss personalities or doings at the Supreme Court, but not affairs in Congress. An exception was the debate on Jay's Treaty, and, even then, what caught his attention was not politics but law. President Washington did not honor the request by the House of Representatives for the treaty's documents and for the instructions that he had given to John Jay. "I forward you . . . the debates on the constitutional powers of the House," Smith told Plumer. That was what interested him: law, the legal right of Congress to be informed—the right being argued against the president's claim to executive privilege. "I take a greater interest in the politics of New Hampshire than those of the United States," he admitted and spent the remainder of his life proving it. He was interested even more in New Hampshire *judicial* politics. Every little aspect held his attention. "I have understood that the Superior Court did not sit at Dover—that Olcott did not attend," he wrote of a recent appointee to the Superior Court, whom he thought not equal to the office. "Pray what was the reason? It is a saying that experience keeps a dear school & that fools will learn no where else. . . . I am sure NH have had experience eno[ugh] of the imperfection of their judiciary to be willing to change it."[3]

"I wish for a few sincere friends & the means of living in a moderate stile & I shall be contented," Smith claimed when he resigned from Congress. "If the duties of an office could insure me this I should prefer it to the practice of the law." Smith had a split legal personality. He detested the practice of law but was absorbed by the study of law. Whenever he had been able to get away from sessions of the House of Representatives, he had attended the United States Supreme Court. "The supreme court are in session," he told Fisher Ames in 1796, "and I am, you know, fond of attending, to learn wisdom." Smith, his biographer said, "constantly attended" Supreme Court sessions and seems to have been obtaining more than wisdom. Surely a reason for going was the sheer pleasure he derived from just sitting in the courtroom and listening to an appellate tribunal. The United States Supreme Court was, in fact, the only appellate court he would ever know. The justices did have to go on circuit and preside at jury trials, but when in the capital all the court's terms were law terms, not trial terms, and just the fact that such an institution existed in American law must have been exhilarating to Smith. At the turn of the nineteenth century, an attorney who had to make a living at the law but did not want to practice either as an office lawyer or as a litigator had few alternatives. There were no opportunities to be house counsel for a corporation as the handful of corporations then in existence did not have counsel; there were no quasi-legislative, quasi-executive bureaus hiring attorneys, no law schools in which to teach, no judge advocate corps, and no agencies—such as the Federal Bureau of Investigation—recruiting young lawyers for a career in law enforcement. For an attorney who did not want to be a practitioner and also did not go into politics or become a writer, little opportunity to use his law training presented itself except to be a judge. Once Smith decided to leave Congress, he knew he had to be a judge, and the judgeship most congenial to his intellectual talents and interests would have been on an appellate court. But the only available court was the Supreme Court of the United States. New Hampshire had no appellate courts, only trial courts. If Smith were to become a judge, he would have to become a trial judge.[4]

After resigning from Congress and returning to New Hampshire, Smith continued to follow the Supreme Court. In 1802, when Plumer, who had been elected to the United States Senate, moved to Washington, Smith asked to be kept informed about what the court was doing. "I wish correct information as to the Business of the Sup Court . . . in the motion of the mandamus to Madison to issue commissions to some of Adams's justices," he wrote in January. "You have, I presume, seen the extraordinary proceedings of the Senate upon the application of Marbury & other justices of this territory [District of Columbia], appointed by the late [Adams] administration, & whose commissions the present [Jeffersonian] administration detained," Plumer answered. *Marbury* v. *Madison* became one of the most famous adjudications in American history, the suppositive authority for judicial review in constitutional law. Smith, Plumer, and most lawyers of the time were not interested in that aspect of the case but in the possibility that the hearing might cause serious damage to the judiciary. To them, *Marbury* was an episode in the political struggle over the Republican program to destroy, or at least curtail, the autonomy of the judiciary on both the federal and state levels.[5]

Marbury v. *Madison* was a case of original jurisdiction, and the Supreme Court had called the attorney general as a witness. After being sworn in, he declined to testify, and the justices gave him a day to think about the issue or, more precisely, as Plumer explained to Smith, not "to consider whether he would answer, but *what* answer he would make." Most people expected he would refuse to answer, "& that if the Court committed him for contempt, measures would be taken to get rid of them," meaning the justices. "Indeed," Plumer concluded, "it has been intimated in [congressional] debate, *that the judiciary feel too independent, & that their proceedings* are extraordinary." Smith was alarmed. "[W]hat you mention of the doings of the senate in relation to Marbury &c I did not expect," he wrote in reply. "What will the sup ct do *in the Premises*? There seems to be hostility brewing between the judiciary and the legislature. It is easy to see which will fall." Then, as was characteristic of him, Smith became facetious. "Why might not the business of the sup court be done by a joint Committee" of the two Houses of Congress, he asked, suggesting several senators and congressmen to be committee members. "We would save expense and their proceedings would be more easily comprehended by your Logans your [unclear] your Jacksons &c."[6]

We should not be surprised that Plumer and Smith did not understand the case of *Marbury* v. *Madison* in the way that the case has become known in American law as the cited precedent for judicial review. Even after Marshall published his decision in the matter, most contemporaries did not think he had said anything significant about judicial review, or any other legal doctrine for that matter.[7] What is worth noting is that Plumer and Smith were worried that President Jefferson could manipulate Attorney General Levi Lincoln's subpoena in the *Marbury* trial as an opportunity to attack the judiciary. There were two reasons why they thought so. First, they were New England Federalists and honestly believed that Virginia Republicans opposed "law" as New Englanders defined "law" and that Virginians thought of the federal judiciary not as separate and independent but just another political element of the national administration.[8] Second, both their definition of law as the knowledge of the legal profession and their expectation that law could become a barrier against republican excesses led them to think that judicial autonomy was fundamental to the survival of American constitutionalism. Urging a fellow Federalist to become a candidate for the Superior Court of Judicature, Plumer outlined his theory of the judiciary as a watch and ward over democracy. "At all times . . . we must place great reliance in the Judiciary," he insisted. "In addition to their administering justice according to law, . . . they will, if they do their duty, be a formidable check to the many wanton abuses that a Legislature dependent upon annual elections, & too often influenced by popular passions, may commit."[9]

There was a third, and personal, reason Plumer and Smith were angered by the national administration's offensive against the judiciary. Jeremiah Smith himself had been a victim of Jefferson's first attack. When Jeremiah Smith resigned from Congress, he did not leave office empty-handed. President John Adams appointed him United States district attorney for New Hampshire. In addition, he was soon rewarded for leaving Peterborough and settling permanently in Exeter by being named probate judge for the county of Rockingham. Opening a law office in Exeter, he had plenty of time for his studies of law, as neither the district attorneyship nor the probate office made many demands and did not interfere with his private practice.[10] In fact, he had the leisure to pursue his hopes of improving and reforming New Hampshire law by writing a treatise on probate, *An Essay on the Law of Descent and of Last Wills and Testaments,* which was not published in his lifetime but was frequently cited by New Hampshire lawyers who read one of the several copies that circulated in manuscript.[11]

Almost immediately upon arriving in Exeter, Smith was thought by neighbors and other contemporaries to be a very successful practitioner, but just as quickly he was discouraged, if not miserable. He particularly disliked the task every New Hampshire attorney had to perform in that era: going to court—though not to argue points of law to the court but arguing his client's cases before juries. It is likely that from his first months in Exeter, he wanted a judgeship but saw no prospect of getting one. There was only one federal judge for New Hampshire, and that office was filled by a man who, although a hydrophobic, might remain on the bench for a decade, possibility even two. The state courts unfortunately paid a salary far too little to support Smith's young, growing family. He saw no chance to obtain a judgeship and began to fear that, if he was ever to break free of law practice, he might have to become a sheriff or start a bank, when, in February 1801, his greatest ambition was realized. The United States Congress created a new federal court system, and President Adams appointed Smith the circuit judge for the district of New Hampshire.[12]

Smith owed his judgeship to the Judiciary Act of 1801. It had been drafted to replace the act of 1789 that a legal historian recently described as establishing "only a meager federal judiciary." The jurisdiction that the

1789 act conferred on the federal courts had been less than what the constitution authorized, and the structure of the system discouraged growth. The main trial court was not staffed by judges appointed to that court but by justices of the Supreme Court riding circuit out of the national capital and sitting with a district judge. In other words, a justice of the Supreme Court and the judge of the local district court presided over most of the federal jury trials.[13]

The deficiencies of the system became apparent during the earliest days of Washington's first administration when people wanting an effective federal judiciary, especially lawyers serving commercial clients, sought reform. Significant changes were not enacted, however, until the waning days of Adams's presidency. The Judiciary Act of 1801 created a set of new circuit courts presided over by judges who were exclusively circuit-court judges and who did not sit on any other courts but, by being a new intermediate jurisdiction, radically transformed the federal judiciary by relieving Supreme Court justices of time-consuming travel and the duty of presiding at jury trials. This new circuit tribunal, a trial court, was the court to which Smith was appointed.[14]

History has tended to view the Judiciary Act of 1801 as ill-timed legislation with both a worthy purpose of relieving Supreme Court justices of circuit riding and making the federal judicial system more efficient[15] and as less worthy of creating judgeships as sinecures for underachieving Federalists.[16] From the perspective of contemporaries, however, the act was seen as a blatant attempt by the better trained lawyers serving a business clientele to gain the upper hand—at both federal and state levels—over lawyers representing more rural, agricultural, "country" interests. The act vested the new circuit courts with original jurisdiction over private civil litigation arising under the federal constitution and the laws of the United States, power that, in the interest of protecting the authority of state courts, the Judiciary Act of 1789 had not conferred. It also increased federal jurisdiction by reducing the amount needed to bring diversity suits—litigation between residents of different states—from $2,000 to $1,400. Moreover, an alien or out-of-state defendant who had not been served with process or who had not appeared in state court could remove the action to the new circuit court even after judgment, if the judgment of the state court was for more than $400, and any defendant in a federal-question case commenced in a state court could remove prior to trial without regard to citizenship or jurisdictional amount.[17]

The Judiciary Act of 1801 greatly extended the jurisdiction of the federal courts. More important to contemporaries, it did so at the potential expense of state courts, especially by attracting to the federal courts all the diversity litigation involving land titles regardless of monetary amount. "So major a version," Kathryn Turner has observed, "may be interpreted as a result, in part, of the desire of certain interests within the Federalist party to enlarge the amount that could be tried in the federal courts apart from the state courts then dominated by interests considered hostile to their own." The idea is that the act "brought the federal judiciary very close to the average citizen," making it not only more accessible but more useful to the people. "[N]o system could have been better adapted to its time and purposes than that of 1801," Henry Adams believed. "The only solid argument brought against it was that it attained its object too completely, bringing Federal justice to every man's door, and removing every difficulty or objection to suing in Federal courts."[18]

That argument has been frequently made by historians and has the plausibility of familiarity. But from a more contemporary perspective, that is, from the jurisprudential dichotomy dividing legal theorists of the day, the important innovation for lawyers—especially lawyers with commercial clients—was that now they could shop for courts with professionally competent judges.[19] Forum shopping usually was for better remedies, higher damages, or less technical process, but after passage of the federal Judiciary Act of 1801, lawyers who otherwise might have filed actions in state tribunals would be going to the new circuit courts, not for procedural reasons, but to obtain professionally trained judges who would decide cases by the common-law methodology. Federalists and other supporters of the act of 1801 knew that the new federal judges appointed by President Adams would be law-trained lawyers. They did not know, of course, how much longer state courts would be dominated by lay judges who entrusted most questions of law (not just questions of fact) to the final determination of jurors, but after the act of 1801, it mattered much less. They now could turn to federal courts, presided over by learned, even scholarly, judges, lawyers of the caliber of John Marshall and Jeremiah Smith.

The act of 1801 created sixteen new circuit judges to preside over what were to be the major trial courts of the federal system. It was known that New Hampshire would receive at least one, and perhaps two, of the new judgeships. "It certainly is an object of great consequence who shall hold the office of Judge of this Court," Plumer wrote George Thatcher, the Massachusetts congressman representing neighboring York County. "Every man living in the District is more or less interested in the appointment, professional men perhaps more sensibly feel its importance." Saying that he was not a candidate, Plumer urged Thatcher to support Smith. It would, he explained, "afford me much satisfaction if our friend Jeremiah Smith Esq. should be appointed. His talents, integrity, knowledge & industry entitles him to that trust. You know the man & his communications, & nothing I can write will add to your knowledge. The appointment would give general satisfaction to all the friends of order & good government."[20]

New Hampshire's congressional delegation hoped the state might receive two judgeships. The congressmen asked that one go to Edward St. Loe Livermore and the other to Smith. Livermore's father was a U.S. senator, so it was politically likely that he would be the first choice. But Smith had powerful supporters. One was former Senator John Langdon, who one day would run against Smith for governor. He urged Samuel Dexter, Secretary of the Treasury, to recommend Smith to the president. Smith himself wrote to Fisher Ames for his support. Ames was at his Massachusetts home in Dedham. "I wrote for you to Dexter, requesting him to show it to Marshall, and to do all he can for you," Ames replied. Tongue in cheek, he pretended to be annoyed at Smith for failing to answer letters. "I heap coals of fire on your unworthy head. But I will not allow my rage to proceed any further; on the contrary, thank you for early asking my influence, which, as one of the Essex Junto, you know is great, in favor of your appointment. I did not write to Mr. Adams, which piece of neglect he will excuse, and I hope you will."[21]

It was particularly important that the New Hampshire appointment go to a competent lawyer of substance and political standing because the growing mental derangement of John Pickering was making it difficult for him to perform his duties as federal district judge. Smith himself had written to Treasury Secretary Dexter about Pickering's disabilities, warning that execution of federal laws, especially the revenue acts, was seriously jeopardized in New Hampshire. He also wrote to John Marshall about Pickering, offering himself as a judge who could alleviate the problem. Finally, he approached those of his former congressional colleagues still in office, telling them that he was available even before they passed the statute creating the judgeship.[22]

On 29 February 1801, President Adams appointed Smith one of the judges of the circuit comprising Rhode Island, Massachusetts, New Hampshire, and the district of Maine. John Marshall sent Smith his commission. "You will be pleased to inform the president, that I accept the appointment, and that it shall be my earnest endeavor to merit, as far as I am able, this distinguished mark of confidence," he wrote back. Smith always believed that it was Secretary of State Marshall who had been responsible for his appointment. "Allow me to add," he continued, "that I am not insensible, on this occasion, to the kindness and partiality of my friends. My obligations to you are particularly grateful, as affording to me evidence of the regard and esteem it has always been my wish to deserve and my pride to cultivate."[23]

"Mr. Smith has now reached the office to which, above all others, he aspired," his biographer concluded. It was also the office to which William Plumer aspired for him. Both men probably expected that this was the position in which Smith, unless promoted to the United States Supreme Court, would remain for life and where he would both make his reputation and work for the reform of New Hampshire law. It was not to be. Smith was one of the Federalist jurists who became known as "the midnight judges." He had been appointed in the waning days of Adams's administration, months after Thomas Jefferson had been elected president. When Adams had asked Richard Stockton to accept the judgeship for New Jersey, Stockton had declined. "It is true," he explained, "that a Judge cannot be removed from office by a new President but the law under which he is appointed may be repealed by a predominant party—and his life may be embittered by unmerited censure and slander." That was what happened—on both counts.

The Judiciary Act of 1801 was repealed, Smith and the other "midnight judges" were legislated out of office, and the censure of Republicans was turned on him for the remainder of his public career.[24]

The controversy over repeal of the "Midnight Judges Act" produced the first major political debate of the Jefferson administration. It was also the beginning of Jefferson's assault on the judiciary. "No one," Kent Newmyer has recently pointed out, "could attend to the anti-Court tirades of Republican orators and editors without at once sensing that American democracy was at fundamental odds with federal judicial power." In the House of Representatives Roger Griswold of Connecticut certainly thought so, even contending that the Republicans were scheming to convert the United States Constitution of checks and balances into a legislative constitution much like the British constitution or New Hampshire's first Constitution of 1776. They were, he warned, "determined at all events to destroy the independence of the judiciary & bring all the powers of government into the House of Representatives." If he was referring to his fellow congressman, William Giles of Virginia, Griswold was not exaggerating. "The term independence of judges or of the judiciary department was just not found in the constitution but was a mere inference from some of the specific powers," Giles asserted. Federal judges were not only subordinate to the congress that created them but should be kept in their place. Senator James Ross said that was just what repeal would mean. "Instead of an august and venerable tribunal, seated above the storms and oscillations of faction," Ross warned, "you have a transient, artificial body, without will or understanding of its own. . . . It will be the mimicry and mockery of justice. No more will you see in the administration of justice, those men, whose acquirements and talents have called them to eminence at the bar."[25]

In the Senate alone the debate extended from the 8th to the 19th of January 1802. And it was not conducted in isolation. It was extensively and widely published. In New Hampshire the coverage was unprecedented, greater even than the bitter clash over Jay's Treaty. Some newspapers printed all of the debates, devoting up to half their columns to senators and congressmen arguing whether the Judiciary Act of 1801 should be repealed and whether repeal would be constitutional. "[I]t would be agreed on all hands," Senator Jonathan Mason of Massachusetts claimed, "that this was one of the most important questions that ever came before a legislature." Several New Hampshire newspaper printers seemed to agree. "No subject since the late election of [the] President, has so much agitated the public mind as the contemplated repeal of the Judiciary law," the *Newhampshire Sentinel* told readers. "A letter from Washington, mentions that the holders of city lots seem much alarmed. Not a lot has been sold for many days and the prospect of a dependent Judiciary, and of Judges who are to be the creatures of power, prevented the sale of landed property. Many of the sober minded Virginians were endeavoring to sell their lands and slaves, and contemplate removing to New England." Today we cannot understand the humor. But in 1802, New Hampshire Federalists thought Virginians their cultural and political antithesis, ranking just above French Revolutionaries, as the lowest standard against which to compare the superior morality, work ethic, and social virtue of New Englanders. If, to save their property, Virginians would move to New England, then the Jeffersonians' attack on the judiciary was truly turning the world upside down.[26]

Before the debate most people in New Hampshire either had never considered the purpose of judicial independence or they did not think it an important constitutional principle. Whether or not the debate changed many minds, it certainly changed the way the judiciary was portrayed and discussed in the state. After 1802, judicial independence was argued differently than it had been in the 1790s. This change occurred even though the extreme Republican theory in 1802 was not much different from that of New Hampshire's. It was voiced on the national level by William Giles of Virginia, Thomas Jefferson's close ally in Congress, who believed law was not principles, doctrines, and immutable rights but politics, subject to the caprice of the majority. "It appears to me," Giles had written Jefferson when he was president-elect, "that the only check upon the Judiciary system as it is now organized and filled, is the removal of all its executive officers indiscriminately. The judges have been the most unblushing violators of constitutional restrictions, and their officers have been the humble echoes of their vicious schemes, to retain them in office would be to sanction the pollution of the very fountain of justice." Connecticut's Senator Uriah Tracy summed up on behalf of those thinking law more autonomous and immutable. Legislation modifying a judicial system did not always threaten the independence of judges, he admitted, "but if we can, by repealing a law, remove them [from office], they are in the worst state of dependence." So, he asked, "Will it be said, that although you cannot remove the judge from the office, yet you can remove his office from him?" The answer was yes, the *Newhampshire Sentinel* reluctantly concluded. "Not a doubt can be entertained that the Judiciary System will be overturned," it warned. "The Judges of the Federal Courts are not removable by the President; and this is the only method that can be adopted to displace them. Repeal the law, and they are dismissed of course."[27]

On some issues, the dichotomy dividing the two sides was so extreme, a reader could easily have concluded they were arguing about two different constitutions. Any judges, even those appointed temporarily, will claim their tenure is constitutionally protected, Senator Stevens Mason of Virginia asserted. Suppose they were told their terms had expired? "Would they not say . . . though the law that creates us is temporary, *we are in the Constitution?*" That may seem to be an extreme theory of judicial autonomy, he admitted, but it had been recently argued as law in *Marbury* v. *Madison.* Counsel had told the Supreme Court that Congress could create the judgeship but not limit the term of office. Judges might be created by congressional legislation, but once they were commissioned, the constitution made them judges for life. That contention struck Mason as ridiculous, but it was exactly what Tracy of Connecticut had argued a few days before. "[T]he judges of the inferior courts, as soon as ordained and established," he asserted, "are placed upon precisely the same grounds of independence with the judges of the supreme court. Congress may take their own time to ordain and establish; but the instant that is done the rights of independence attach to them." The two arguments were very much opposites of one another, but Congressman Giles, an expounder of the impermanency of legal rules, thought they could be reconciled by the supremacy of legislative discretion.

> It is contended on one side that the judiciary department is formed by the constitution itself. It is contended on the other side, that the constitution does no more than to declare that there shall be a judiciary department, and directs that it shall be formed by the other two departments under certain modifications. . . . The number of judges—the assignation of duties—the fixing compensations—the fixing the times when and places where the courts shall exercise their functions, &c. are left to the entire discretion of congress. The spirit, as well as the words of the constitution, are completely satisfied, provided one supreme court be established. Hence, when all these essential points in the organization and formation of courts is entrusted to the unlimited discretion of congress, it cannot be said that the courts are formed by the constitution.[28]

High Republicans disliked a great deal of the judicial law that Smith and Plumer were hoping to promulgate, but there was nothing that they disliked more than to hear talk of the judiciary not enforcing acts of Congress or of a state legislature on grounds of unconstitutionality. Judicial review was the extreme doctrine of legalists, the antithesis of republicanism. It was, therefore, rather risky for Senator Mason of Massachusetts to premise judicial independence on the possibility that the judges might, and quite likely would, exercise judicial review. Legislatures, he warned, were subject to "violent passions" and could react angrily if the courts were to say any statutes were unconstitutional. "Hence the necessity of placing the judges above the influence of these passions; and for these reasons the Constitution had put them out of the power of the legislature."[29] A few days earlier, Mason had explained what he meant: "Because the duties which they [judges] have to perform, call upon them to expound, not only the laws, but the constitution also; in which is involved the power of checking the legislature in case it should pass any laws in violation of the constitution. For this reason it was more important that the judges in this country should be placed beyond the controul of the legislature, than in other countries where no such power attaches to them."[30]

Congressman James Bayard of Delaware had a different slant on the same argument. The constitution, he insisted, intended courts to rule on the constitutionality of legislation. If so—that is, if the constitution expected the courts to protect the people from Congress—it would not have made the judiciary subordinate to the very body the courts were expected to keep in line. "Can any thing be more absurd than to admit, that the judges are a check upon the legislature, and yet contend that they exist at the will of the legislature?" he asked. "What check can there be when the power designed to be checked can annihilate the body which is to restrain it?"[31]

Today we agree with Mason, the Massachusetts senator, and with Bayard. What they say, after all, has been familiar law since the twentieth century, when the federal judiciary went beyond independence and usurped supremacy in American constitutional law. In 1803 the judiciary was still struggling for independence from the legislative branch and, to his contemporaries, Senator Mason of Virginia made more sense than he would for us when he warned of the possibility of too much judicial independence. "This independence of the Judiciary so much desired, will . . . soon become something like supremacy," he pointed out, not imagining he was foretelling a future that would have amazed him. "They will, indeed, form the main pillar of this goodly fabric, and they will soon become the only remaining pillar, and they will presently become so strong, as to crush and absorb all the others into their solid mass." After all the United States was supposed to be a republican government, and the supremacy of non-elected judges was quite unrepublican. "Though of opinion that each department ought to discharge its proper duties free from the fear of others," Mason claimed, "yet I have never believed that they ought to be independent of the nation itself. Much less have I believed it proper, or that our constitution authorizes our courts of justice to control the other departments of the government."[32]

New Hampshirites who read the debates on the act of 1810 learned much more about the principle of judicial entrenchment than they had in 1791–1792 when it remained more or less a hidden issue, not submitted to the voters when they adopted Plumer's constitution, and, therefore, not debated in public. Again, it was Virginia's Mason who explained the doctrine to Congress.

> With regard to the institution of the Supreme Court the words are imperative; while with regard to inferior tribunals they are discretionary. The first *shall*; the last *may* be established. . . . When, therefore, the constitution, using this language, says a supreme court *shall* be established, are we not justified in considering it as of constitutional creation; and, on the other hand, from the language applied to inferior courts, are we not equally justified in considering their establishment as dependent upon the legislature, who *may*, from time to time, ordain them, as the public good requires. . . . [A]mong the enumerated powers given to Congress, while there is no mention made of the supreme court, the power of establishing inferior courts is expressly given. Why this difference, but that the future supreme court was considered by the framers of the constitution as established by the constitution; while they consider the inferior courts as dependent upon the will of the legislature.[33]

Within a little more than a decade, Mason's words would be echoed in New Hampshire political arguments. If William Plumer read them, he learned again how serious his failure to entrench the Superior Court of Judicature into the New Hampshire constitution might become. Applying Mason's interpretation of the law to the constitutional situation of the New Hampshire courts, the difference was that in New Hampshire, because none of that state's courts were created by the constitution, none were constitutionally protected from legislation abolition. Plumer had anticipated that an occasion might arise when a political party would be tempted to replace the sitting state judges with new appointees by abolishing the state's judiciary. That was why, in 1791–1792, he sought to entrench, if not all the courts, the highest court at least. When his amendment was rejected by the constitutional convention, all New Hampshire courts—not just the inferior courts, but the Superior Court as well—were exposed to the same legislative elimination as the U. S. Circuit Court on which Jeremiah Smith sat in 1802.

Many answers were offered to Senator Mason's legal doctrine. One of the most thoughtful, published in New Hampshire, was written by HAMPDEN. His argument is memorable in part because everything he said was so contrary to the Jeffersonian-Republican constitutional interpretation that it is possible he was trying to irritate the other side of the debate.

> That all the courts except the supreme, are created by the legislature, I admit. But what creates the legislature; and what gives it power to create courts? Verily the constitution. But the constitution does not make courts, so created, subject to the legislature, which is only made the instrument of creating and establishing such courts. . . . The constitution gives the legislature power to make grants of land, or other property, and appropriate of money. But when it has granted or sold a tract of land to an individual, or to companies, it cannot vacate the grant: —nor can it repeal a law which appropriates money. If this construction should be put upon the constitution, contracts would be broken at pleasure, and society and government would soon be at an end.[34]

Supporters of the repealing act of 1802, in general, interpreted the constitution strictly. Like Virginia's Senator Mason, they insisted on finding articles, sections, or words that specifically conferred independence on the judiciary, or, they contended, the principle of judicial independence could not be a constitutional imperative. Opponents of the act, more likely to be loose constructionists, said that there were at least two specific constitutional provisions securing judges from congressional abolition. One was the mandate that judicial salaries shall not be diminished during a judge's term of office. "This provision is directly levelled at the power of the legislature," Congressman Bayard asserted. "They alone could reduce the salary. Could this provision have any other design than to place the judge out of the power of Congress?" He thought the provision made proponents of repeal look ridiculous. "You cannot take the compensation from the judge, but you may separate the judge from the compensation." That construction was far too loose for Jeffersonians repealing the act of 1801. "We are so enamoured with the salutary and practicable independence of the English judiciary system, that in infusing its principle into our constitution, we have stampt it with the proverbial folly of the Medes and Persians!" Congressman Giles explained. "If this principle had been introduced into the constitution in express words it would have formed an unfortunate contrast to all other parts of the instrument; yet gentlemen make no difficulty in introducing that principle by construction, which would have appeared stupid and absurd if written in express words in the body of the instrument."[35]

The second constitutional provision that, along with the "salary" clause, opponents of the act of 1802 claimed secured judicial immunity from legislative abolition was the clause granting judges tenure during "good behavior." That provision was in both the U. S. and the New Hampshire constitutions and would be frequently cited when the General Court debated abolishing the state's highest court in 1813 and 1816. Senator William Hill Wells of Delaware, a Federalist, enunciated the theme that would become the favorite argument of New Hampshire Republicans in 1813. "The constitution provided, that the judges of both the inferior and superior courts shall hold their offices during good behavior; but may be removed on impeachment, by the House of Representatives and conviction by two thirds of the Senate," he pointed out. "What words can go stronger to any dependence of that department upon the pleasure of any other?" he asked. Put another way, because Jeremiah Smith and his fellow circuit judges had tenure during good behavior, it would not matter if repeal of the Judiciary Act of 1801 was constitutional legislation; constitutional or unconstitutional, the repeal would not affect their tenure. If the act of 1801 could be repealed constitutionally and the judges removed, Wells warned, judicial independence was destroyed. "This however is a new way of getting at the judge without affecting his independence. We will not touch the judge but we will slip the office from under him."[36]

Wells postulated one constitutional result of repeal. If the Judiciary Act of 1801 was repealed and the circuit courts abolished, the "good behavior" provision preserved the tenure of the circuit judges. Wells's fellow Federalists suggested three alternatives to his rule. The first was that the "good behavior" provision prevented a legislature from constitutionally abolishing any court once it had been created and staffed with judges. The second, a more narrow contention, held that a legislature could abolish any court it had created, but abolition would not destroy the tenure of the sitting judges (which was Wells's argument) and also not affect their right to compensation. And third, although a legislature could eliminate a court and take the office from the judge, it had to continue paying him for the duration of his term.[37]

Some lawyers argued for the first alternative. One was Richard Bassett, former governor of Delaware, one of the Federalists along with Jeremiah

Smith who had been appointed a circuit judge. Congress, he contended, might create judicial offices, but it was the constitution that created judicial tenure. "As soon as congress have executed their power of *establishing the* court, and the *officer* is appointed," he claimed, "the provision in the constitution respecti[ng] his *continuance* attaches upon the law. It is identified with it, and secures the office to the possessor by its own immutability." It was an extreme contention, but one aspect of it—that the judge had a property in the office—was plausible enough in the jurisprudence of that day to have worried Thomas Jefferson. When the judiciary bill of 1801 was pending in Congress, he had written to James Madison that he was more apprehensive about its passage than any other action being contemplated by the out-going Adams administration, "because appointments in the nature of freehold render it difficult to undo what is done." That was why Mason of Virginia objected to senators on the other side of the debate using the words "his office" when speaking of a judge. "[I]t is not *his office*; but the office of the people," Mason insisted. "[I]t is complained of," Gouverneur Morris of New York answered, "that in speaking of the office, we say it is *his* office. Undoubtedly the institution is for the benefit of the people. But the question remains how will it be rendered most beneficial? Is it by making the judges independent, by making it *his* office, or is it by placing him in a state of abject dependence so that the office shall be his today and belong to another to-morrow?"[38]

The way to dispose of the "good behavior" argument, Senator Brackenridge of Kentucky suggested, was not as property but by the canons of constitutional construction. "[B]ecause the constitution declares that a judge shall hold his *office* during *good behaviour,* can it be tortured to mean, that he shall hold his office after it is abolished?" he asked. "Can it mean, that his tenure should be limited by behaving well in an office, which did not exist?" That was only one interpretation of the "good behavior" provision, Congressman Bayard answered. "Has the constitution said, that he shall hold the office during good behavior, unless Congress shall deem it expedient to abolish the office? If this limitation has been omitted, what authority have we to make it a part of the constitution?" he wondered, as if to show that both sides could play the game of strict construction.[39]

The outcome was a foregone conclusion. The Republicans had won the election; they controlled both houses of Congress and were not about to leave sixteen Federalists in judicial office when they could be removed so easily. The Judiciary Act of 1801 was repealed and with it Jeremiah Smith's judgeship.

The debates over repeal of the Judiciary Act of 1801 had little impact aside from educating Americans about the doctrine of judicial independence. They were valuable for doing that, at least in New Hampshire, but they had no effect on Congress. Both sides were closed minded; neither could have persuaded the other. But if the two sides would not hear each other for political reasons, they also sometimes could not hear each other because of the jurisprudential dichotomy dividing them. Quite often they were speaking from opposite principles: the Federalists from a law that was autonomous and occasionally immutable, the Republicans from a law that was mutable, political, and often fashioned by legislative direction. The member of Congress who made the most extreme use of immutable doctrine seems to have been Senator Morris of New York when he asserted that Congress was estopped *by law* from repealing the Judiciary Act of 1801. He directly took on the principle of legislative supremacy and challenged its validity by postulating an autonomous immutable, nonpolitical legality. "When the legislature have created, by law, a political existence, can they, by repealing the law, dissolve the corporation they had made?" he asked and answered by raising four high Hamiltonian or receptionist questions that Jeffersonian legal theorists would have answered differently than he did. "You say you can undo whatever your predecessors have done. Your predecessors have borrowed money at high interest; can you now reduce the interest? You have funded the national debt; have you now a right to abolish that debt? Under a pressure of necessity, you have given an usurious consideration of eight per cent. to obtain money; can you now, (because it is onerous) annihilate that contract? When, by your laws, you have given to any individual the right to make a road or a bridge, and take a toll; can you by a subsequent law, take it away?" A lawyer of the school of Jeremiah Smith and most other members of the Rockingham County bar such as Daniel Webster, John Pickering, and Jeremiah Mason would have answered "no" to all these questions. And, of course, Senator Morris answered no to all of them. "No; when you make a compact, you are bound by it," he insisted. "When you make a promise, you must perform it. Establish the contrary doctrine, and mark what follows. The whim of the moment, becomes the law of the land." Lawyers who thought of and defined "law" differently than did Morris, lawyers such as Thomas Jefferson, Samuel Livermore, and William Giles, would have scoffed at that argument. The whim of the moment, they might have said, if it is the whim of the legislature duly enacted into legislation, should be the law of the land.[40]

That was just what bothered Daniel Webster. Congress's repeal of the Judiciary Act could mean that every court not constitutionally entrenched now existed at the whim of some legislature. "Federalists looked on, while this act of desperate vengeance was executed, with awful presentments of the consequences," he said in his *Appeal to the Old Whigs* of New Hampshire. "They foresaw, that this repeal, while it annihilated one of the most esteemed provisions of the Constitution, would leave alive a spirit that would triumph over the remnant. . . . The man who mentions it seriously is ridiculed."[41]

William Plumer could take the ridicule. In a pamphlet he stuck out his neck, charging that Congress had violated the constitution by removing "Judges from office, against whom no charge of misbehavior was ever suggested, notwithstanding the Constitution expressly declared 'they shall hold their office *during good behavior.'"* He went further. Jefferson himself, Plumer charged, had made a direct attack on judicial independence. The repeal act had been passed, he said, "to affect the independency & endanger the security of the judiciary." Even as late as 1804, not long before Plumer switched to the Republican Party, he was saying that Jefferson was not only capable of deliberately destroying judicial independence—he intended on doing so. "Men of discernment at that time, considered the measure as a fatal stroke at the constitutional authorities & liberties of the country; but others . . . considered the justices of the Supreme Court perfectly secure," he charged. "Let such men remember that the destruction of the Inferior Courts in 1802 was but a part of a ruinous system which is to terminate in the removal of other judges both of the inferior and supreme Courts."[42]

A measure of how strongly some New Hampshire Federalists reacted to the repeal of the Midnight Judges Act is the election sermon of 1802. One election sermon was delivered each year. The audience was the officials of all branches of the state government: the governor, councillors, senators, representatives, militia officers, and judges. The sermons were supposed to be instructional and inspirational, not political and certainly not partisan. In 1802, however, the preacher, a Congregational minister from Sandbornton, departed from tradition with a long condemnation of the legislation repealing the Judiciary Act of 1801. The repeal, he boldly asserted, was part of a political plot to render the national judiciary "wholly dependent" on the pleasure of the president and Congress. "Every attempt," he concluded, "whether directly or indirectly, to destroy the independence of the Judiciary, is a fatal stab at the very vitals of the Constitution, and in its tendency and consequences subversive of an impartial administration of justice, the importance of which every one will readily perceive, when he considers that property, personal liberty, and even life itself, in many cases, depend upon the decision of the judiciary."[43]

New Hampshire Republicans, by contrast, simply did not think the principle of judicial independence important. The repeal of the Judiciary Act of 1801, they seemed to say, was purely a matter of politics, not of constitutional law. "[I]n case any falling administration shall in future," a pamphleteer wrote, "attempt to prop itself against the rising administration by the creation of new courts, and by an unseasonable and indecorously hasty appointment of judges, it is to be hoped that the above removal may be made a precedent during all generations." If any individual should be faulted, that person was Jeremiah Smith. He had accepted a midnight appointment and had received a princely salary for supposedly doing no work. He had, the public was reminded many times, "received from the *unnecessary and useless office* of judge of the late circuit court of the United States *two thousand dollars per annum.*" New Hampshirites could not contemplate anyone being paid so much. No official in the state government got anywhere near that amount of money. The chief justice of the state, for example, did not make half that sum.[44]

Jeremiah Smith's reaction was surprisingly muted, especially as he would later say "it was the only office that he ever greatly desired." Believing it would be his life-long employment, he had devoted three months to legal study. "Though always a hard student," his biographer claimed, "he now regarded his former attainments as of no account, and afterwards looked back on those three months as the beginning of his legal education."[45]

Perhaps Smith's self-instruction had led him to a deeper understanding of substantive law and legal theory, and he might have been a better judge for it, but his new learning did not prevent him from making a strikingly strange legalism when answering an admonition from Samuel Dexter. After hearing that Smith might be appointed chief justice of New Hampshire, the former secretary of war and the treasury had written to him that he must resign from the circuit court before accepting the chief justiceship. Smith expected that he would not be able to accept the appointment as chief justice because the pay was far too low, but he had no intention of resigning, even though the circuit court had been abolished.

> I certainly believe that I shall continue a circuit judge *de jure,* and it is equally certain that I shall cease to be a judge *de facto.* The office of supreme judge in this state, by our state constitution, is incompatible with the holding of a living office under the United States. But as I am to receive no salary, and am in no immediate expectation of a pension from the United States, I do not conceive that it is incompatible with my titular office of circuit judge, according to the spirit of our constitution. . . . In the constitution of the United States, I find nothing which renders the two offices incompatible. If I viewed it in this light, I should decline, at all events. I conceive that there is still a faint glimmering ray of hope, that the circuit judges will be restored. I am well assured (in confidence) that measures will be taken to try the validity of the repealing act. I do not conceive that accepting an office in the state incompatible with that of circuit judge, according to the state constitution, would be evidence that I consider the office as extinct, in consequence of the repealing law. It would only be evidence that I consider its duties and emoluments as suspended, and chose to make myself useful during the suspension.[46]

It defies belief that Smith thought there was any chance of being reinstated on the federal court, but possibly he did. William Tilghman seemed to hope so. President Adams had appointed him chief judge of the third circuit, and, along with Smith, he had been legislated out of that office. He wrote to Smith suggesting that all the judges who had been removed should meet to discuss what could be done to regain their offices. "Believing as we do, that the repealing law is a violation of the constitution," he told Smith, "we feel ourselves impelled by sacred obligations, to take legal measures for disputing its validity." Smith replied that "some steps ought to be taken to obtain a constitutional decision on the late act of congress."[47] He apparently was thinking of a lawsuit, testing the constitutionality of the repeal. That would have put the United States Supreme Court in a very un-comfortable position, a consideration that may explain why the other mid-night judges decided not to sue.[48] The only action that asked the United States Supreme Court to rule on the validity of the Judiciary Act of 1802 did not involve a midnight judge as a party and, therefore, did not raise the is-sues of judicial tenure and independence.[49] In New Hampshire there seem to have been expectations that Smith would, at least, join other midnight judges to sue for their salaries. When a federal case was reported at Hartford that challenged the validity of the repealing statute, the *Newhampshire Sen-tinel* told its readers that the issue of judicial independence—at least for the federal judiciary—would be decided. "Nothing so interesting to the people of the United States has occurred since the existence of our government," the printer editorialized. "If bro't before the court, the question must be de-termined, whether one *distinct, independent* branch of our constitution has not been madly sacrificed at the shrine of Democracy."[50]

William Plumer thought that Smith and his midnight colleagues should have sued. Reflecting on the question two years later, he concluded: "When the Judges of the Circuit Court were removed by the repeal of the law of 1802, then was the time for the Judges of the Supreme Court, to have taken their stand against the encroachments of Congress & of the Executive. That Court ought to have declared the repealing law unconstitutional—they ought to have refused to have held Circuit Courts— & the Judges of the Circuits ought to have continued to have held their Courts the repeal notwithstanding."[51]

The midnight judges decided not to file a lawsuit. Instead they submitted to Congress a memorial, in which Smith joined. "That judges should not be deprived of their offices or compensations without misbehaviour, appears to the undersigned, to be among the first and best established principles in the American constitutions," they told the legislators, the majority of whom they knew believed otherwise. They asserted that they had been "vested" in their judgeships and, therefore, were entitled to the compensation that went with the offices, "notwithstanding any modification of the judicial depart-ment, which, in the opinion of Congress, public convenience, may recom-mend." The petition was obviously a compromise; even so, it is politically puzzling why the former judges pursued it. Challenging a statute ostensibly to defend judicial independence, they went not to the courts but to the legis-lature, the authority, against which, in the United States at least, the doctrine of judicial independence was supposed to defend.[52]

"Your memorial, & that of ten other of the late Circuit judges was in-stantly rejected in the House, 61 to 37," Plumer wrote Smith from Wash-ington. He expected the senate committee to which the memorials had been referred would "make an able report, which will be eventually re-jected."[53] Jeremiah Smith was deeply affected by the loss of his circuit judeship. When Smith was an old man, his biographer recalled, "he looked back on no part of his public life with so much pleasure, though it was a pleasure accompanied always by the feeling, that in losing the office he had been thrown out of the place best fitted for his improvement, distinction, and usefulness."[54]

Although he knew that there was no chance he would be restored to the federal bench, Smith apparently never resigned. New Hampshire Republicans were amused. "The office being vacated by the repeal of the federal judiciary law, he again descended to the bar," *People's Advocate* wrote of Smith in 1816, "but he still claims his salary as a judge, and were federalism restored to power he might obtain the smug sum of *seventy-five thousand dollars* as the salary of an office which has not existed for the last fifteen years!" Poor Smith, he received neither the judgeship nor the money, and the laugh was on him.[55]

Five

A Hydrophobic Judge

"The affair of the Circuit judges turned out as I expected," Jeremiah Smith told William Plumer. Plumer had also known how it would turn out and thought repeal of the Judiciary Act of 1801 only the first step in the president's campaign to destroy whatever independence American judiciaries possessed. "The removal of the Judges, & the destruction of the independence of the judicial department," he lamented, "has been an object on which Mr. Jefferson has long been resolved, at least ever since he has been in office."[1] Actually, Jefferson had been planning his attack on the judiciary even before he took office. He had ample reasons, he believed, especially after passage of the act of 1801 and the appointment to the newly created circuit courts of professional, common-law oriented judges, all of whom were Federalists. "On their part, they have retired into the judiciary as a strong hold," Jefferson wrote to John Dickinson shortly after his election. "There the remains of federalism are to be preserved and fed from the treasury, and from that battery all the works of republicanism are to be beaten down and erased. By a fraudulent use of the constitution, which has made judges irremovable, they have multiplied useless judges merely to strengthen their phalanx."[2]

After he had joined the United States Senate and met Jefferson, Plumer became even more convinced that the Republicans were out to thwart the judiciary. The president told him that the federal constitution should be amended so that judges could be addressed from office, as in New Hampshire. "This business of *amending* the constitution is found to be a tedious process," Jefferson complained. "[T]he good work of *reform* cannot be delayed." Regrettable as the fact was to the president, if he wished to remove judges, especially Supreme Court justices, they could not be legislated from office, the process by which the midnight judges had been removed by repealing the statute that had created the court and thus abolishing both the court and the judgeships. Rather, the only constitutional process for dismissing a United States Supreme Court justice or a circuit judge whose office had not been eliminated by statutory repeal was impeachment. It was cumbersome, but there was no other choice. "The president & his Cabinet agree that impeachment conviction & removal from office is necessary," Plumer recorded. "A triumphant majority in each House are devoted to their views & will carry them into effect." Believing that he knew Jefferson's program, Plumer was not surprised when the Republicans struck their second blow against the judiciary. What did surprise him was the target. It was not a Supreme Court justice, as he had expected, but the federal district judge from New Hampshire. Having removed Jeremiah Smith from office, the Jeffersonians next went against another of Plumer's personal friends.[3]

There may have been no resident of New Hampshire whom Plumer admired more than John Pickering, considered by many people to be Rockingham County's most outstanding citizen. "No lawyer in the state advocated so many causes as he did, or received so small a compensation," Plumer wrote of Pickering many years after the events discussed here. "To avarice and economy he was a stranger, and with all his professional business acquired little more property than he expended to support his family." As soon as Pickering had become an attorney "he promptly assisted the poor, & those from whom he never expected any other reward than thanks. . . . He is a man of strict integrity, unblemished honor & of great humanity," Plumer had noted while still a law student, perhaps indicating the type of lawyer he hoped to emulate once he was admitted.[4] "He has a retentive memory, & possesses a vast fund of humour & pleasantry. His company is much sought for, & . . . he does more business, particularly as an Advocate, than any other in the State; but obtains much less money from his practise than some little contemptible pettifoggers." It was an admiring appraisal, completely the reverse of what the Republicans would present to the nation on impeaching Pickering. "His conduct was so fair and honorable that the tongue of slander seldom reproached him," Plumer wrote, describing Pickering before his mental illness. "His temper was placid, his disposition benevolent, his manners gentle, and his habits social."[5]

Pickering was probably the most popular lawyer in the state. Although Josiah Bartlett was elected president by the General Court in 1790 when no candidate had a majority of the popular votes, Pickering had received a substantially higher plurality from the people.[6] His public service was distinguished. As noted, he was the chief author of the Constitution of 1784, so much so that Jeremiah Smith concluded that he regarded the document as "a favourite Child of his own begetting," which, Smith said, explained why Pickering had taken the lead to oppose some of Plumer's reforms at the constitutional convention of 1792.[7]

He might have been much better known outside New Hampshire but for his fear of crossing water. He was elected to the Continental Congress, the Annapolis convention, and the federal constitutional convention, but his phobia kept him at home.[8] His only national service was as federal district judge for New Hampshire, an office local in reputation, in function, and in influence.

The United States District Court for New Hampshire had a remarkably sparse docket during its first decade of operation. At the July 1790 term held in Exeter, for example, no cases were heard, leading a Portsmouth newspaper to remark, "Happy State indeed, where Courts are rendered unnecessary by the virtue and patriotism of its inhabitants." It was also happy for Pickering as it meant he encountered few litigations during his first five years as a federal judge. In fact, relieved of riding circuits and crossing rivers, he did quite well. But as the docket of the court began to grow, so did Pickering's "nervous complaints," and, Plumer explained, "his rational facilities were impaired, and such a degree of mental derangement followed, as rendered him incapable of transacting any business which required the exercise of reason and judgment." By the time Thomas Jefferson became president, John Pickering was also an alcoholic.[9]

It is remarkable, but Pickering's problem was not unique. John Sullivan, Pickering's predecessor, was appointed district judge in 1789. Almost immediately his "health began to decline into premature senility." The senility may have triggered alcoholism, for, by 1792, he had reached such a state of drunkenness and mental deterioration that, after May of that year, he was no longer capable of presiding at court. In 1794 Sullivan "went mad." Asked to do something about the problem, President Washington is reported to have said "there is no man in the country he would not sooner remove than General Sullivan." The only constitutional means was impeachment, but that was not available, people thought, because insanity was not an impeachable offense. Temporary legislation provided the solution. Congress passed a law transferring the jurisdiction of the court from Sullivan to a judge appointed by the circuit court for the New Hampshire district, "until the next session of Congress, or until a new district judge be appointed in that district, and no longer." In less than nine months, Sullivan was dead.[10]

When Pickering reached the final stages of mental incapacity, there was no need for special legislation. The Judiciary Act of 1801 had been recently passed and was already in operation. It authorized the newly created judges for the New England circuit to appoint one of their own number to take the place of an incapacitated district judge. On 23 April the three circuit judges, holding court in Portsmouth, appointed Jeremiah Smith to "perform the duties of the said district Judge during the period the inability of the said district Judge shall continue." Smith successfully assumed Pickering's duties, although there was one slightly embarrassing incident that demonstrated how much Pickering needed relief. Unlike Sullivan, who had lived in Durham, Pickering was a Portsmouth resident who could easily get to court by simply walking there. One day, when Smith was presiding at a jury trial, Pickering came in, took a seat on the bench, and assumed direction of the proceedings. When counsel had finished offering evidence, the confused judge started to charge the jury, although he did not know what the case was about. "He was, however, soon perplexed, and being unable to proceed with his charge, uttered a short prayer and retired." Smith then took up the charge and "went on, as if nothing had taken place."[11]

Once the Judiciary Act of 1801 was repealed, Smith held his last session either as circuit judge or as substitute district judge. Whether they had realized it or not, the Republicans had, by repealing the law, forced John Pickering back on the bench, for he was now the only judge who could lawfully sit in New Hampshire's federal district court. By that time, the summer of 1802, he was completely deranged, and by October it was evident that he had lost all control. On the fifteenth of that month, the Republican surveyor of customs for Portsmouth seized *Eliza,* a brig belonging to a prominent Federalist, Eliphalet Ladd, for being unladed contrary to law. When the matter came to trial, Pickering entered the courtroom thoroughly intoxicated. Edward St. Loe Livermore, Ladd's attorney, obtained a postponement, but the next day Pickering was even more inebriated. Over protests— and without listening to the testimony—the judge ordered the case dismissed, returning *Eliza* to Ladd. The district attorney, John Samuel Sherburne, protested that the ruling would injure the national revenue. "Damn the revenue," Pickering shouted; "I get but a thousand of it," he said, referring to his annual salary. Sherburne threatened to appeal, but Pickering did not care. "Yes, appeal," he announced, "and let old Wig try it, but by God he shan't alter the decree, for I will be alongside of him." Old Wig was Justice William Cushing of the Supreme Court with whom Pickering sat to form the circuit court, the original federal circuit court now restored after the midnight judges' court had been abolished.[12]

Pickering's courtroom had been packed with spectators who came to watch the fun of an intoxicated, insane judge browbeating customs officials, court officers, and the federal prosecutor, all of whom were Republican officeholders, with curses. The United States district attorney, John Samuel Sherburne, at whom Pickering shouted, claimed he was humiliated. When the judge ruled for Ladd, the claimant, Sherburne objected that the court had not heard any of the government's witnesses. Pickering jeered, "You may bring forty thousand & they will not alter the decree."[13] Sherburne immediately collected depositions and wrote a detailed account describing Pickering's antics on the bench. He sent the documents to the administration in Washington, in effect an indictment of the federal judge, to be used to remove him from office.

There was no need to persuade President Jefferson. Sherburne's accounts provided him a far better opportunity than surely he had ever expected to obtain for beginning his program of removing Federalist judges from the bench. Instead of attacking through the political front as he had against the act of 1801, he could now proceed, as Eleanore Bushnell suggests, "under dignified constitutional process," against a target ideally suited for prosecution, "a grossly defective jurist for whom no one would make a plea of competence, who was no longer qualified to be on the bench, whether he belonged to the Federalist or to the Republican party." Lynn Turner had less kind thoughts of Jefferson's motivations. "The whole machinery of the federal government," he contended, "was brought to bear with crushing force upon an unfortunate old man whom the administration wished to remove from office, partly in order to reward unscrupulous party hacks in Portsmouth, but chiefly to establish a precedent which would serve in subsequent attacks upon the members of the Supreme Court." Turner may have been too harsh on Jefferson but only because he did not ask whether the president had any choice except to remove Pickering from the bench.[14]

Plumer had just arrived in Washington, newly elected to the Senate, when Sherburne's papers were received. At the Treasury Department, where he went to pay his respects to the secretary, Albert Gallatin, he was told of the *Eliza* trial. Gallatin warned him that severe measures would be taken unless Pickering could be persuaded to resign. Plumer should have followed through and written the Federalist leaders in New Hampshire that, for his own sake, the judge had to resign. Twenty-five years later he would say in his autobiography that it would have been better to have done so. In 1802, however, he urged his friends in Portsmouth to stop all talk of resignation. It is possible he told or hinted to the secretary of the treasury that was what he would do, for Gallatin did not wait to see if Pickering would resign before he started the process of impeachment. Perhaps he never intended to, or, more likely, Jefferson insisted on using Pickering to create a precedent for impeaching other judges. As soon as all of Sherburne's depositions were received, the president sent them to the House of Representatives. The "matter of complaint against John Pickering," he explained, "is not within the executive cognizance." It was, rather, the lower house "to whom the Constitution has confided a power of instituting proceedings of redress if they shall be of opinion that the case calls for them." He was saying that he wanted the house to remove the judge by using its authority to impeach. The congressmen understood his intentions.[15]

When Plumer first wrote to New Hampshire, urging that Pickering not resign, his friends did not know what was occurring. Only Sherburne and his associates knew. Referring to what he called "the attack which appears by the last papers to have been made on Judge Pickering," Jeremiah Smith complained of being in the dark. "We are not informed from whence the complaints came & *what* it is. The newspapers only mention that the President communicated the complaints as to his incapacity. Will he be turned out? Or will the duties be assigned to another Person?" Plumer was unable to enlighten anyone. "[T]he Secretary of the Treasury made a communication which was sent to the house of representatives stating that Judge Pickering was incapable of executing the office he now holds," he wrote James

Sheafe, who had preceded him as senator from New Hampshire. "I tho[ugh]t it would, with the accompanying documents be printed: but the Clerk, yesterday told me there was no order for it, but that it was referred to a select committee." The most he could learn was that "the [district] attorney, marshall & clerk of your district has certified that the judge is incapable, & that his incapacity is the effect of inebriation." It apparently did not occur to Plumer that the case was being kept under cover, because Sherburne had collected evidence only of Pickering's drinking, with no mention of mental illness.[16] Undoubtedly under instructions from Jefferson, Gallatin also emphasized only the alcohol problem, ignoring mental competency.

Richard E. Ellis has written that Plumer had three reasons for not urging Pickering to resign. First, "he shared the High Federalists' belief that the administration was plotting to overturn the Constitution. He believed they had already started by repealing the Judiciary Act of 1801, and to allow them to force a judge to give up his office would weaken the independence of the judiciary still further." Pickering was the perfect judge with whom to start. There was no doubt he should not be in office. Once he was convicted, the Republicans could go after the Supreme Court justices with more likelihood of success.[17]

Second, Plumer was concerned that "if Pickering resigned, his successor would be District Attorney John Samuel Sherburne, who was not only a Republican but also Plumer's personal enemy." Ellis is right that Plumer believed Sherburne would succeed Pickering. "You well know that his successor will be a man whom we cannot approve," he told the judge's brother-in-law. "You can be at no loss to determine who is the principal agent," he wrote a client, "& what is the strong motive that propels him to act." He became even more upset when told that the evidence Sherburne had collected against Pickering "conveys in strong terms the idea of his being a very *unwilling witness* against an intimate friend." Knowing how willing Sherburne was to climb to the bench over the back of his mentally ill mentor, Plumer was struck by Sherburne's hypocrisy, but he was not surprised by it.[18]

If asked whether he was saying Sherburne was being devious, even dishonest, Plumer would have replied that, for Sherburne, such behavior was nothing new. "He was devoid of moral principle, and restrained by nothing but the fear of *shame*," he wrote twenty-four years later. "He did not live quietly with his wife, and to his children he was a tyrant. He was as eccentric as he was unprincipled, and . . . his hand was against every man. He had no friends, and had no friendship for any man, not even for his children." Although Sherburne had a successful law practice, Plumer would not even say he was a good lawyer. "Tho[ugh] possessed of considerable talents, he was too indolent to be considered a thorough well read lawyer," he believed. "As an advocate he was above mediocrity. But being passionate and very irritable on being interrupted by the court or opposing counsel, in the examination of a witness, or in an argument, he often became so angry and intemperate as to injure his client."[19]

Whether Plumer was fair or not, his appraisal of Sherburne is about all that we have, and it has set the tone for the few historians who mention Sherburne. Lynn Turner certainly swallowed it. To him, writing in the twentieth century, Sherburne was "a Portsmouth lawyer whose guile and hypocrisy were especially distasteful" and who "seemed to inspire widespread distrust and hostility." One contemporary who knew Sherburne as well as Plumer and disliked him as much was benignant, generous Jeremiah Smith. He had served with Sherburne in Congress, but they might as well have represented different states. There was no collaboration between them. "I cant associate with [him]," Smith explained. "I hate him with a pure heart fervently." Smith understood that in 1795, when other Federalists were urging Pickering's appointment to the federal district court, Sherburne had been seeking the appointment for himself. Now he was trying to take the judgeship from Pickering by being his principal accuser, a turn of events many in New Hampshire found particularly distasteful as it was well known that he had studied law in Pickering's office and had frequently been befriended by him.[20]

Ellis's third reason why Plumer did not ask Pickering to resign was friendship. The judge was an old, close acquaintance whom Plumer "was unwilling to desert in his time of need." About the time when Gallatin was hoping Plumer would encourage Pickering to resign, James Sheafe, the judge's brother-in-law, wrote to thank Plumer for the attention "you are paying to the family of Judge Pickering as well as to himself." He assured Plumer that "there is no probability Judge P will resign his office. He is very feeble & weaken and I think he will not remain long in the way of the seekers of his office." Besides, his children would not let him resign so soon after losing the family home in the great fire of Portsmouth that had recently wiped out entire sections of the town. "It would be distressing indeed to them to be deprived of the sum they receive for his salary more particularly at this time among others they have been deprived of their habitation lead by the dreadful calamity that happened to us by the fire on the night of the 25th inst[ance] they have been obliged to leave this Town to seek a house at Dover at this inclement season of the year." After Plumer received that letter, there was little chance he would urge the judge to resign.[21]

There was yet a fourth reason that may have persuaded Plumer not to urge resignation. On talking to his fellow senators, he discovered that some northern Republicans were reluctant to condemn an insane man. These conversations encouraged him to hope impeachment might fail. He was confident enough that the defense could possibly win that he asked some of the Federalist members of the Rockingham County bar to provide Pickering's family with sufficient financial support so that they had the means to contest the impeachment, warning that if the judge was convicted the way would be open for the Republicans to remove Justice Samuel Chase and all the remaining Federalist judges. Apparently no one responded, for the family received scant monetary assistant, if any. Having no resources, Pickering's relatives had to defend him alone, against the witnesses whom Sherburne had rounded up and whose expenses were paid by the federal government.[22]

One question Plumer does not seem to have considered: whether resignation from office was a rational act that an insane man was legally capable of performing. If he did ask it, Plumer may have concluded that it was irrelevant as the administration never acknowledged that Pickering was mentally ill.

It is too late for us to discover whether there was collusion between the Jefferson administration in Washington and John Samuel Sherburne in Portsmouth. It may be coincidence that all the stories that Sherburne collected contained the incidents that Jefferson preferred to use and avoided the evidence that the administration did not want brought before the bar of the Senate. It blamed all aspects of Pickering's behavior on his inebriation. No mention was made by any of the deponents that the judge was well known to be mentally ill, or, at the very least, hydrophobic.[23]

One story that Sherburne did not tell Washington occurred when the sergeant of the United States Senate arrived in New Hampshire and went to the judge's house to serve the summons. Pickering was clearly out of his mind that day. "[T]he Judge expressed his determination of claiming his trial by *battle,* and that all things might be prepared in due form, requested the Sergeant to be the bearer of his challenge to Jefferson," Plumer was told. "The Judge says he is entitled to this mode of trial and will have it. That he will soon come on to Washington and convince Jefferson if he does not again retreat beyond the Allegany that other men besides Cornwallis can fight." There is no evidence that the sergeant-at-arms delivered the challenge to Jefferson or reported the judge's outburst to anyone in the Senate. The official line among Republicans was that the judge was not insane, so the less said about his unusual behavior the better. Jeremiah Mason, the leading member of the Rockingham County bar, thought if only Pickering could be in Washington, no one could deny his condition. "I sincerely wish Judge Pickering's health would permit his going to Washington," Mason told Plumer. "His appearance & conduct would instantly make such a defense as none but madmen like himself could resist." Pickering, Mason concluded, was to be tried "for the crime of Insanity."[24]

Mason was right. Insanity was what Pickering was tried for, except that insanity was not mentioned before the prosecution. The pattern of trial had been set by the administration, and the House of Representatives fell in line. The articles of impeachment discouraged the Senate from taking the broad view and interpreting the impeachment clause of the constitution to allow the removal of an incompetent judge from office. Mental illness was not mentioned, and Pickering's conduct was attributed to voluntary drunkenness and public blasphemy, both punishable as misdemeanors in New Hampshire.[25] The first three articles charged that Pickering, in wilful contradiction of United States law, wrongfully delivered *Eliza* to Eliphalet Ladd without proper customs certificates or hearing the government's witnesses, "wickedly meaning and intending to injure the revenues of the

United States, and thereby to impair their public credit." The fourth article said the judge presided at trials in a state of "total intoxication," and, "being a man of loose morals and intemperate habits," when speaking from the bench, profanely "invoke[d] the name of the Supreme Being." The expressions "wickedly meaning and intending" and "loose morals and habits" pointedly described a defendant of rational faculties who was capable of making choices.[26]

The administration's strategy was challenged at the start of the proceedings. Congressman Samuel Tenney, a member of a Federalist clique known as the Exeter Junto, called for a reading of Sherburne's depositions. He did so, he explained, "to show that Mr. Pickering had sustained a respectable character, and that his recent conduct had arisen from insanity." Joseph Nicholson of Maryland, who drafted and introduced the articles, immediately stated the administration's answer: insanity was irrelevant. He then told the house that "[w]hether John Pickering was insane or not, it was not for him to decide, but he was clearly of the opinion that the insanity stated by the gentleman from New Hampshire proceeded from constant and habitual intoxication."[27]

Nicholson meant that drunkenness was sufficient grounds for impeachment, and Jefferson agreed. Before the trial began in the Senate, Plumer dined at the White House. "Speaking of the impeachment of Pickering, I observed I had no doubt that the judge was *insane,* & asked him whether insanity was a good cause for impeachment & removal from office." According to Plumer, Jefferson replied, "If the facts of his denying an appeal & of his intoxication, as stated in the impeachment are proven, that will be sufficient cause for removal without further enquiry." That, Plumer reflected, was not federal constitutional law, although it was good New Hampshire constitutional law. "If a judge is insane, if he is inflicted with a disease that renders him incapable of performing his duty, and there is no probability of his recovering; if he is grossly and habitually intemperate . . . either of these disqualifies him for being a judge and is sufficient reason for his removal," the senator reasoned. "To remedy these evils, our [New Hampshire's] constitution provides, that the governor, with consent of the council, may remove judges upon the address of both houses of the legislature." That New Hampshire solution was the better procedure—to address a mentally incompetent judge from office, not impeach an insane judge for high crimes and misdemeanors. "Had the constitution of the United States," Plumer later observed in his autobiography, "given authority to congress to have removed a judge by *address,* as that of New Hampshire does, I believe every senator would have voted for Pickering's removal. Tho it was wrong for him to remain in office, yet it was a violation of the principles of our government, to convict & remove him on an impeachment on account of his insanity." That was why the administration did not mention mental illness, and the Federalists tried to make it the one probative fact. The correct constitutional principle, New Hampshire friends of Pickering maintained, was that mental incapacity was an addressable, but not an impeachable, offense.[28]

The matter was not settled, although Plumer claimed that it was. At this point he interpreted the United States constitution by what it did not provide. The fact that it did not have a clause for addressing judges from office, yet limited impeachment to high crimes and misdemeanors, was evidence that the framers intended that mental incapacity was not a cause for removal. "[W]ho will pretend that old age with its attendant infirmities, or the loss of understanding," he asked many years later, when writing of Pickering, "are crimes or misdemeanors for which a judge shall be impeached, convicted and removed! It is doing violence to our reason, as well as language, to consider *misfortune* and the *infirmities of age* as *crimes,* or *misdemeanors.*"[29] But, as was previously noted, the addressing clause had been rejected by the constitutional convention on grounds of judicial independence. Morris and Wilson had said that judges who could be addressed from office would not hold their judgeships by the tenure of "good behavior."[30] The "high crimes and misdemeanors" clause had been narrowly worded to protect the tenure at "good behavior." It was adopted at James Madison's urging instead of "maladministration," which quite likely would have been interpreted to encompass mental incapacity. "So vague a term," as the word "maladministration," Madison had objected, "will be equivalent to a tenure during pleasure of the Senate," further evidence that the framers of the federal constitution contemplated a judiciary more independent of legislative control than did most state constitutions, including New Hampshire's. William Plumer, of course, was applying the same concept of judicial independence when he claimed that "it is requisite to allege & prove crimes and misdemeanors in the accused." Otherwise, he warned, "a judicial officer will hold his office not by the tenure of *good behavior,* but the *pleasure of the legislature*—a tenure fatal to the independence of an important department in the government."[31]

In *Federalist* #79, Hamilton contended that a constitutional provision authorizing removal of judges on account of *inability* "would be more liable to abuse than calculated to answer any good purpose." But he drew a distinction between *inability* and *insanity.* Legislative power to remove a judge for insanity would not risk the abuses that might be incurred with removal for inability. To allow a judge to be removed for inability could "give scope to personal and party attachments and enmities." Power to remove an insane judge was not so likely to be abused. "[W]ithout any formal or express [constitutional] provision," insanity "may be safely pronounced to be a virtual disqualification."[32]

Senator Richard Wright of Maryland agreed with Hamilton, but he came to his conclusion from contrary legal premises. The "good behavior" clause did not protect the tenure of every judge, he contended, only those judges whose behavior was *good.* "If judge Pickering was now here as mad as Bedlam it would make no difference," he told the Senate. "I would remove him—he holds his office during good behavior—Madness surely is not good behavior." Perhaps all Wright meant was that the absence of good behavior was impeachable, not that the reverse of constitutional good behavior was judicial misbehavior. That was what Senator David Stone of North Carolina said. "To what source, then, shall we resort for a knowledge of what constitutes this thing, called misbehaviour in office?" Stone asked. "The constitution, surely, did not intend that a circumstance so important as the tenure by which the judges hold their offices, should be incapable of being ascertained," he answered. "*Their misbehaviour* certainly is not an impeachable offence; still it is the ground upon which the judges are to be removed from office. The process of impeachment, therefore, cannot be the only one by which the judges may be removed from office, under and according to the constitution. I take it, therefore, to be a thing undeniable, that there resides somewhere in the government a power to declare what shall amount to misbehaviour in office by the judges, and to remove them from office for the same without impeachment."[33]

Had Jefferson developed Senator Stone's premise and utilized the power Stone said resided "somewhere in the government," he might have obtained from the Pickering prosecution the precedent he sought for impeaching Justice Chase and Judge Richard Peters, if not Chief Justice John Marshall himself. But it would have been too loose construction for strict constructionists such as Jefferson and William Giles of Virginia to find in the clause guaranteeing tenure for good behavior an intention that the absence of good behavior vested the legislature and executive with authority to address a judge from office. An alternative might have been to ask the Senate to convict Pickering and at the same time declare that the term "misdemeanor" covered all cases of misbehavior where criminal intent was not proven. But the Republicans would have had to have been certain that evidence of mental illness was not made public if they wanted Pickering's conviction to become a precedent for the impeachment of Chase. For the most extreme among the Republican senators, there was no need to do any of this. Certainly Giles, who claimed the constitution's impeachment powers were "without limitation," saw no such need. Besides, "[i]mpeachment was not a criminal prosecution; it was no prosecution at all," he told the Senate. "A trial and removal of a judge upon impeachment need not imply any criminality or corruption in him. And a removal by impeachment was nothing more than a declaration by Congress to this effect: You hold dangerous opinions, and if you are suffered to carry them into effect you will work the destruction of the nation." Impeachment, then, was not a hearing about the conduct of a jurist but a legislative mechanism for keeping judges in line.[34]

Judge Pickering had been ordered to appear before the Senate on 2 March 1804. He never went to Washington. Even if he had had the money for the trip, he would have had difficulty crossing the Delaware River, not to mention the Hudson or the Connecticut. Instead of hearing Pickering, the Senate received a petition from his son, Jacob, praying the court for a postponement to allow the defense to collect evidence and that it hear Robert G. Harper on his behalf. That is, to hear Harper for Jacob Pickering, not for his father, for, as they were expecting to defend on grounds of insanity, they could not have anyone acting as the judge's attorney as an insane person could not appoint an agent.[35]

Harper was both a bad and a strong choice for defending Pickering—bad because he was thoroughly partisan and detested by Republicans and strong because he was one of the great advocates of the day. When he obtained permission to speak, the managers of impeachment who were conducting the trial on behalf of the lower house walked out of the Senate. They knew he would offer evidence of insanity and did not want to sanction it with their presence. And evidence of mental incompetency was what the Senate heard. Harper presented depositions from the judge's physicians, one of whom deposed that Pickering was "very hypochondriacal, and subject to nervous complaints, but, as far as my knowledge extended, very exemplary and correct in his morals until within about three years, when he discovered symptoms of mental insanity, and consequent intemperance and profanity in some instances." The lawyers who deposed were in private practice and supported the medical people. In the deposition he gave Jacob Pickering, Edward St. Loe Livermore, who had represented the libelee in the *Eliza* case, came close to saying that Sherburne lied in his statement. "I am sensible that it has been reported that Judge Pickering injured himself by the too free use of inebriating liquors," Livermore deposed, "and it has been the opinion of some not so well acquainted with him, this was the principal cause of his distraction. I think it was very erroneous and the supposition uncharitable. It is possible at times he may have drank too freely, but I think I have good reason to conclude it was the consequence of his insanity." Harper wanted time to obtain more depositions but was told he was not permitted to file motions. He concluded by saying that he had presented enough evidence to prove Pickering incapacitated, that an insane man "is incapable of committing any crime" and "cannot be put upon his trial."[36]

The proceedings made Senator John Quincy Adams impatient. Coming from neighboring Massachusetts, he had personal knowledge of Pickering and knew that he was mentally unbalanced. He was, moreover, intrigued with the reasons why James Jackson did not care to hear evidence of insanity. The Georgia senator knew how to be rid of Pickering. "He said the House of Representatives were at this moment debating whether they would not impeach another Judge," Adams recorded, "and by-and-by we should have Judge Chase's friends come and pretend he was mad." Adams thought the Georgian amusing, but Jackson was one senator frank enough to say what was really important. At least, Adams's grandson, Henry, suggested as much when he observed that "Acquittal of Pickering would probably be fatal to the impeachment of Chase."[37]

The trial of Pickering by the Senate was marked by a number of peculiarities, diminishing its value as a precedent for impeaching Samuel Chase and other Supreme Court justices. The defendant never appeared, and he was unrepresented by counsel, for Harper had represented the judge's son only, not the judge personally. No member of the family, apparently, could afford the trip to Washington, not even James Sheafe, the judge's brother-in-law, who had been a United States senator. As a consequence, no witnesses were called for the defense, though a few depositions, testifying to mental instability, were submitted. Senator Samuel White of Delaware had a point when noting that without appearance, plea, or defense, the proceedings scarcely deserved the name of a mock trial.[38]

Several witnesses who appeared for the prosecution were another peculiarly of the trial: with no defense counsel to cross-examine or object that certain evidence was inadmissible, they were free to give roaming, opinionated testimony. Moreover, Plumer observed, they "were well chosen & prepared for the purpose for which they were called." Put another way, they were careful not to discuss Pickering's mental condition. There were seven in all, five of whom had been appointed to public office by Jefferson. Most telling were two—Sherburne, the district attorney, and Jonathan Steele, the clerk of the district court; both expected to be appointed district judge once Pickering was removed. Everyone in Washington seems to have known this, so their testimony must have appeared self-serving, if not tainted evidence. As Plumer put it to Smith, they "discovered a great forwardness in testifying against the accused."[39]

As the trial neared its end, the Federalists found a way to produce evidence on Pickering's behalf and, also, to introduce testimony about his mental competency. After the prosecution rested, Senator Uriah Tracy of Connecticut asked that New Hampshire's two senators testify. No one objected, and they were allowed to express opinions that were entered on the official trial record. It was yet another event marking the trial as peculiar. After all, both men, Simeon Olcott and William Plumer, were judges in the case. They were sworn to be impartial, yet they were permitted to give evidence in support of one side, the defense, and then to vote their judgments, which, of course, were for the same side.[40]

Olcott, who had known Pickering for over thirty years, had been an associate justice on the Superior Court when Pickering was chief justice. He refuted the claim that the judge had been a drunkard before appointment to the federal bench. "He was often affected with a nervous complaint, or what was called hypochondria, which sometimes produced extraordinary effects," Olcott related, "but he never saw the effect of spiritous liquors, which he thinks he should have noticed, if true, as his seat was generally next to said Pickering, while on the bench."[41]

Following Olcott, Plumer testified that he knew Pickering well and that his mental illness had begun about four years earlier. "I never heard a suggestion of his being intemperate, until after I was informed of his insanity," he explained. "I have seen him many times within the last four years; sometimes he was intoxicated, at other times he was sober; but when wholly free from intoxication, he appeared to me to be in a state of insanity." Plumer ended his testimony by observing that Pickering's "insanity was the cause of his intemperance. Though I think it not improbable that, after his insanity had produced a degree of intemperance, the intemperance and insanity might then act mutually as cause and effect." The next day, Senator John Smith interpreted the last remark to mean that Plumer had said that "the insanity proceeded from the intemperance of the Accused." No, Plumer corrected him, "I have no hesitation in saying that I fully believe that his hypochondriac complaints produced the delirium & insanity— & that his insanity caused his intemperance."[42]

Another peculiarity was the form in which the question of guilt was put. The senators did not vote whether Pickering was guilty of high crimes and misdemeanors as the constitution seemed to prescribe. They answered, rather, whether he was "guilty as charged." The wording was designed to draw in moderate Republicans who were reluctant to call Pickering a criminal but felt he had to be removed from the bench. "This form, by blending all the law and facts together under the shelter of general terms," John Quincy Adams suggested, "put at ease a few of the weak brethren who scrupled on the law, and a few who doubted of the facts." It was also another factor depriving conviction of some value as a precedent for impeaching other judges.[43]

The wording eased the conscience of several senators. Pickering was convicted by a straight party vote, and it is evident that some who pronounced him guilty thought him a mentally ill person whose insanity produced his intemperance, not a drunkard whose drinking produced his incompetency. One was Senator Robert Wright of Maryland. "If it should appear that the Judge is insane, that will not decide the impeachment," he contended. "[W]e can remove from office the insanity notwithstanding—His not discharging the duties of a Judge is good cause of conviction & removal altho' he is not guilty of any corruption or improper conduct in office." A somewhat stronger theory of senatorial authority to convict was suggested by Pennsylvania's George Logan. "We have been led into an error by considering this Court as a court of *criminal jurisdiction*, & Judge Pickering as a *criminal*," Logan pointed out. "This is a *court of enquiry only*. —If the Judge is *insane*, whether by *the act of God*, or his *own imprudence*, is immaterial—for in either case he is incapable of discharging the duties of a Judge—And being unable to do his duty, & a complaint being made to us, it is our duty to remove him."[44]

Many years later William Plumer would look back and conclude that Pickering had been "wholly unfit to be a judge," and, although he had to be removed, the Senate acted "with great reluctance." At the time, however, Plumer had an entirely different perspective. The arrogance of the Virginians had overwhelmed him with bitterness, and for the first time in his life he contemplated disunion. The day before the conviction he wrote a long letter to Jeremiah Smith. "Tomorrow, no doubt, an insane man will be convicted of high crimes & misdeamers [*sic*]; & probably the next day John Samuel Sherburne will be announced as his successor," he told his friend.[45]

Ten days after Pickering's removal, Jefferson sent to the Senate the nomination of John Samuel Sherburne for United States district judge for New Hampshire. Jonathan Steele was promoted from clerk of court to Sherburne's vacant position of district attorney. The third main witness against Pickering was rewarded with Steele's former office of clerk of court. "Thus is the man who advised & promoted as far as he was able the impeachment of Judge Pickering, rewarded by being appointed his successor," Plumer wrote, knowing that Sherburne was well satisfied. Three days later he learned that Steele was not satisfied. He had expected to become judge and had refused the consolation prize. He tried to save some of his self esteem by taking the high road of principle. "I was unwillingly made a contributory instrument in creating vacancies, and a due regard to my own reputation forbids me to profit by that achievement," he told the public. Although Plumer thought the statement was "intended as a sarcasm upon the president for making the appointments, and a reproach upon Sherburne, whom he hated," most New Hampshirites undoubtedly saw it as sheer hypocrisy. Steele, however, enjoyed more public respect than did Sherburne.[46]

Sherburne's own hypocrisy stirred some hostility among the people, most likely lowering still further the public's respect for the judiciary. When, after about two decades on the bench, he, too, became insane—or, as Plumer expressed it, "he became an *idiot*"—some people in Portsmouth said it was God's judgment for his treatment of Pickering. Justice Joseph Story, holding court in New Hampshire, "adjudged that Sherburne was incompetent, and by visitation of providence was disable to hold a district court, and perform the duties of judge of that court," Plumer later wrote with what must have been some satisfaction. "Sherburne was the third district judge of the United [States] in New Hampshire," Plumer noted, "and it is a singular fact, that each of them, when they died were either *idiots or insane persons.*"[47]

The impeachment of Judge Pickering filled Plumer with greater apprehension for the independence of the judiciary than had the repeal of the Judiciary Act of 1801. That Pickering had been found "guilty as charged," without proof of a crime, Plumer feared, meant that state judges as well as federal judges would hold office "not by tenure of *good behavior,* but the *pleasure of the legislature.*" True, that was somewhat similar to the conditions of tenure in New Hampshire, but he wanted to strengthen judicial tenure in the state, not see New Hampshire tenure standards spread to other jurisdictions. The day after the conviction, he wrote a long account of the trial for the Boston *Repertory.* The article ended with pessimistic foreboding. "How far these proceedings will form a precedent to establish the doctrine, that when requested by a majority of the House, two thirds of the Senate can remove a Judge from office without a formal conviction of high crimes and misdemeanors, time alone can develope," Plumer warned. "I really wish those in New England who are boasting of the independence of our

Judiciary would reflect on what a slender tenure Judges hold their offices whose political sentiments are at variance with the dominant party. The House of Representatives have this day impeached Judge Chase."[48]

Plumer meant Justice Samuel Chase of the United States Supreme Court. When, in January, Congressman John Randolph of Virginia had first demanded an investigation of Chase's judicial conduct, Plumer had written to Smith that "the attack on the judiciary has now commenced." Chase's impeachment following immediately on Pickering's conviction was, to both Plumer and Smith, a second step in a Republican campaign to make certain that the judiciary remained subject to the legislature. "It is time to leave the Pumps & take to the long Boats," Smith replied. "A majority must & will do what they please, a paper constitution affords no security to a minority."[49]

With Jefferson in the White House, Plumer feared, federal judicial tenure was precariously slender. The impeachments of Pickering and Chase, he supposed, were "parts of a vicious system, which extends to the removal of every Federal judge from both the Supreme and inferior Courts." After learning that Randolph was investigating Chase, Plumer wrote to Jeremiah Smith: "I think the other judges will not be impeached *this session*; but in due time they will & must be denounced & fall." It is telling that he had said the same the year before, on first arriving in Washington. "The judges of the Supreme Court must fall," he then assured Jeremiah Mason. "They are *denounced* by the Executive as well as the House. They must be removed; they are obnoxious and unyielding men; & why should they remain to awe & embarrass the administration. . . . Our affairs seem to approach an important crisis." Smith, too, was certain the independence of the federal judiciary was doomed. "They hate Marshall, Paterson, etc. worse than they hate Chase because they are men of better character," he replied to Plumer. "To be safe in these times good men must not only resign their offices but they must resign their good names. . . . Tell me what the judges say—are they frightened?"[50]

Had they been asked, Republicans would have answered that they had valid grounds for impeaching and convicting Chase. They were not attacking the courts but exposing a political judge who had abused his life-tenured office for party ends. There is no need to go into the evidence; it is enough for us to study Republican beliefs about the grounds on which it was legitimate to remove judges from the bench by impeachment to understand what alarmed lawyers who espoused the legal philosophy of Plumer and Smith. Plumer was then having his first doubts about the future of Federalism as a political party, but he would never have doubts about Federalist jurisprudence, and, as his son said, the Chase impeachment "touched him at a tender point." Telling Jeremiah Smith of Randolph's speech demanding an investigation of Chase, Plumer emphasized matters at the center of the dichotomy dividing the two main schools of legal thought in the early republic. One of Randolph's accusations, he wrote, was that Chase at "the trial of Fries . . . had prohibited his [the defendant's] counsel from stirring a question of law to the jury which had previously been settled by the Court." Randolph, although not a lawyer, was a somewhat extreme adherent of the Virginia or Republican theory of law. He, of course, thought Chase's ruling an abuse of judicial power. Plumer did not have to ask Smith; he knew Smith would not agree with Randolph. Smith, like Plumer, wanted judges and not juries to decide questions of law. At another trial, Randolph complained, Chase had "exercised too much authority over the prisoner's counsel, by obliging them to argue the question of fact, and prohibiting them from arguing the law to the jury." That, too, by the notions of lawyers who viewed law as did Jefferson, Samuel Livermore, and Randolph, was improper judicial interference with the right to jury trial. But to Plumer and Smith it was a rule of judicial conduct they hoped to make standard procedure in New Hampshire courts. By their jurisprudence, Randolph was accusing Chase of acting as a judge should act, or, at least, as they hoped would become the judicial norm.[51]

Daniel Webster, a fellow Federalist member of the Rockingham County bar, wrote from the same jurisprudential perspective. "If any one, at this day, doubts it to be an object with the Democrats to humble the Judiciary in the dust before their feet, let him consider maturely the treatment of Judge Chase," he warned the Federalists of New Hampshire. "Unfortunate Judge! He mistook the temper of the times. He imagined he was living in the days of a virtuous Republic, when the Laws are more powerful than the *offender*." Webster meant that Chase forgot he was living during the administration of Thomas Jefferson, a time when the legal theory of the dominant political party held that the majority in Congress could, by legislative fiat, change what he, Plumer, Smith, and Chase regarded to be "law."[52]

Republicans were feeling their way with impeachment. They were hoping, Plumer was certain, to create a constitutional precedent making impeachment an instrument by which the political majority could remove a judge for any reason it pleased. Randolph, Plumer informed Smith, contended in the House of Representatives that the tenure the constitution conferred on federal judges, of "*holding their offices during good behavior,* was designed only as a bar a[gains]t Executive removal, & not to prevent him [the president] from removing from office when requested by a majority of the representatives of the people."[53]

Now a member of the upper house, William Giles of Virginia was Jefferson's leader in the Senate, and when he spoke he was speaking for the administration. Senator Albert J. Beveridge later said that Giles thought impeachment a legal "method of ousting from the National Bench those judges who did not agree with the views of the Republican Party." John Quincy Adams recorded a conversation in which he overheard Giles arguing that "[t]he power of impeachment was given without limit to the House of Representatives; the power of trying impeachments was given equally without limit to the Senate. . . . And a removal by impeachment was nothing more than a declaration by Congress to this effect: You hold dangerous opinions, and if you are suffered to carry them into effect you will work the destruction of the Nation. *We want your offices,* for the purpose of giving them to men who will fill them better."[54]

We can assume Adams heard correctly, because Plumer wrote in his diary that Giles said the same to him. "We have authority to remove a judge," he explained to Plumer in a private conversation, "if he is disagreeable in his office, or wrongheaded, and opposed to the administration, though not corrupt in conduct. Judges ought not to be independent of the co-ordinate branches of the government; but should be so far subservient, as to harmonize with them in all the great measures of the administration." Adams noted that, in the conversation he overheard, Giles "treated with the utmost contempt the idea of an *independent* judiciary." In his conversation with Plumer, Giles went even further, Plumer reported. He maintained that the judiciary should be political. He was attempting to persuade the wrong lawyer.[55]

Plumer was astonished when Justice Chase was acquitted. He had not expected it. He, of course, voted to acquit, but a majority of his colleagues were for conviction on at least one of the articles of impeachment. It required, however, the concurrence of two-thirds of the members present to convict, and the leadership could not muster that many. "This acquittal of Judge Chase was a great point gained in support of the Constitution, and the independence of the Judges," Plumer concluded, with much relief. "A prosecution commenced in the rage of party, and impelled by the whole influence of the administration, was arrested; and, to the honor of the accused, he owed his acquittal to the votes of his political enemies." It is possible that the acquittal reconciled Plumer to some of those enemies or, at least, caused him to think of them less harshly.[56]

Talking with Plumer while the Chase trial was still pending, Jefferson complained that impeachment was "a bungling way of removing judges." After the acquittal of Aaron Burr for treason, the president lamented that Chief Justice Marshall, who had presided at the trial and whom Jefferson blamed for Burr being freed, was "protected [from impeachment] by the Constitution itself; for impeachment is a farce which will not be tried again." Jefferson had hoped to remove by impeachment the judges appointed by Washington and Adams. But when his congressional supporters started the process with the trial of Chase, Jefferson did not become active and assert party leadership. He seldom took the lead in matters that were controversial or might fail. He had long realized that impeachment might be too clumsy a procedure to be used for purely political purposes. On the day that a House committee reported that Judge Pickering should be impeached, Plumer and Jefferson had a conversation. "It will take two years to try this impeachment," the president regretted. "The Constitution ought to be altered, so that the President should be authorized to remove a Judge from office, on address of the two Houses of Congress." Unlike Giles, Jefferson knew there had to be an amendment to introduce into federal law the process of addressing judges from office.[57]

Other Republicans agreed with Jefferson that addressing out of office was better than impeachment. John Randolph again took the lead. In the House of Representatives, he moved that the United States Constitution be amended to authorize the removal of federal judges by the president on the joint address of both houses of Congress. Reaction in New Hampshire was along party lines. When Vermont proposed a similar amendment, the lower house of the General Court, controlled by Republicans, voted 79 to 76 to support it. Federalists' reaction was stronger than might be expected, at least in New Hampshire. If addressing from office became part of the national constitution, John Hubbard Church exclaimed in a Fourth of July oration, "will not one branch of our National Legislature be, in effect, destroyed? And will not the Judges of our Supreme and other Courts be dependent upon the caprice of any number who form a majority of Congress? Will not the independence of the Judicial Department be destroyed, and the Judges be subject to removal, at the arbitrary pleasure of the Legislature, without impeachment or trial?" Some members of Church's audience had to wonder if he knew anything of New Hampshire law. After all, none of the legal mischiefs he mentioned had occurred in New Hampshire, yet the authority of legislators to address the executive for removal of judges from office had been in the state constitution since 1784. But then he may have been referring only to the federal government and Jefferson as president.[58]

It has been conjectured that Chase's acquittal was not the stunning defeat for the Jefferson administration that it appeared to be in 1804. The Republicans, the argument contends, got all they really needed from the Chase impeachment. Before the impeachment, Chase and other Federalist judges had politicized the federal courts, using the bench as a pulpit to attack Jefferson. After seeing Chase undergo the ordeal of a trial, the federal judges became less openly political, much less outspoken, more reserved, that is, more judicial. With federal courts no longer acting as Chase had acted, it is said, Jefferson, Giles, and their cronies had obtained all they could have expected, and so the impeachment of Chase was a victory, not a defeat, for the administration.

The prosecution of John Pickering belies that supposition. Pickering himself was hardly worth the effort spent to convict him. He easily could have been superseded on the bench had the Republicans passed legislation similar to the provision in the Judiciary Act of 1801 that had authorized the judges of the New England federal circuit to substitute Smith for Pickering. That provision was omitted from the Judiciary Act of 1802, despite the fact that, at least twice, federal judges—Sullivan and Pickering—had been so deranged that they had to be relieved of their duties. Even after the *Eliza* case, the Republicans could have eased Pickering aside by passing similar legislation. The Federalists would have supported them. Jefferson rejected that solution, and one reason has to be the political advantage he sought by convicting Pickering of high crimes, giving the Republicans political momentum for impeaching Chase. And it was not just Chase and John

Marshall to be removed but also Justices William Cushing, Alfred Moore, and William Paterson. Beyond the justices of the Supreme Court were other federal judges to be removed: John Davis of Massachusetts, Elijah Paine of Vermont, John Sloss Hobart of New York, Robert Morris of New Jersey, and, of course, Richard Peters of Pennsylvania. They certainly, and perhaps other judges as well, would have been removed, and the doctrine of judicial independence would have lost whatever significance in federal constitutional law that it still retained after 1802.

Ironically, the administration may have been too successful against Pickering. The moderate Republicans who had reluctantly voted that New Hampshire's insane district judge had been guilty as charged may have experienced a touch of conscience. The administration's projected theory of judicial dependence was not quite persuasive enough to make them comfortable convicting a "political" justice of high crimes and misdemeanors for being too partisan and too outspoken. The federal judiciary, which had been weakened by the repeal of the act of 1801, was not further diminished. It did not, however, regain during the nineteenth century the strength it would have obtained had the circuit judges created by the act of 1801 not been legislated out of office. For most of the nineteenth century the justices of the Supreme Court had to take to the road—going as far as the Pacific Coast—to preside at jury trials and hear appeals. The federal judiciary did not operate efficiently until the high court justices no longer went on circuit and no longer sat on lower trial or appellate courts. It was not until then that it shook itself free of Jeffersonian limitations.

Six

A Dependent Court

In twenty-first-century American constitutional law, few principles are more encased in platitudes than the principle of judicial independence. That was not true during the early decades of the republic, certainly not in New Hampshire. "No government, without an independent Judiciary as a co-equal and co-ordinate branch, can long retain its freedom," William Claggett told the House of Representatives in 1813, seeking to persuade the members to respect judicial autonomy. "Nothing," the German lawyer and American law professor Francis Lieber agreed some years later, "is of so vital importance, of so momentous influence, as the independence of the judiciary. . . . It is at once the noblest and most conciliatory principle in the state."[1]

It is no surprise that judges have believed that American liberty depends on their independence from the executive and legislative powers of the government. After all, it is not just a legal principle they celebrate but their own autonomy, their freedom from interference, and, quite frankly, from being second-guessed and corrected. The judges of Virginia worried about political and social pressure on their decisions as early as 1788. "The propriety and necessity of the independence of the judges is evident in reason and the nature of their office; since they are to decide between government and the people, as well as between contending citizens," the Virginian judges contended, "and, if they be dependent on either, corrupt influence may be apprehended, sacrificing the innocent to popular prejudice; and subjecting the poor to oppression and persecution by the rich.

And this applies more forcibly, to exclude a dependence on the legislature; a branch of whom, in cases of impeachment, is itself a party."[2]

What may be surprising is how much the notion of the judiciary, whether independent or not, as the guardian of rights had seeped into the collective unconscious of the general American population during the period of the early republic. "The judiciary is the last resource and hope of expiring liberty and life," *The Farmer's Cabinet* in Amherst, New Hampshire, editorialized, "and should not be approached by public caprice or individual pique or derision." The public did not need the reminder. Although the electorate was ever ready to subject the judges to the politics of the day, a mystique had already developed about the judiciary as liberty's sentinel. For evidence, consider four toasts offered at Fourth of July celebrations— Republican celebrations as well as Federalist:

"The Judiciary. A necessary barrier against Tyranny and Licentiousness" (Pembroke, 1809).

"An enlightened and Independent Judiciary—The only safe barrier against licentious liberty and oppressive power" (Londonderry, 1815).

"The Judiciary—Independent of party influence, may it ever protect right, punish iniquity, and prove the safeguard of liberty" (Amherst, 1808).

"The Judiciary of a free Government—The great fortress which alike protects the Government from the outrage of the People, and the People from the oppression of the Government" (Portsmouth, 1810).[3]

Most Americans at that time believed that the doctrine of judicial independence was a constitutional principle inherited from England. They were wrong. In the mother country it had not been the judiciary that had been independent of governmental manipulation but the common law. The common law, after all, was a law of process, not substance, of technicalities, not principles, and of rules, not theory. Many elements of common-law practice and procedure were so complex that specialists—trained in its vocabulary and formulae—alone could master it. They formed a detached profession whose reasoning and methods of reaching conclusions were so obscure to the uninitiated that the government had few officials competent to interfere with its rulings. Land law is a good example. The judges deciding cases of real property were left alone both because their work was essential to society and because no one but common lawyers understood what they were doing.[4] After Lord Chief Justice Coke thrust the common law into the politics of his day, making it the constitutional mechanism for limiting prerogatives claimed by James I and VI as well as Charles I, common-law judges became embroiled in the political struggles between Parliament and the Crown. People charged with seditious libel and other state crimes eventually looked to juries rather than judges for protection.

The English constitutional innovation making the greatest impression upon Americans during the age of the early republic had been relatively recent, a legacy of the Glorious Revolution. It was a provision in the Act of Settlement giving English judges, for the first time, good-behavior tenure. It provided that "Judges Commissions be made *Quamdiu se bene gesserint* [as long as he shall behave himself well] . . . *but* upon the Address of both Houses of Parliament, it may be lawful to remove them." For Americans, that provision was the "original intention" of their right to judicial independence. But in their haste to embrace this new right, they missed something. They did not give heed to the purpose of the new tenure. It gave judges—if they behaved well—protection against the Crown, not against Parliament.[5]

While North America was governed by Great Britain, judicial tenure existed at the Crown's pleasure. By the 1760s the perceived insecurity of judicial tenure "at pleasure" became a colonial constitutional grievance. Some historians believe that this grievance should not be taken seriously. "Judges in colonial America," Gordon S. Wood has written, "had been relatively insignificant members of government." That statement is not correct. For much of the population, especially for rural people living away from the few larger towns, the judiciary was the only government they ever experienced. The lower judiciary set many of their taxes, laid out highways, determined where bridges should be built, licensed ferries and taverns, checked to see if the licensees were serving the public, administered poor relief, and received the presentments of grand jurors, reporting nuisances, hazards, and crimes in their county. Moreover, the judges were secure in their offices, at least under the appointed governors. Joseph H. Smith found that in the colonies there were none "of the wholesale dismissals from judicial office that characterized the reigns of Charles II and James II in England." Rather, Wood pointed out, it was the colonial legislatures that intervened with the judiciary, "either by direct interference in the process of adjudication or by the correction and amendment of court-administered law by statute."[6]

Whether or not they were satisfied with the degree of political independence enjoyed by their courts, the constitutional inequality of their judges' tenure grated against Americans' constitutional sensibilities. Quite a few colonials, including some polemical whig writers, demanded that their judiciary have the same tenurial protection enjoyed by English judges. In 1759 the Pennsylvania Assembly voted to create its own constitutional equality, enacting a statute granting provincial judges the "good-behavior" tenure that English judges had received after the Glorious Revolution. The change was vetoed by London, and the issue of judicial tenure was pushed forward as a major topic of political agitation in the colonies. In what is generally considered the first pamphlet of the pre-revolutionary controversy, Joseph Galloway contended that Pennsylvania had to obtain sufficient judicial independence to be able to resist imperial erosion of customary constitutional rights. "The men therefore who are to settle the contests between prerogative and liberty, who are to ascertain the bounds of sovereign power and to determine the rights of the subject, ought certainly to be perfectly free from the influence of either," he asserted. Unless judges in the colony enjoyed "good-behavior" tenure, Pennsylvanians would not be able to "look for strict impartiality and a pure administration of justice," or to "expect that power should be confined within its legal limits, and right and justice done to the subject by men [judges] who are dependent."[7]

In December 1761, London instructed the colonies not to enact more statutes like the one Pennsylvania had attempted. They were forbidden to issue judicial commissions on any tenure but "the pleasure of the crown." The colonists obeyed. The edict by itself did not threaten their constitutional position as it did not change any existing privileges but required rather that the status quo of the customary colonial constitution remain in force. Eleven years later, however, Parliament promulgated that Massachusetts judges would be compensated by the Crown, no longer by the provincial assembly, which had been paying the judiciary from "time immemorial." It was a stunning constitutional innovation, driving Americans to defend a constitutional stance from which, most colonists believed, they could not afford to retreat. "[W]hile judges hold their commissions during pleasure," the Massachusetts House resolved, "any one of them who shall accept of . . . the crown for his support . . . will discover to the world that . . . he is an enemy of the constitution and has it in his heart to promote the establishment of an arbitrary government in the province." Combining the judicial tenure grievance with a judicial salary grievance took the pre-revolutionary constitutional controversy beyond the pale. American judges could become too dependent on Parliament if paid directly from London when serving only "at pleasure." If any judges would *not* be independent, it was these judges. "The British Parliament have shewn their wisdom in making the Judges there as independent as possible both of the Prince and People, both for place and support," Bostonians voted. "But our Judges hold their Commissions only during pleasure." They were dependent for "support," if not "place." Before very long other colonies had the same grievance as Massachusetts. That was what the Declaration of Independence meant when charging that the king "has made judges dependent on his will alone, for the tenure of their offices, and the amount and payment of their salaries."[8]

The era of writing and adopting the first American constituent constitutions, during and following the Revolution, brought new dimensions to American meanings of judicial independence. "[T]here is no liberty," Baron de Montesquieu had warned, "if the judiciary power be not separated from the legislative and executive."[9] John Sullivan urged the drafters of New Hampshire's first written constitution to pay no heed, and agreeing with Sullivan, they wrote a constitution without a trace of Montesquieu. But theory changes, and in the years following that first constitution, thanks to John Adams's genius for constitution making, Americans began to understand what Montesquieu meant. By the time Plumer helped write the third New Hampshire constitution, even many radical republicans were persuaded that government could be restrained by being divided into separate branches and yet remain republican. More remarkably, there was now a new measure for determining and defining judicial independence: the degree by which the judiciary was separated from the other branches of government.

The drafters of the first separation-of-powers clauses in state constitutions, Gordon Wood contends, "never meant to create the kind of independent judiciary we have today. All they wanted to do was separate the judges from the corrupting influence of the governors; no one as yet had in mind separating the judges from the control of the legislatures."[10] Although it is certainly true that no one in that generation wanted judicial independence to develop into the judicial supremacy of today, it was not long before some constitutional framers became aware of the equally corrupting influence of political faction. James Kent was only paraphrasing what had been said since the 1780s by legal commentators who thought of law as he did, when he observed that republicanism had increased, not decreased, problems of influence by adding the element of popular corruption. Alexander Hamilton had made the point in 1788 when he infused the concept of judicial service at good behavior with a new, republican meaning. "In a monarchy," he said of good-behavior tenure, "it is an excellent barrier to the despotism of the prince: In a republic it is a no less excellent barrier to the encroachments and oppressions of the representative body."[11]

Legal theorists of the Jeffersonian persuasion dissented from Kent and Hamilton. They disagreed with the Hamiltonian or "receptionist" principle that judicial independence was integral to separated powers, not because they preferred a judiciary dependent on the executive but because, by the 1810s, they believed the principle of separation was being misconstrued into the notion that the judiciary was independent from everything, including the people themselves. "In a government founded on the public will," Jefferson eventually would write, judicial independence "operates in an opposite direction, and against that will."[12]

In New Hampshire neither the Constitution of 1784 nor Plumer's Constitution of 1792 distinguished between independence from the executive and independence from the legislature. They provided that citizens were entitled to impartial judges and nothing more. Both copied their judicial independence provisions from the Massachusetts Constitution of 1780. The clause in the Massachusetts constitution is printed here. Words omitted from the two New Hampshire versions are in italics. Words that were added by Plumer and his colleagues in 1792 are in bold type.

> It is essential to the preservation of the rights of every individual, his life, liberty, property and character, that there be an impartial interpretation of the laws, and administration of justice. It is the right of every citizen to be tried by judges as *free*, impartial *and independent* as the lot of humanity will admit. It is therefore not only the best policy, but for the security of the rights of the people, *and of every citizen*, that the judges of the supreme judicial court should hold their offices as long as they behave *themselves* well; **subject, however, to such limitations on account of age as may be provided by the constitution of the State;** and that they should have honorable salaries ascertained and established by standing laws.[13]

The puzzle that cannot be resolved is what we should make of the fact that the New Hampshire framers did not think the right to be tried by *free* and *independent* judges important enough to be retained in the constitutions. It was sufficient for them that judges be *impartial*. Chief Justice John Pickering undoubtedly had a reason for dropping the words "free" and "independent" in 1784, but he left no record telling us why. That, however, is not the interesting question. It is, rather, considering that Plumer and Smith went to the constitutional convention in 1791–1792 to strengthen the independence of the judiciary, why they did not put one or both words back in?

There is no answer. The most we know is that Plumer thought judicial independence best protected by the clause that judges "shall hold their offices during good behavior," also lifted from the Massachusetts constitution. After all, he pointed out, the judiciary is the weakest branch of the government. "They have no command or influence over the physical force of the nation—no control or direction of the public treasure. . . . It therefore appears to me important that judicial officers, especially those of the higher tribunals, should hold their offices during *good behavior*."[14]

The other clause in the constitution which, together with good-behavior tenure, defined judicial independence was a provision that judges "have honorable salaries ascertained and established by standing laws." Hamilton had placed it below tenure in importance. "Next to permanency in office, nothing can contribute more to the independence of the judges than a fixed provision for their support," he argued. "In the general course of human nature, *a power over a man's subsistence amounts to a power over his will.* And we can never hope to see realised in practice the complete separation of the judicial from the legislative power, in any system which leaves the former dependent for pecuniary resources on the occasional grants of the latter." Hamilton contended that Massachusetts and New Hampshire too easily evaded this constitutional duty because they did not supplement the "honorable salaries" provision with a supporting provision that the compensation of judges "shall not be *diminished* during their continuance in office."[15]

At the turn of the nineteenth century, American legal theorists found it easier to agree on what made courts independent than on what courts should do with independence. Those who were law oriented said independence was to protect the laws from the people; others who were more republican oriented said it was to protect people from government. "In monarchical governments, the independence of the judiciary is essential to guard the rights of the subject from the injustice of the crown," James Kent suggested, "but in republics it is equally salutary, in protecting the constitution and laws from the encroachments and the tyranny of faction." James Madison sought to justify the principle to Jefferson (who would never agree with it). "In our Governments," Madison explained, "the real power lies in the majority of the Community, and the invasion of private rights is *chiefly* to be apprehended, not from acts of Government contrary to the sense of its constituents, but from acts in which the Government is the mere instrument of the major number of the Constituents."[16]

William Claggett told the New Hampshire House of Representatives in 1813 that it was more likely people needed protection from their elected officials, that is, from what Madison termed acts of government. "Suppose that the Legislative and Executive departments should pass a favorite measure which trenches upon the rights of the people," Claggett asked. "Have the people any security, if the Judges are not independent of the influence or denunciation of these departments, and cannot take up the act and declare it not law, and therefore void?" Two years earlier *The Farmer's Cabinet,* with a good deal of exaggeration, suggested that this had already become the judiciary's constitutional role. "Our judicial tribunals are daily growing more and more important in proportion as tyranny and usurpation are spreading over the earth, and the consequent disregard to justice and equity," it editorialized in a notice about the Superior Court convening in the town of Amherst. "In times like the present, when we are tossed about upon the 'tempestous [*sic*] ocean' of political tolerance and innovation, the judiciary is our *sheet anchor* of hope, and should be preserved free, uncontaminated and independent."[17]

Not every commentator on the judiciary in the early republic was concerned about protecting judicial autonomy from either the legislature or the executive. Some observers were fearful of too much independence, afraid that courts free of legislative supervision could get out of hand. When the draft of Massachusetts' seminal constitution was submitted to the public in 1780, several towns voted that judicial autonomy was being carried too far. The town of Greenwich objected to salaries "Established by Standing Laws—Because in our oppinion it ought always to be in the Power of the Legislative to grant, Annually, all Salarys or Wages to all Publick officers of this State." Wilbraham wanted judges of the Supreme Judicial Court "Annually Elected at large through the State." The reason why, the town meeting explained, was that "it keeps each Branch more Immediately Dependent upon the People—and therefore will Serve to keep the three Branches Distinct and Independent of each other and as each Branch are the Substitutes of the People according to the Declaration of Rights."[18] During the period of the early republic there were state court systems without the security of judicial tenure. In neighboring Vermont, as well as the two other New England states, Connecticut and Rhode Island, judges were elected annually by the legislature, and further south one jurisdiction's judges served "during pleasure."[19] We do not have returns from New Hampshire towns as we do for the two in Massachusetts, Greenwich and Wilbraham, but there is enough evidence to be confident that a sizeable number of people in the state were opposed to many, if not all, elements of judicial independence; to what degree they were opposed, however, cannot now be known.

Although the drafters of the Constitution of 1784 established tenure during good behavior, they weakened much of the potential for independence—as implied by the words "good behavior"—by vesting the legislative and executive branches with power to remove judges by address without cause, no matter their behavior. And, although the drafters of the Constitution of 1792 readopted the good-behavior provision, they weakened it further by doing nothing to end the established legislative practice of annually voting fluctuating salaries, sometimes even decreasing salaries that the constitution mandated should be "permanent." The delegates to the Constitutional Convention of 1791–1792 also showed their lack of enthusiasm for judicial independence by refusing to entrench the Superior Court into the constitution and by rejecting the amendment depriving the General Court of authority to restore litigants to their law. The better view of judicial independence, MARCELLUS pointed out in 1813, was to think of judges' dependence —a dependence on the legislature that "may remove them by address, and repeal old law constituting Judicatories [i.e., courts] and establish new ones." The *Portsmouth Oracle* thought it more exact to say the judiciary was dependent on *both* the legislative and executive branches. The constitution "will be found to make the Judiciary . . . totally dependent upon the other two branches of the Government," the *Oracle* theorized. "They are dependent for their offices, their powers, and their emoluments. For their offices, because the Constitution expressly provides, that the Legislature and the Executive may remove every Judge in the State, whenever they please. For their powers, because the Constitution confers none. Whatever jurisdiction they have, is conferred by law—of course the Legislature may grant to any particular Court little, or much or none at all at pleasure. For their emoluments, because the Constitution expressly leaves them to the discretion of the Legislature."[20]

The constitution's judicial independence clause, commentators frequently contended, was best interpreted by its original meaning created during the Glorious Revolution: that is, to establish independence from the Crown, not from Parliament. "[T]he commission of a Judge during good behavior, was to protect him against the Executive, not against the *Legislature*," MARCELLUS concluded. "The framers of the [New Hampshire] constitution and the people who ratified it, in ordaining the commission of Judges to be during good behavior, had no other idea, than the preventing their removal by the *Executive*. They did not mean to place them out of the reach of the General Court."[21] Just to recite the ways the legislative branch could make judicial rules showed how much the constitution did not place the courts out of reach. The legislature was empowered to create and abolish all New Hampshire courts, including the highest; to define and regulate their jurisdictions; to designate when the courts sat, for how many days, and where; to determine the judge's financial and personal support, such as sheriffs, clerks, and other officers; to set the number of judges who must preside at each jury trial (first four, then three judges during Smith's first term); to authorize or forbid law terms at which the court, without juries, heard appeals, errors, and arguments of law; perhaps to prescribe rules of procedure; and, until 1819, to entertain petitions to overturn adjudicated verdicts and restore litigants to their law.

New Hampshire proponents for a judiciary more dependent than independent often claimed that dependency was good republican theory. "Those who effect to scout the phrase 'sovereign people' ask much in a jargon, understood by none but themselves, about '*the independence of the Judges*,'" the *New-Hampshire Gazette* explained. "Are they to be independent of THE PEOPLE? If they are to be independent of the people, and the people are not also to be independent of them; we may as well call them *superior to the people*, at once, and [be] done with it." The trial of Aaron Burr clinched the argument. Chief Justice John Marshall ruled that the article in the United States Constitution defining treason as "levying war" meant that to be guilty Burr had to have committed an overt act, and that restrictive interpretation, excluding any notion of constructive treason, resulted in Burr's acquittal. "The conduct of Judge Marshall is a handsome comment upon the *independence* of the Judiciary," the *Gazette* continued. "Had he known that at the end of five or seven years, he must account for his official behavior, does any one believe he would have acted as he has done? . . . Depend upon it, this independence, this irresponsibility, will make tyrants of bad men and bad men of good."[22]

The *Gazette* warned against thinking that impeachment could be a device to police an otherwise independent judiciary. The failure of the Jefferson administration to remove any judge except the insane John Pickering proved impeachment too clumsy to do the political job Republicans wanted done.[23] New Hampshire officials did not need Pickering's conviction to learn that the procedure of impeachment was unwieldy. The trial of Woodbury Langdon had made that evident. Charges had to be preferred against the judge, the impeachment had to be voted by the House of Representatives, managers had to be selected to conduct the prosecution, briefs had to be written, the senators had to be sworn in as judges, then they were instructed as to how to conduct a trial, at which the defendant was represented by attorneys who were entitled to present a full defense. In New Hampshire, however, the difficulties of impeachment were relatively unimportant if the Republicans wanted to remove judges from office. It was just one of three procedures that could be used. The other two, "addressing out" and "legislating out," were much more efficient. They are the reason why impeachment was not the method of choice for removing New Hampshire judges from office.

Addressing out of office was more direct, faster, cheaper, and far less complicated than impeachment. A clear and easily implemented provision of the New Hampshire and some other state constitutions, it is not a well known procedure, in part because it was rejected by the framers of the United States Constitution. For purposes of this discussion, the most interesting argument made in the constitutional convention at Philadelphia against adopting an "addressing" article was advanced by Gouverneur Morris. He insisted that the "addressing" authority would destroy judicial independence. It was, Morris contended, "a contradiction in terms to say that the Judges should hold their offices during good behavior, and yet be removable without a trial." That reasoning has been persuasive to many lawyers but not to the legal historian Barbara Black. She claims the opposite: that the authority to address judges from office is "the safety-valve approach to judicial independence," one way to make "good behavior" mean what it says, for it allows a judge to be removed who is competent, honest, and expert but not, in the judgment of the legislature and the executive, *good* according to how they define the word. In Massachusetts, for example, Edward Greeley Loring was addressed out of the office of judge of probate for Suffolk County for serving as United States Commissioner enforcing the Fugitive Slave Act of 1850. Abolitionists and other anti-slavery factions did not think that remanding fugitive slaves to their owners was *good behavior.*[24]

While still a Federalist, William Plumer had been troubled by the ease with which judges could be addressed from their courts, without either accusation or hearing, just by a vote cast on the spur of the moment with no requirement that the addressers *publicly* explain why they were addressing out the addressee or even that they had reasons. After he switched to the Republicans, Plumer began to see addressing out in a more positive light. "Our governor, councillors, senators and representatives are annually elected by *ourselves,*" he wrote, using his favorite pseudonym, ARISTIDES, "and to extend the principle of frequent elections, a principle so favorable to republicanism, our constitution reposes the authority of removing even our judges from office whenever a majority of the legislature request the governor, and he with consent of the council concur with that request." Judicial independence was lessened, Plumer admitted, but not more than sound republican principles called for, because, after all, the practical and political result of addressing judges from office "was to render the tenure of judicial officers as permanent and as independent of the legislative and executive authority, as the nature of a free government would permit."[25] At the time he wrote these words, Plumer was not only a member of Jefferson's party; he had also assimilated a good degree of Jefferson's disdain for judicial independence. No other New Hampshire governor would exercise the authority of addressing judges out of office as many times as Plumer would.[26]

The most drastic method of removing judges was to legislate them out of office. It entailed removing the entire bench, and, as a result, it was also the most political procedure as it allowed the governor and Council to appoint an entirely new court. The process of legislating out was even easier than addressing out. The legislature simply repealed the statute that had created the current court. If the governor concurred and signed the bill, the court was abolished and the judges were removed from office. Although previously quoted, it is worth repeating what Senator Uriah Tracy said, for he had the best summary of how legislating out operated as procedure: "although you cannot remove the judge from office"—that is, a judge serving at good-behavior tenure—"yet you can remove his office from him." Other observers thought that the legislative power of legislating out could "entirely destroy" the "independence of the judges." It destroyed, in other words, the intention of good-behavior tenure, as Governor John Taylor Gilman was told after he and the two houses legislated out of office the New Hampshire Superior Court in 1813. "The Constitution expressly declares the Judges *shall* hold their offices during good behavior," THE PEOPLE protested. "But, Sir, according to *your* doctrine, this means as long as the *Legislature* shall say; or until any dominant faction, shall see fit to indulge, or remove them." Not so, a Federalist had argued three months earlier. Legislating an entire court out of existence did not effect a judge's tenure, only his office. "[A] judge's commission is created and given him as a judge by and under the act or law of the General Court, (not by the constitution) and when that law is abolished, the tenure of his commission is also abolished; he is no longer *the judge* or *a judge.*"[27]

Virginia's St. George Tucker was the first jurisprudent to acknowledge that good-behavior tenure could not be reconciled with the power to legislate a court out of office. "[A]lthough the tenure of office be, *during good behaviour,* this does not prevent the separation of the office from the officer, by putting down the office." Tucker continued, "but only secures to the officer his station, upon the terms of good behaviour, so long as the office itself remains. Painful indeed is the remark, that this interpretation seems calculated to subvert one of the fundamental pillars of free governments."[28]

Only courts not entrenched in a constitution can be legislated out of office. "The practical rule, which governs the whole subject, is that every court may be abolished by the power which established it, but not by any lower power," Justice Horace Gray explained. "The [United States] Supreme Court, therefore, established by the people in their Constitution . . . can be reached only by an amendment to the Constitution. But all inferior courts, being but the creators of the Legislature, may be abolished by the same power which created them." That was the legal rule that cost Jeremiah Smith his office as a midnight judge. It is also the legal principle that motivated Plumer and Smith to argue so hard to entrench the Superior Court into the New Hampshire Constitution of 1792. Their failure meant that all New Hampshire state courts could be legislated out.[29]

Removal of Smith and the other midnight judges had persuaded many New Hampshire people that legislating an entire court out of existence was constitutional. In the politics of the day, however, constitutionality was not the question debated. The question that interested most commentators was whether New Hampshire's judiciary was independent. No one examined the issue more closely than the committee on the judiciary for the House of Representatives in June 1816. It voted that legislative power to legislate the courts out of office meant that the judiciary was *dependent* and, worse, it was dependent on the caprice of partisan politics.

If the legislature can at its will and pleasure abolish a court, and thereby remove the Judges from office, then it is clear that the Judges, instead of holding their offices by a permanent tenure, are mere tenants at the will of the legislature, and the general court has a control over the other courts wholly inconsistent with the independence which the constitution intended to give to the Judges. In all free states a diversity of sentiment upon public measures will exist; and this diversity of sentiment will constantly engender party heat and intemperance; and the public mind will at times become too much agitated for calm and sober reflection. Amid these agitations, it is of infinite importance to the community, that the men who are to settle and finally determine rights involving the characters, the fortunes and the lives of individuals, should be placed as far as possible from the control of those, who are actively and warmly engaged in maintaining the ascendency of a party. For if the court are to be changed with every change of popular opinion, the Judges will of course be selected from the dominant party, and the most zealous and active partizans will be the most likely to be placed upon the bench; and the court thus become an engine in constant activity to maintain and support the preeminence of a party, instead of a tribunal calmly and soberly engaged in the administration of fair and impartial Justice.[30]

The committee's reasoning was persuasive as law and agreeable to the politics of New Hampshire, yet members of the House of Representatives who voted to accept the report did not take to heart the words quoted. Just five days after they approved this report, the members of the house adopted an opposite policy. They concurred with the Senate and voted to legislate the Supreme Judicial Court out of existence. Then for good measure they addressed the same judges out of office. In other words, they addressed out the judges of a court that no longer existed.[31]

Seven

A Man for One Office

Despite the legislative authority to both address and legislate judges from office, New Hampshire lawyers working to reform the state's judicial system did not think judicial independence the main difficulty that they faced. It was a very serious matter, especially the ease and willingness with which the legislature assumed the right to restore litigants to their law, but it was not their most pressing challenge. A greater problem was the compensation New Hampshire paid to its judges. After that, perhaps not quite as serious but nevertheless quite troublesome, was the public-policy theory, shared by a number of state officials, that some high court judges should be nonlawyers. It was not just a matter of New Hampshire politics. It was even more an articulated principle of New Hampshire jurisprudence to have laymen on the bench.

Jeremiah Smith might have become chief justice as early as 1795 had New Hampshire paid judges reasonably decent salaries. He would have had to leave Congress, of course, but there is convincing grounds for believing he would have done so had he been named chief justice. But, planning to get married and raise a family, he could not have accepted the office at the salary it paid. When he did leave Congress and set up practice in Exeter, his net income for his first year, ending on 1 September 1799, was $2,351. For the next two years his net income was $3,018.69 and $3,077.60. In 1797, the compensation for the chief justice of the Superior Court was raised to $850; an associate justice netted $800. That was up from $600 for the chief and $466.67 a year for each associate. Yet even that small amount was not a judge's take-home pay. While on circuit he had to absorb all of his expenses; he was not reimbursed by the state. And these costs—transportation, bed and board, livery stable—were expected to rise substantially in the next two decades as New Hampshire would surely be adding at least four new counties and, therefore, more terms of courts and more towns to which to travel.[1]

The better lawyers with successful law practices simply could not afford to become state judges unless they had other sources of income. That fact was especially true for judges of the Court of Common Pleas. Their pay was lower than that of Superior Court justices. "The Legislature have virtually said, by the small salaries allowed them," A FRIEND TO TRUTH concluded, "that it was not expected that they would be lawyers by profession."[2]

It might be thought that the two problems were related. Had New Hampshire paid adequate salaries, more attorneys surely would have been willing to be judges, and there would have been no need to appoint non-lawyers to the bench. But cause and effect was not that simple. The fact that good lawyers were unwilling to serve was not the only reason why laymen were appointed. There was a prevalent theory in turn-of-the-century New Hampshire, shared by many important state officials and not just by agrestic members of the general public, that not every judge should come from the ranks of the practicing legal profession. In fact there was an argument, quite often stated, that it would be a better court if some of the judges were not legal practitioners but came from a more practical line of work. It was a theory of judicial governance that Lynn Turner did not credit. He preferred to think the policy was due to antilawyer bias. "The two factors that seemed most influential in guiding legislative and executive policy towards the judiciary," he observed, "were niggardliness and a prejudice against lawyers," adding that "[n]either of these was confined to one party." Turner is certainly right if all he meant was that there was a very strong strand of antilawyer sentiment in turn-of-the-century New Hampshire. But there was also a political theory, perhaps not peculiar to New Hampshire, yet widely shared within the state, that there were other experiences besides legal training that fitted a man to be a judge.[3]

A measure of just how strongly some officials felt that only lawyers should not be appointed to the state's highest bench surfaced in 1798 when a vacancy occurred on the Superior Court. Jeremiah Smith said he would have become a candidate, except that the salary was just too low for his needs, and, besides, he realized he did not have sufficient political backing. Instead he supported Arthur Livermore, perhaps the only young lawyer in the state with sufficient income to serve on the bench. "Judge Edward St. Loe Livermore consents to sit this week at Dover, and then leave the bench," Smith observed. "I shall use all my endeavors that Arthur Livermore succeed his brother."[4]

Edward St. Loe Livermore and Arthur Livermore were sons of Samuel Livermore, who had been attorney general and chief justice of New Hampshire and currently was representing the state in the United States Senate. A well trained lawyer from a politically powerful family, Arthur Livermore was, for Smith and Plumer, the logical person to be appointed to the court. He was not so obvious a choice to the governor, and one reason was prejudice against lawyers. Both of New Hampshire's chief executives of the 1790s, Josiah Bartlett and John Taylor Gilman, did not favor placing lawyers on the bench. They preferred, as one historian put it, "to select judges on the basis of their military or genealogical records rather than their legal attainments."[5]

"The governor and council have just dispersed, and monstrous to relate, have appointed Paine Wingate and Ebenezer Smith," Jeremiah Smith wrote to an acquaintance. "If you are curious to know why it was that Arthur Livermore was not appointed I will tell you what they say. That Arthur Livermore was too young; that there have been two of that name and family on the court before, and that the bar were universally for him, and therefore they could not appoint him." Plumer was more blunt. "Previous to this," he observed, "the governor had been considered by lawyers as being hostile to the bar; these appointments confirmed that opinion."[6]

It would be impossible to measure the depths of antilawyer feeling in New Hampshire when Plumer and Smith were at the bar. It is, however, telling that the governor about whom they complained was a Federalist, the leader of what was correctly known as the lawyers' party. It was their opponents, the Republicans, who were vocally antilawyer. "Much of this opposition to the Barr proceeds from a few restless antifederal men," Plumer had written a few months earlier, referring to Republicans. "They think, & justly, that the Barr are opposed to their measures & that we have much influence in the State." Another reason, Turner pointed out, was that lawyers "played an important part in giving the Federalist party that intellectual superiority which it enjoyed almost to the end of its existence." As New Hampshire turned more and more Republican, their leadership among the Federalists made lawyers "the more unpopular with the mass of the people."[7]

In retaliation, Federalist newspapers regularly counted the number of lawyers whom the Republicans nominated for public office, but, of course, the Federalists ran many more. "Are not four lawyers out of five candidates rather too many to have on one list?" QUERIST asked of the Federal congressional slate in 1808. "Would it not be *republican,* to have some merchants and farmers, as well as *lawyers?*" Three months later Jeremiah Smith was a Federalist candidate for presidential elector along with six other lawyers. There were no lawyers among the Republican nominees, but there were "five substantial, honest Farmers." "Men of Newhampshire," ROCKINGHAM asked, "will you choose Lawyers or Farmers?" The "men of Newhampshire" answered two years later by electing Smith as governor and filled other state offices, RATTLE thought, with too many lawyers. "Behold at the head of our government is a lawyer, the secretary is a lawyer, the treasurer of the state is a lawyer, and some say a speculator, the speaker of the house of representatives a lawyer, the president of the senate a lawyer, and a great proportion of the justices of the peace in the state are lawyers," he complained in the *New-Hampshire Gazette*. "Now is it not high time that the people should awake from their slumber and prevent themselves from being trodden under foot by lawyers who are mostly educated in the jurisprudence of Great Britain."[8]

It was very rare for the Republican press to praise a lawyer for serving as a lawyer. Usually Republican newspapers were panning lawyers, and there were few sins that Republican writers did not lay on lawyers. "[A]s a profession or society of men, a more intolerant and persecuting is not to be found," the *Patriot* complained. "The business of nearly one half of our attornies is made up of unprincipled speculation and persecution." "Lawyers in this State," a Portsmouth newspaper lamented in 1805, "a few years since, were very scarce, and poor, for want of business, and since they have increased, and are increasing, like the locust in Egypt, their business has become very lucrative, (what is that a sign of?) now all the youth, are studying law, instead of divinity—what is that a sign of?"[9]

During the years after Jeremiah Smith left Congress and was practicing law in Exeter, the Republican newspapers in the state became more politically vocal, which meant criticism of attorneys became even more public and partisan. One complaint they frequently voiced was that lawyers were a profession, and any profession, by being an exclusive, separate class, was out of place in a republican society. Because of their education, their professionalism, and the fact that they did not work with their hands, they stood out with clergymen and merchants, apart from the remainder of the population. "There are three classes of people, *viz.* The *priests,* the *lawyers,* and the *merchants,* who complain of our low salaries," a Republican newspaper explained. "The most of these, some how or other, create to themselves great estates; but how much does any of them, who follows his profession exclusively, add to the real wealth of the community? The first is a tax on the vices, the second lives on the distresses, and the third piles up wealth by pampering the luxuries, as well as supplying some [of] the necessities of the people."[10]

Lawyers and clergy were always linked as two parts of the nonproductive trio, although sometimes the third group was physicians rather than merchants. A toast at a Fourth of July celebration at Plainsfield in 1809 explained that connection. "*Professional characters, Clergymen, Lawyers and Physicians.* May they never forget that their main support is from independent farmers, mechanics, and laborers." Five years later, in another Fourth of July toast, the three were still together. "*Professional Characters.* Clergymen, Physicians and Lawyers—May they not inter meddle in cases where their knowledge does not extend." It was a Republican Fourth of July celebration, and people in attendance knew what was meant. It would not have been offered at the Federalist celebration.[11]

A Republican complaint that had much substance was that lawyers were pro-British. Republicans said it was due to lawyers' training, and they may have been partly right. "[T]he profession of the law, considered as a body, is devoted, heart and hand, to the support of British principles and British politics in the United States," Decius asserted. "The causes of this attachment to England will be found in the *nature of their studies* and the *objects of their pursuit*. These studies are the laws of Great Britain. . . . The praise of British jurists, consistently sounding on their tongues, soon finds its way into their hearts. Immured in these pursuits, and seeing nothing beyond, they contract by degrees, a habit of admiration for the celebrated men whose opinions they adopt; and of attachment for the country where those laws were first enacted, from the explanation of which, their own respectability and importance have arisen."[12]

Identified with the Federal party, lawyers were tarred with all the evils that the Republican press visited upon the Federalists, especially the fear that lawyers were conspiring to create a monarchy and introduce a hereditary aristocracy. Rockingham demonstrated how easily one favorite argument—that lawyers were pro-British due to their education in English law—led to the conclusion that lawyers were plotting the downfall of republicanism. "The men of the law, whether Judges or practitioners, are early habituated to receive information and instruction from British authorities," Rockingham argued; "they study British law; quote British writers; imbibe British personalities; and fancy the British form of government, the most stupendous fabric of human wisdom. From ideas and opinions such as these, the transition to anti-republican sentiments is natural and easy. *Men of this description*, whatever they may pretend, hold the Constitution of the United States and the principles in which it is founded, in utter contempt. *They* wish to assimilate the political institutions of our Country with those of Great Britain."[13]

It is difficult today to imagine that the Republican writers were serious, but they repeated the accusation so often, it is likely they thought there were people who believed it. The contention was most concisely summed up by A Dover Farmer. "The RIGHTS and LIBERTIES of this happy country, are a nuisance and an eye sore to the Judges and Lawyers. They wish to remove them, to overthrow them, to trample them under foot, and on their ruins to establish a monarchy and an aristocracy." After Plumer converted from the Federal party to the Republicans, Veritas, writing in the *Concord Gazette*, accused him and his eldest son of repeating the same charge of conspiracy against his former friends, which he would have dismissed as nonsense just three years earlier. "Lawyers seem to be particularly obnoxious to them," Veritas wrote of Republican propagandists. "No class of men (*old tories* only excepted) are pointed out as irreconcilable enemies to the union and the liberty and rights of the people. The Epping lawyer and his son, previous to the March election, trimmed the mid-night lamp to persuade the good people of this State that lawyers were conspiring with British agents to overthrow our government, and they must not be trusted with any office."[14]

Anyone sifting through New Hampshire newspapers, Federal as well as Republican, for the first two decades of the nineteenth century is surely struck by how much antilawyerism was part of the political culture. When, for example, PHILO criticized the writing style of JUSTITIA, he felt he did not have to explain his criticism. Rather, he took for granted that his readers disliked the way in which lawyers constructed their arguments. "As a writer you possess the merit of ingenuity and the astuteness of legal science," PHILO told JUSTITIA. "Despairing of vindicating your friend against most of the charges alledged against him, you discover the cunning of the shuffling lawyer, by selecting the most favorable points in your defence, while you declare it "needless to notice all the *trivial* items objected against our chief magistrate.""[15]

Writers simply assumed that newspaper readers had internalized a distrust of lawyers and introduced remarks disparaging lawyers without any attempt to explain why they were doing so. They expected readers to know what they meant. Urging voters to elect George Sullivan to Congress, the *Concord Gazette* claimed, "He is a lawyer, who studied the profession as a noble science . . . not as an art, that he might more easily pray on his fellow man." A law student was reported by the *New-Hampshire Gazette* to tell his father that he was ready to practice law because his studies "had initiated him in all the sophistical chicaneries of the Lawyers, and that he now perfectly knew how to make right wrong, and wrong right." Some writers utilized the antilawyer culture to create interest. An example is LUCIUS, a Portsmouth commentator, who tossed out the following remark in a newspaper article when making a point that had nothing to do with lawyers: "Who ever heard of a client looking out for a new lawyer to transact his business because he found from experience (if the thing be possible) that his present attorney was honest and faithful."[16]

The antilawyer culture was not based on unreasoning bias. There were many people in New Hampshire who could recite a list of reasons for mistrusting lawyers. Consider CIRCULAR, who thought lawyers a class apart, spending their professional hours "misleading the people of this State, and making their fortunes, on the sins of the people."

[C]an a free government possibly exist, where any one class of citizens are commissioned, or tolerated by authority, to lord it over, or to mislead, any other class? Can it be consistent in a free government, to tolerate any class of citizens, to excite law-suits among the ignorant people, and be the real cause of, perhaps, two thirds of the actions that are commenced in the State yearly, and to pay very little attention, to the solemn oath they have taken, or to the Table of Fees, made by authority, to govern them in their charges for services? can it be consistent, for them to be active, in making laws, to govern a free people, and to make them lengthy and mysterious, and then to take the lead, in the bar, and on the bench, to explain those laws, their own way, to deceive the Jury, and to take turns, to fill the bench for awhile, for the honor, and then resign, and take the bar again, for the sake of the profits, and have their technical terms, and masons signs, as it were, to carry their part, with a full design, to get the cause, right or wrong, for their client, to make themselves popular, in their calling.[17]

CIRCULAR's chief complaint, that lawyers formed an exclusive group socially and politically out of place in a republican society, was, perhaps, the deletion most frequently voiced against attorneys during the years Plumer and Smith were in practice. "That *Lawyers* esteem themselves a privileged order—an *Aristocracy!* admits of no dispute," the *American Patriot* complained. A few months after printing those words, the owner sold the *American Patriot* to Isaac Hill, who would take the newspaper to new heights of partisan journalism, making it, in only two to three years, the most influential Republican organ in the state. He changed the name to the *New-Hampshire Patriot* and began thrashing lawyers, constantly and relentlessly. His favorite word for describing a political enemy was "pettifogger." One major theme Hill reiterated was "the interests and rights of the people are adverse to the interests and prosperity of the lawyers." Many New Hampshire citizens seem to have agreed, especially after being served with papers in a lawsuit. Defendants assumed they never would have been sued if a lawyer or two had not moved into the vicinity where they and the plaintiffs lived. It was an assumption that Hill readily turned into a certainty. "Towns which before they [lawyers] were introduced lived in peace and quietness, without quarrelling or litigation of any kind, are now kept in a continued scene of uproar and confusion, without any other visible means than the introduction of a lawyer."[18]

There were other commentators who complained about New Hampshire lawyers as forcefully as Hill. Perhaps no other Republican commentator stated the case against them as an economic class apart more forcefully than did A DOVER FARMER. "What interest have the Lawyers in common with the rest of the community?" he asked. "None. If the merchants loose their property by capture or shipwreck; what harm does the Lawyer suffer? None. If by frost, by drought, by blast or mildew, the fruits of the earth are destroyed and the Farmer is disappointed in his expected harvest; what injury does the Lawyer sustain? None. —He is totally unconnected with the rest of the community. His views, his wishes and interests are distinct and separate from theirs."[19]

A DOVER FARMER lay bare the heart of the case against lawyers in New Hampshire during the era of the early republic. Lawyers were a breed apart from the general population. That was a key complaint of people fearful of outside economic forces they could not control or those who were nostalgic for the more communal, less individualistic society they recalled from their youth. They remembered a colonial past when, in their town meetings, they voted where a local turnpike would be located, set tolls on bridges and ferries and, when serving as jurors, decided such matters as the law for the enforcement of agreements to deliver crops to market after the harvest. If there had been a drought, or blast, or mildew so that crops had failed or in some way did not meet the contractees' expectations and could not be delivered as promised, jurors applied rules of fairness and did not enforce the agreement or enforced it differently from how the parties had intended. Now the turnpikes over which they sent their produce to market had most likely been financed by a partnership in faraway Portsmouth or Boston, and moneymen never seen in town, unknown strangers, laid out the routes, determined the quality of repairs, and set the tolls. Judges were now beginning a "reform" effort to take questions of law away from jurors and, when crops failed, attempting to enforce contracts as the parties had intended, not by community values of what was fair or what was just, as once had been the rule. People living in rural areas or in small towns knew that it was lawyers who served the outsiders by reshaping, remaking, and taking over their lives and livelihoods. It was the lawyers who were the local agents for these new manipulative economic forces they could not control. It was lawyers, as A DOVER FARMER said, who were "totally unconnected with the rest of the community."[20]

Bad economic times made such fears even more acute and complaints even more frequent, as when New Hampshire suffered greatly from the twin blows of the national embargo and the War of 1812. "The whole-sale merchant called upon his debtors, the petty traders in the country, and they in turn upon their customers," the *Patriot* expounded, "and, on failure of prompt payment, recourse was had immediately to a lawyer, or more properly a collector, for the knowledge of many who assume the name of lawyers, extends no further, than to commence a suit on a note of hand or account, prosecute the same to judgment, collect a few dollars from some unfortunate or negligent man, pay it over to their employer, and tax an exorbitant fee for their services. If any fault is found with one of them for extortion, the reply is—'I gave two thousand dollars for my *knowledge*, and I cannot afford to do business for nothing.'"[21]

At a time when the population of New Hampshire was 214,000, and there were 130 lawyers in the state, the *Patriot* lamented that that number was far too many. "If lawyers multiply as fast in years to come as in the few years past," it complained, "farewell to the prosperity and peace of our citizens —farewell to industry and enterprise. Simple justice is requisite to the happiness of the State; and so far as lawyers are instrumental in facilitating this, so far they are beneficial to society. More than simple justice is oppression, and less than this, is injustice."[22]

So many lawyers, Republican printers feared, not only meant that a multitude of lawsuits would be filed but also that there would be too many poorly paid, yet greedy attorneys causing the bar to degenerate into mere bill collectors. "The Courts of law would never be so constantly crowded with petty, vexatious and disgraceful suits," PUBLICOLA complained, "were it not for the herds of pettifogging Lawyers that infest them. . . . They are in law what quarks are in medicine; exciting the malady for the purpose of profiting by the cure, and retarding the cure for the purpose of augmenting the fees." William Plumer did not deny there were such lawyers, saying they were not lawyers of the better class but "the third and fourth ranks" of the profession. "These men assume the names of lawyers, though they are profoundly ignorant of the first principles of law and government. Their knowledge is confined to a few technical terms, to the forms of declarations and pleas in plain simple cases, and the taxing of bills of cost. They are, in fact, mere *collectors of debts.*" Plumer was remarkably critical. "They have an interest directly opposed to that of the people," he insisted, "that of multiplying suits and increasing fees. . . . Too many of them take much pains to promote litigation and increase the number of suits, by purchasing demands and urging the people to sue, by engaging to carry on suits without fees if their clients should not recover, or by making the amount of their fees altogether dependent upon the result of the suit."[23]

Plumer did not say so, but other people, mostly correspondents writing to Republican newspapers, charged that lawyers made litigation more expensive than it should have been. One popular accusation, which many people believed, was that lawyers had formed a conspiracy to keep the law complicated and known only to themselves. "Their interest, as a profession," PHOCION alleged, "requires that laws should be obscure, tautological, contradictory and uncertain, so that to understand them should be a labor of a life—that the path which leads to the temple of Justice should be crossed and indented, so winding, perplexed and involved, that none but themselves should be able to find their way through it."[24]

There is little evidence what New Hampshire lawyers thought about their bad press. It is not mentioned by Plumer or Smith, nor in Daniel Webster's correspondence, and, as yet, there were no bar association publications to defend the profession. Lawyers may not have felt harassed, but they could have been annoyed, especially when antilawyer sentiment hurt the profession. Just as, on one hand, it was charged that the only reforms lawyers permitted were those that increased the "glorious uncertainty of the law" and, of course, increased their fees, so on the other hand the only legal reforms Republicans supported were those that suppressed the practice of law, such as allowing defendants to avoid trial by jury by electing arbitration at which neither side could be represented by an attorney. Writing to Smith in 1797, Plumer attributed enactment of some reforms he had sponsored in the House of Representatives to the fact that country legislators assumed they "would lessen the business & influence of lawyers." And, of course, as in all the other states, there was strong opposition to efforts by the bar to form associations and to set standards for admission to law practice. "The rules and regulations of the practitioners at our judicial courts, and commonly called 'bar rules' are oppressive and unconstitutional," JUNIUS objected. Because they were "made by a class of men, whose interest is to create a monopoly of practice," they violated the right of the people to equality.[25]

There is no evidence that antilawyer politics damaged law practice or even effected the income of New Hampshire attorneys. True, we know little about the economics of law offices for there are no collected papers of a practitioner except for Daniel Webster's younger years. Nor do we know much about its impact on the courts. But it is reasonable to suggest that the vigorous antibar press, at the very least, diminished respect for the judiciary among the population and, therefore, harmed the judiciary. Persistent trashing of the bar surely rubbed off to some considerable extent on the judges. Although it also cannot be measured, even for purposes of specula-tive history, the antilawyer atmosphere of New Hampshire politics surely had a negative effect on Plumer and Smith's program of judicial reforms. Consider, for instance, how mistrust of the bar made it difficult to persuade the public that only trained lawyers who were leaders of the profession should be appointed to either the Superior or Common Pleas courts. There is no need to trace the controversy through every appointment of a layman to the bench. The debate over whether judges should be lawyers received its most extensive public airing in 1809 when Governor John Langdon ap-pointed Richard Evans to the state's high court. Jeremiah Smith, who had been chief justice of the Superior Court since May 1802, had just been elected governor, defeating Langdon (who had stood for reelection), and was due to be sworn into office the day after Evans's appointment. He was an-noyed not only because Langdon had made an appointment that Smith had expected to make but also because Evans was a nonlawyer. In Smith's guber-natorial address to the General Court the next day, he asserted that the time had come when only lawyers should be appointed judges. Some Republicans were furious. "If the late Chief Justice thinks *himself* the only correct standard of justice—if he supposes law was never properly dispensed except when he was on the bench—then may he justify himself in saying that only lawyers ought to be judges," the *New-Hampshire Patriot* replied.[26]

Smith was politically crucified by the ensuing controversy. It was an ar-gument he should have gone to every length to avoid. Instead, he started it. That he did so is indicative of his incredibly poor political instincts, so different from his judgment concerning judicial and legal matters. He would serve only one term as governor because of that problem. Just about every gubernatorial policy he initiated—and every speech he gave—opened him to more criticism and fresh attacks, so badly did he gage public reac-tion and the cleverness of his opponents, for they twisted almost every-thing he said by convulsing his meanings or deliberately misquoting a word or two. Despite his successful terms as a congressman and his valu-able service in the state House of Representatives, he barely functioned in the executive chair during his one year as governor, developing no pro-grams and accomplishing none of the reforms of the judiciary that had been his main purpose for becoming govenor.

Of course, the time in the executive chair was but a temporary sideshow. Smith's failure as a one-term governor hardly matters to legal historians or even to New Hampshire political historians evaluating his contributions to the growth of New Hampshire or the stability of the state's economic development. He belonged in a much different office, and in it his talents shone. He was the first of the four outstanding New Hampshire chief justices who have, over the last two centuries, been the leaders of the bar and the makers of state law. Smith had been sworn into his judicial office during the summer of 1802, on a day that Daniel Webster would later recall was one of the most memorable dates in New Hampshire legal history. "[W]hen Jeremiah Smith became chief justice," he would exclaim, "it was a day of the gladsome light of jurisprudence." As Webster well knew, jurisprudence was Smith's forte, not politics. Smith never, for example, spoke publicly against legislative dominance of the courts. That the judicial branch of the government was administratively controlled by the legislative branch disturbed Smith much less than lawyers in the twenty-first century would think. It was a fact of political life, and he knew better than to fight it. His interest was the development of state law and, especially, legal theory. Deciding disputes of citizens and promulgating rules to govern the solution of future litigations was his professional strength. The gage of his success would be eventual official publication of judicial opinions, the creation of an appellate law term, and replacing jury-dominated common-sense jurisprudence with judge-dominated common law. They would be his legacy, not just to New Hampshire lawyers, but to all the receptionist lawyers of the United States.[27]

Remembering Smith's stellar accomplishments supporting the great jurists such as John Marshall, James Kent, and Joseph Story to shape the future course of American law, it is possible to overlook that when he became chief justice of New Hampshire, he not only inherited a judiciary of dependent constitutional status; he took over a court system that was in turmoil. During an eight-year period the previous decade, Lynn Turner has pointed out that the Superior Court "had suffered seven resignations, one impeachment, and innumerable threats [from the legislature] of removal" of judges under investigation. Turner identified several causes for the turmoil, but an old one alone told a good part of the story: money. New Hampshire continued to pay salaries too low to attract professionally trained lawyers to the bench. Not as serious but still damaging considering the courts' dependent status were the politics of the day. "The spirit of party ran high," Plumer recalled a quarter century later. It "divided families, neighborhoods, towns & states; &, blind to public interest, embittered the sweets of social life, & hazarded the rights of the nation." Even if it had not been so dependent on the political branches of the government, the judiciary had to be affected by the bitterness and animosity. At the turn of the nineteenth century, moreover, even the New Hampshire judiciary was not apolitical.[28]

At the time Smith became chief justice, New Hampshire had been a solidly Federalist state for over a decade. John Taylor Gilman, the governor who appointed Smith to the Superior Court, had been in office since 1794, but the political configuration that ensured his annual elections was most unusual, and the Republicans needed only competent leadership and a vote-getting gubernatorial candidate to challenge Federal ascendancy. Portsmouth, the largest town and only center of shipping, shipbuilding, and mercantile interests, was also the center of republicanism, and it was the merchants and traders who furnished the leadership of the Jeffersonian party. Federal strength lay inland where nine-tenths of the population were farmers. In most other states they were the people who furnished the base of Jefferson's strength, but fear and hatred of "atheist" France, driven and preached by the Congregationalist clergy, had kept the agricultural yeomen of New Hampshire voting for the Federalists, keeping Governor Gilman in the gubernatorial chair so that he was able to appoint Smith chief justice.[29] Soon the Federalists would discover that Jeffersonian gains and Federal decline were unavoidable.

Plumer led the Federalists through the first several elections of the century as their majorities steadily declined. His service was remarkable, keeping the party in office even after it lost its majority. He was owed much and received his reward when he was elected United States senator, beginning in 1802. The new chief justice, his friend, was delighted but wondered if the Federalist cause might have been better served had the Republican incumbent been reelected rather than Plumer. The month that Plumer was sworn in as a member of the Senate, the political fortunes of New Hampshire Federalism crumbled even more. A few weeks before Plumer arrived in Washington, John Langdon, at that time the only Republican senator from New England, left the capital. He had been the first New Hampshirite to serve the full term of six years and the first to be elected to a second term. His reelection had been opposed by most Federalists, but not by Jeremiah Smith. Langdon, he warned in 1795, would be much less dangerous to the Federal party staying in Philadelphia than returning to New Hampshire, where he would furnish Republicans with the political leadership they then lacked. Smith wrote Robert Fletcher, soon to obtain notoriety as the plaintiff in the famous constitutional litigation of *Fletcher* v. *Peck*, that if he had the choice he would have returned Langdon to Philadelphia where he could do less harm to New Hampshire Federalism. "If he is not elected, he will, I fear, be soured, and rear up an anti-federal party in the state; set up democratic clubs, poison the pure principles of our virtuous citizens," Smith predicted. "Let our people fall into the hands of the devil, but let them not fall into the hands of these men; famine, plague, and pestilence are nothing to it."[30] Smith was apocalyptic. Langdon returned to his Portsmouth home and in a short time, just four years, led the Republican party to triumph.

Smith would continue in that political vein throughout his career on the bench, a strong political partisan all his years as a judge. But he did not belong in politics. He was a man only for the law. Still there is a surprising dimension to his judicial career. A chief justice in a jurisdiction in which the political branches of the government exercised control over the judiciary and in which his political opponents went into the ascendancy five years after he was sworn into office, he might well have failed as a judge but for one consideration: he was respected. We must not attribute this to his caution, even though, considering his partisanship, he was very cautious. As chief justice, he did not quarrel with the legislature. He even acquiesced in the General Court's authority to restore to their law litigants who had lost a cause before a jury and petitioned to try the case again before another jury. Even lawmakers who were not lawyers and did not understand what he was accomplishing somehow recognized that he was truly the competent lawyer that New Hampshire needed on its court. They might be suspicious of his jurisprudence, but somehow New Hampshire politicians understood that he was the jurist to put the state on the path to legal stability and legal predictability. That was why he was respected. It was his competency, his leadership, and the confidence of the bar, not his legal theory, that won him respect. To keep him on the bench, even rabid Republicans were ready to go to lengths that surprised them, increasing his salary more than they had thought anyone could be worth. In this regard, Smith's judicial reputation was in striking contrast to that of his colleague Arthur Livermore. He was a judge lawmakers did not respect.

Eight

An Impetuous Judge

Long before the watershed election of 1805, Jeremiah Smith knew that the Federalists would certainly be swept out of office. "I wish a happy new year to you," he wrote William Plumer, "& to Messers Chase, Shippen, Yeats, Smith, & all other Judges laboring under impeachment. . . . In party times miserable is the condition of a Judge." It was the first day of 1805, and he was saying that the Republicans, after the spectacular gains made in 1804, would capture the governorship, the Council, perhaps even the two houses of the General Court, and, once they did, they would surely legislate his court out of office, taking for themselves control of the entire government. He did not expect that he would be impeached as were the judges he listed in his New Year's greeting to Plumer.[1] But he was certain he would soon be either addressed or legislated out of his chief justiceship.

The year 1805 did not turn out entirely as Smith anticipated. When John Langdon became governor, he introduced few changes to the government. There was, in fact, very little he could have done about the Federalist officeholders, especially judges. Aside from militia officers and justices of the peace, the New Hampshire executive had few appointments, and some of the best, on the judiciary, could have been filled only if the legislature first abolished the Superior Court and the Court of Common Pleas. "The judges of our Courts of law are appointed," Plumer explained to Senator Tracy of Connecticut: *"none of them will resign, & but few die."*[2]

Returning to New Hampshire from Washington, two months after Langdon was overwhelming reelected in 1806, Plumer was surprised to discover that a new political atmosphere prevailed. "The rage of party appears to have spent its force in this State," he concluded. "Langdon is re-elected without a real rival—a large majority of the legislature are of that party. The federalists are silent quiet & submissive. The violent Democrats [are] obliged to own that the change of men has produced but little change in the public measures."[3] Most surprising to Plumer and Smith, and probably to most New Hampshire lawyers, there had been no changes in the judiciary.

While still living in Washington, Plumer had contacted Langdon and asked him to open a correspondence to keep him informed of state affairs, especially about proceedings of the General Court. "I am anxious on the subject & feel interested in their doings," he explained, and then in the next sentence he revealed what really interested him. "Will a reform in the Judiciary be effected this session?" He may not have been asking whether the Republicans would address Smith's court from office. Judicial reform had been talked of during Gilman's penultimate term as governor, a year when the Federalists had still a slight edge in the lower house. Legislature committees had been appointed, the *Farmer's Cabinet* had reported, to study the administration of justice and "take into consideration the laws of this State respecting the jurisdiction of the Justices of the peace in criminal causes" and for both the high court and the justices to "report by bill" such "alterations and amendments as shall be judged necessary." Plumer did not expect the justices' court could be reformed—"No essential change can be effected but with the approbation of the Justices of the Peace"—but he hoped for changes in the Superior Court. The chief justice had requested them.[4] Smith wanted the powers of the justices on his court "enlarged" and the Court of Commons Pleas extensively restructured. Unfortunately the lawyer who wrote the reform bill, Jonathan Steele, followed his own notions of what should be done, not what changes were likely to be adopted by the legislature. His bill, Jeremiah Mason complained, was not supported by more than twenty votes. It would have abolished the Common Pleas. That part of the plan had much support. What few members liked was the court he would have substituted in place of Common Pleas. "It was essentially defective," Plumer complained after it was defeated. "It trusted too much not only to the skill & integrity of *one* man in each County but to his *health*. For should one of these County Judges happen to be sick at the time established by law for holding his Court every action in the County must be continued for six months. This delay would work great injury & manifest injustice."[5]

Chief Justice Smith seems to have been the only lawyer of influence in the state supporting Steele's bill. He wanted trial courts presided over by a single judge, especially trials conducted in his own Superior Court. Most lawyers opposed Steel's bill because they knew the new Common Pleas judges would be laymen and thought that nonlawyers were incapable of presiding alone at trials. Smith agreed, but he had another object in mind. Since first becoming chief justice, he had been seeking legislative authority for single-judge trials, at least on the Superior Court level. Due to tenets of republicanist legal theory, the legislature not only refused to authorize single-judge trials, but when he introduced them, apparently by a rule-of-court, the two houses enacted legislation mandating that all sitting judges had to preside together at each jury trial.[6] Steel's bill looked to Smith as though it was opening a new opportunity for reform. If single-judge trials were authorized for Common Pleas, it would become difficult to deny them to the Superior Court. More important to Smith, if the Common Pleas became one-judge courts, and the judges in most counties were laymen, Smith could hope that the public would soon see that nonlawyers were not competent to preside at jury trials. That would provide a major boost for the reform to which he gave the highest priority: appointing only lawyers to the judiciary.[7] He must have supported Steele's bill only for that reason—because of the single-judge provision—for he could not have thought there was any chance it would become law. Experience had taught him only too well that New Hampshire Republicans would never permit trials at which only one judge presided.

Considering the politics of New Hampshire in 1805, defeat of the reform bill was of little consequence compared to the fact that Governor Langdon showed no interest in removing Jeremiah Smith or any of his associate justices from the bench. It was not what Smith or most other Federalists had anticipated. "We shall remain in session till Saturday morning," he had written Plumer from Portsmouth two or three weeks before the election of 1804. "Much pains are taken to find occasion to blame the court, but I am determined no just cause shall be given. We will be faithful even to the end. As to myself I think my time is short, & I am determined to leave the office with a conscience void of offence." Starting another paragraph, he added: "These are times of great searching of hearts. You will therefore excuse this self approbation."[8]

As quickly as possible on becoming president, Thomas Jefferson had removed the midnight judges. Langdon, it was expected, would remove the Federalist judges once he was governor. A decade later MARCELLUS, a strong Republican partisan, recalled Langdon's first term: "the Judges were federal, . . . the Constitution was not then violated to drive them from office," he boasted. He does not tell us why, nor did any of his contemporaries or subsequent historians. But MARCELLUS may have given us a good hint when pointing out that his party did something much more than merely leaving the tenure of Smith and his colleagues undisturbed; they actually "increased the salaries of federal Judges to retain them in office." That claim was only partly true. In 1804, the year Plumer's genius for organizing election campaigns had denied Republicans complete victory, that party had nonetheless won most offices, including control of the House of Representatives, electing Langdon speaker. Led by Langdon, 28 Republicans joined 73 Federalists to raise the salary of Jeremiah Smith, who had told friends in the legislature that he would have to resign if his pay was not increased to a specified amount. They had only one purpose: to keep him in office as chief justice. It cannot be said that in that highly bitter partisan era Smith was politically popular, not in the sense that popularity crossed party lines. As previously stated, the better explanation is that Smith was admired as a professional. Legislators of both parties knew that for the first time, both in colonial and state history, New Hampshire's court was headed by an outstanding student of law, a reformer who cared deeply about improving the legal institutions of New England. Smith was valued and appreciated. It may have been, too, that he was personally popular with some legislators, but that was secondary.[9]

In May 1802, when Smith was first named chief justice, his yearly salary was $850, and each of the three puisne justices was paid $800. Keenly as he desired to be chief justice, he reluctantly declined appointment, informing the governor and Council that he could not afford to mount the bench unless he received a higher remuneration. In an unprecedented response, the legislature demonstrated how much value politicians attributed to Smith's reputation as the state's most learned lawyer by raising judicial compensation to $1,000 for him and $900 for each of the associates. These sums had been voted by the legislature despite knowing that most of their constituents would be astonished. Had they been told that Massachusetts judges made more than twice that amount, most New Hampshirites would have said Massachusetts was irrelevant: $1,000 was simply unbelievable pay for a New Hampshire officeholder. Yet the problem of salary was not solved even with this remarkable sum. After about a year's experience on the court, Smith discovered that expenses traveling circuit amounted to about $300 a year, leaving him with a real income of just $700. He could have made well over three times that amount in law practice; with a growing family, it would be depriving them of subsistence if he stayed on the bench. When the General Court convened in June 1804, he informed both houses that he would have to resign. Again the legislature demonstrated how much they valued having him as chief justice by voting the princely addition of $500 to his salary as long as he continued to occupy the office. It was an increase for him alone; the others on the Superior Court remained at the former scale of $900, which meant, if their living expenses on circuit were also $300, that their take-home pay would be exactly half that of Smith's. It was a great tribute to him but an insult to the three puisnes, especially to the two who were lawyers, Arthur Livermore and William King Atkinson.[10]

The three associate justices petitioned the General Court for pay raises proportional with Smith's, "lest in the public view our office should become degraded and rendered comparatively insignificant." The petition caused anxiety among members of the bar, fearful that one or both of the two puisne judges who were lawyers would resign, closing the court for several terms and leaving vacancies that no competent attorney would fill at the current compensation. By a vote of 23 to 119 the House of Representatives refused to raise the associates' salaries, and Judge Atkinson resigned.

To the great relief of the bar, Arthur Livermore did not retire. But he was very unhappy and showed his anger by not going on circuit one or more times.[11]

Livermore had a double grievance. In the very act telling him that he was worth much less than Chief Justice Smith, the legislature not only failed to raise his salary but it also increased his duties substantially. Remarkably, New Hampshire's reputation for niggardliness did not suffer when Smith was voted his portentous salary. The legislature did not appropriate funds from general revenues to increase his pay; it was too crafty to find the money in so obvious a place as the state treasury. It compensated him not from current taxes but from the *judiciary itself*. The statute raising Smith's salary was coupled to a companion bill reducing the membership of the Superior Court from four judges to three upon the death or resignation of a current judge. When Atkinson retired, Smith's additional $500 was taken from the salary of $900 that would have been paid to him, and, of course, the state profited by keeping for itself the remaining $400. Livermore was now on a court with one less associate yet had his labors substantially increased, for now he was responsible for one third of Atkinson's former duties. From the time of its first establishment after independence from Great Britain, the court had always had four justices. It did not revert to four members until 1833, when the population was not only larger but the growth of manufacturing brought an astonishing increase in litigation.[12]

Livermore's discontent sparked the first political crisis of Smith's chief justiceship. Livermore did not attend the spring 1805 circuit of the Superior Court. At the next session of the House of Representatives, William White, member for Wentworth, moved that a committee be appointed to investigate. Before the committee could contact him, Livermore wrote a letter to White that he apparently also gave to the *Courier* of Concord, for most legislators first read the text in that newspaper. Livermore complained that he had learned of White's motion from "the public prints" and asked why he was the only judge being questioned. "I think, that whoever will inspect the record of the Superior Court, will find that *no other judge* in this State *ever attended* as many days & hours of the Bench in the period of six years, *as I have*," he insisted. "If I am correct in this, . . . it must be allowed to be rather singular, that the imputation *of negligence should first fall on me*. If, in discharging the duties of my office, I have at any time been less faithful than *others*, I expect no *favors*, & in the sight of *him* who sees all our motives, I declare that I wish none." Livermore had said what had to be said, but in a much more belligerent tone than other lawyers would have used. Everyone acquainted with him knew he would not stop after writing only what was necessary. He was then the most contentious person in state government and in fact proved to be New Hampshire's most disputatious nineteenth-century high-court judge. He had genuine complaints about salaries and about the unfairness of New Hampshire lawmakers, and no matter how unwise it was to raise issues publicly, he was impetuously unable to remain silent. Moreover, he was confident about what should be criticized: it

was not the General Court so much as its control over and constant supervision of the judiciary. He did not say so, but after the grievance of unequal
salaries, he was complaining most about judicial dependence. No other
lawyer stated the complaint so bluntly or so insultingly.

> The whole Judiciary of the State is *feeble* in the hand of the Legislature. Far be
> it from me, as a member to think of resistance, whenever that body, *whether
> from one motive or another,* choose to *drive* me from office; because I know that
> the only alternative will be, to hold the office in *such disgraceful terms as they
> may* think proper to impose. The conduct of the last legislature, in creating an
> *unusual inequality* in the compensation of the Justices, such as does not exist,
> & never did exist, in any other of the United States, was *calculated to cover with
> dishonor all the Court, but the Chief Justice.* When or how I ever *deserved such
> censure* is to me unknown.[13]

New Hampshire people—strangers in the general public, as well as politicians and legislators who knew Livermore personally, or by reputation—
expected outbursts from the judge. Even so, this letter caused astonishment. "Is it not extraordinary to hear of a *Judge* complaining of enquiry, because he has not been *more negligent* than other judges?" Plumer asked.
"Are the crimes of others sufficient to exempt us from censure & from pun-
ishment?" Plumer may have been more legally positivistic than justified by
the laws existing then, but he made a persuasive point by contending that
Livermore had no grounds for questioning the legality of the General
Court's investigation of his circuits. The authority had been settled by the
Woodbury Langdon impeachment. That precedent required that he answer
every question he was asked. If Livermore wanted to make a different defense, Plumer concluded, he would have better been advised to concentrate
on the unequal compensation alone. It was a much sounder ground for
complaint. "Whether he intended to complain that his salary is too low, or
Judge Smith's too high is uncertain," Plumer wondered. "One thing is certain
—his pride is wounded at the inequality of the salary between him & the
Chief Justice. Whether he intends to resign or still hold a seat on the bench
which the Legislature has according to him *dishonored* & rendered *disgraceful* appears from the letter uncertain."[14]

Livermore had been on the court since the last month of 1798. He had
gotten there with the support of Plumer and Smith, who worked harder to
have him appointed than they did any other judicial candidate. "He was
then about thirty years of age," Plumer would recall, "& I thot he was an
honest[,] honorable man, of decent talents, & a correct lawyer; but he was
naturally arbitrary, sometimes imprudent, & did not possess those finer
feelings which are requisite to constitute a first rate character." Not able to
find a better lawyer willing to be a judge at the low salary, Plumer "recommended him to the governor and council, who received his name with
coolness." It is no mystery why. At that time, members of the Livermore

family were not in favor. Arthur's brother, Edward St. Loe Livermore, had been the chief associate of Plumer's at the Constitutional Convention six years earlier, when Smith had been away at Congress. He was the man who cost Plumer much support when, angry at the opposition, he personally and publicly insulted many of the leading men in the state. Arthur's father, Samuel, a former chief justice, was then a United States senator seeking re-election to a second term. Arthur and his brother spent much of the June 1798 session of the General Court badgering members to reelect their father, losing their tempers too many times, and abusing legislators—most of whom were without enthusiasm for reelecting the senator. The upshot was that some councilors were "violently opposed to Arthur Livermore," and, when they adjourned without appointing him, it appeared that his chances of becoming a judge were over.[15]

By the time of the December session of the legislature, much of the anger had subsided. Pressured by lawyers who wanted a law-trained judge, the governor and Council gave in and appointed Livermore to the Superior Court on the same day his father was reelected to the Senate. Less than two months later Plumer reported that "his conduct, thus far, is very commendable. . . . I was & still am pleased with his appointment. He will give a legal tone to the decisions of the Court." Smith took a few more months to reach the same conclusion. "Arthur Livermore makes a good judge," he said.[16]

"Although by nature imperious, Arthur Livermore was an able and usually an upright judge," a biographer insisted. "His impatience and pride would, however, break out at times." That temper was a Livermore family trait that for at least two or three decades caused constant distress to members of the New Hampshire bar. Samuel, the father, even though a respected and successful officeholder, including those of attorney general and chief justice, "was a man of strong intellectual powers, but arbitrary, imprudent, & too often governed by his passions." The brother, Edward St. Loe, was the most rash Livermore—"haughty, irritable, & imprudent," according to Plumer. "His passions were strong & often governed him more than his reason." Once he "greatly insulted & abused O[liver] Peabody & myself in open Court," Plumer told Smith. "He is too haughty, too insolent & over-bearing to be a friend. This is the 4th time he has quarreled [sic] in Court with gentlemen of the Bar." Yet, when serving on the bench, his personality was surprisingly transformed. As a presiding judge, "he was modest, calm, & patiently attentive to business," exceeding "the raised expectations of his friends, & by his judgment & conduct mortified his bitter enemies, for such he had."[17]

Unlike his brother, Edward, Arthur Livermore did not discard his abrasive personality when on the bench. He took it with him right into the courtroom. "As a usual thing," a biographer observed, "the lawyers stood in fear of him, for he never hesitated to speak his mind, and his sharp tongue and fearless bearing always added double force to the castigation." Once opening court at Hopkinton, he learned that the lawyers who had filed cases were not in attendance. He summarily dissolved the session, "taunt-ingly remarking that by the next term the counsel would probably be ready to begin work." By 1806 Plumer, having lost patience with him, was no longer a supporter. "Judge A. Livermore's conduct, like himself, is singular & extraordinary," he wrote to James Sheafe, the man he succeeded as U.S. senator. "He is eccentric, unacquainted with the world, with business, & I believe, *with himself.*"[18]

Both branches of the General Court implemented William White's mo-tion of enquiry by appointing committees to ask Livermore to explain why he had missed his circuits. On receiving the official letter from the commit-tee of the lower house, Livermore became even more precipitate, putting his effrontery on display for all the state to observe. "The insinuation it contains, that I have neglected the duties of my office is groundless," he replied, referring to both the letter and to a resolution of the General Court. "For nearly seven years I have held a place in the judiciary; & during that time, the court of which I have been a member has been regularly holden in all our Counties. . . . [O]f the services incident to the Court, I have contributed my part."[19]

The letter to the house committee mostly repeated arguments Livermore had made to White. At best, he showed slight interest in replying to the legislature's enquiries. Writing to the committee, but really addressing the general public—that is, everyone in New Hampshire who read newspapers —he added scorn to disdain, attacking both houses for promulgating un-equal salaries and blaming the lawmakers, while exonerating the judiciary, for cancelled circuits. The conclusion was as predictable in its complaints as it was insolent in its tone. If he was negligent, Livermore contended, it was not his fault considering the peculiar circumstances of his hapless pay. It was, rather, the General Court that was to blame. If the legislative branch of the government expected him to travel all his circuits, it had to give him and his colleagues financial incentives. "It is well known that formerly in this State, the extreme parsimony of those who composed the General Court had effectually cooled the zeal of most judges for the public service, & tended powerfully to put down the whole government of New Hamp-shire to the level of contempt," he charged. "And it is a fact that the little glimmerings of liberality that have at times appeared in the Legislature have uniformly been harbingers of encreased assiduity in judges and other officers, & productive of much good to the community."[20]

There is no extant evidence whether the letter passed through more than one draft or whether Livermore edited it in order to tone down the bluntness of his words. Surely the mere task of writing provided time to cool his anger and realize what he was saying and how he was saying it. Yet he does not seem to have reflected or to have tempered his enmity. Consid-ering the standards of official communication, what he had written could hardly have been more insulting. Even the conclusion—what he wanted legislators to think about—owed more to his anger than to his reason. After

all, to say that the General Court would see him travel every circuit required by law once it increased his salary was saying that if he got a sufficient increase, he would do the work he already was being paid to do.[21]

The committee of the House of Representatives receiving Livermore's letter must have decided that he was challenging the entire legislative branch
of government and that his answer was just too contentious for the committee alone to handle. It reported that no further legislative proceedings
were called for, which was a way of passing the problem on to the full
house. As the committee expected, its report was rejected. A motion was
made to address the governor and Council to remove Livermore from the
Superior Court. That, too, was defeated. The Senate, however, voted to address the judge off the court, sending the house a resolution saying Livermore's letter was "unsatisfactory, and indecorous: *Therefore, resolved,* that
the Legislature address the executive to remove Judge Livermore from office." In the debate that followed, the question was raised for the first time
in the printed record: what was the legislature's authority to investigate and
supervise the judiciary? Some members (we may assume they were Federalists) contended "that the legislature had exceeded its authority in instituting an enquiry of Judge Livermore respecting his non-attendance at the circuit; that the Judge was not amenable to the Legislature, in its legislative
character; and by no means bound to answer, where he might criminate
himself." Of course his letter had been highly offensive, these members admitted, but Livermore's scurrilous tone was not an issue the house could
consider constitutionally. The proper question was "whether the absence of
Judge Livermore from the courts, is a sufficient cause to justify the Legislature in an address for his removal." The members raising the question answered that it was not.[22]

The December session of the legislature for 1805 was held in
Portsmouth, which may explain why the *New-Hampshire Gazette* reported
the debates. For the newspaper's printer it was a local event, so either he attended in person or arranged for someone else to take notes. It is somewhat
striking, moreover, that the article, although addressed to "Messrs. Printers," is not in the form of a letter, the usual practice when inserting in the
press special news items. Also, it is quite long for a newspaper account of
that period, running across two-fifths of the page, instead of being printed
in two columns, perhaps to call attention to its uniqueness. Whatever its
origins and no matter how the *Gazette* obtained it, history benefits by having it. The details it reports of the debate over Livermore's letter is the only
account extant from the era of the early republic of any theory explaining
why members of the General Court understood that they had constitutional authority to supervise the judiciary. In support of the resolution to
join the Senate in addressing the governor and Council to remove Livermore from the Superior Court, members of the house (Republicans, we can
assume) argued: "That, although the constitution, did not expressly authorize the Legislature to enquire of a Judge respecting a supposed neglect or

misdemeanor on his part; yet, that such authority was inferred, from the power which is invested in the House of Representatives to impeach, and in the Senate to try an impeachment for crimes and misdemeanors; and further, that as the legislative body is the immediate representative of the people; so it has a right of enquiry into the conduct of judicial officers; and, although Judge Livermore was not bound to furnish evidence against himself; yet, it was incumbent on him to explain to the people, the causes which led to a seeming neglect in him of official duty."[23]

That statement summarized the constitutional theory, and it was supported by a majority of the representatives. Power to impeach officials, including the judiciary, was vested by the constitution solely and completely in the two houses of the legislative branch. The full and exclusive authority to impeach members of the judiciary unquestionably encompassed the much more minor authority to investigate judicial conduct, including attendance at circuits. In addition, judges were public officials, and as public officials, judges were responsible to the people for their conduct. From that constitutional principle it followed that judges were answerable to the people's representatives, the two houses of the legislature. After he had once been questioned by "the people," Livermore had a duty to answer, but he had not done so. Neither of his two letters had responded to "the people" or addressed their concerns. As a consequence, his replies were voted "unsatisfactory." As both letters were "degrading to the majority of the people," neither was, as a matter of law, a proper answer. Therefore, the house ruled, the letter addressed to the committee should neither be laid on the table nor put out of sight, because "it discovered [i.e., revealed] the man."[24]

At the time of this debate, December 1805, New Hampshire had not yet addressed a judge from office. Members of the house who were defending Livermore claimed that addressing from office was a more limited power than its subsequent development as law in the nineteenth century proved it to be. The addressing power, they argued, was available only "in case a judge had become *non compos.*" If that were true, Livermore could not have been removed from the court by addressing out but only by the more cumbersome, more technical, and more time-consuming procedure of impeachment. True, the members wishing to discipline Livermore replied, impeachment was an option, but address was also available. They explained the process of addressing out broadly, as it would soon develop in New Hampshire law, encumbered by no rules and no restrictions, except that the governor and Council had to concur with the General Court. "The people in appointing a judiciary wisely reserved to themselves the right of address to the Executive; and the same people gave the Governor, united with his Council, a discretionary power to remove a judge," the majority reasoned. "The Legislature as representing the people, must exercise its authority with discretion; but a sense of moral obligation alone in each individual member of the legislative body, can controul this authority; no bounds are prescribed in the constitution; and the right of the Legislature to address the Governor is by no means limited, as has been asserted, to the case of a Judge under mental derangement; it extends to all cases where the man is unfit for a Judge."[25]

This report was one of the few occasions when New Hampshire legislators discussed the process of addressing out, and, as the debate progressed, the truth began to be realized. The power of addressing from office had no limits—the judiciary was completely dependent on the General Court because legislators could exercise the authority to address whenever they needed to remove a judge or they wished merely to be rid of a judge. "Should the executive appoint to the office of Judge, a man without ability, or without morality; the Legislature are authorized to address the Governor to remove the Judge from office," the representatives voted. "And where a Judge in his official station has acted with ability and integrity, yet in his private conduct was notoriously unjust and vicious; in that case it would be the duty of the Legislature to address the Governor for his removal, as much a duty indeed, as if such Judge had become *non compos mentis.*" And of course they could do so in the case of an extremely obnoxious, arrogant judge, who, when described, it was assumed, fit the case of Arthur Livermore exactly: "where a Judge discovers a proud and imperious disposition; an intemperate zeal in his own cause; a vindictive spirit against every one who opposes his views; and, (after his passion subsides) an impertinent contempt for the people, in their Representatives." This last supposition, of course, stated Livermore's offense. "That the voice of the people from which all power proceeded, was entitled to the most respectful attention; and that Judge Livermore, by disregarding that voice, had rendered himself culpable." The question was put, "shall this House concur with the Hon[orable] Senate in its Resolve," to address the governor and Council to remove Livermore. The motion was defeated, 64 yeas and 71 nays.[26]

From the perspective of party politics during that partisan era, the vote was stunning. "At a time when the Jeffersonians were straining every nerve to remove a Federalist judge from the [United States] Supreme Court," the historian Lynn Turner observed, referring to the impeachment of Justice Samuel Chase, "New Hampshire Republicans thus refused to exploit a promising opportunity to begin a local purge. Although removal of a judge required only a majority vote of both houses, the advice of the Council, and the signature of the governor—all of which the Republicans could have delivered—they allowed the state judiciary to remain solidly Federalist."[27] A political historian writing in the twentieth century, Turner took the long view, and he was right: the most striking fact about the New Hampshire judiciary in January 1806 was that both Jeremiah Smith and Arthur Livermore remained as judges, undisturbed by the Republican party despite its distrust of the judiciary. They might have stayed on the court their entire careers if Smith had not run for governor. The shorter view was taken by Livermore's contemporaries, and because he was not popular, they were more critical of him than of the Republicans. We need only the example that follows. It is significant because it is from *Farmer's Cabinet* of Amherst, just about the only newspaper in the state not affiliated with either political party: "Whatever provocation he may have had," it said of the letter Livermore had written to the committee of the House of Representatives, "it is certainly a production far beneath the dignity of the office he holds, and must be generally condemned. We think it honorable of the Legislature, that it was not made a cause of address for his removal."[28]

The most prestigious trial lawyer at the New Hampshire bar agreed with the *Cabinet*. Jeremiah Mason, a Federalist, had been apprehensive that the judiciary could be seriously damaged had Livermore been addressed from office. "They made a very devious and persevering attack upon Judge Livermore," he wrote Plumer who was in Washington, telling him about Livermore's complaints of unequal salaries. "The members were exasperated and in fury declared war against him. If his enemies had procured an immediate division I think the Judge would have been removed from the Bench. But it was delayed till their fury subsided in some degree. . . . I am very glad this attempt failed. It would have done much mischief & no good."[29]

No other lawyer, except possibly Smith, had been more successful in convincing New Hampshire legislators of the merits of judicial independence than Plumer, but he did not agree. He now knew Livermore much better than he had in 1798 when he and Smith used all their powers of political persuasion to have him appointed to the bench. Now he faulted both the jurist and the House of Representatives. "The conduct of the General Court & of Judge Arthur Livermore appear to me of a very extraordinary kind," he replied to Mason. "The [General] Court, tho' not without precedent, proceeded irregularly in appointing a Committee of enquiry. If the non-attendance of the Judge, at the Spring Circuit, merited legislative notice, impeachment, or removal by address, was, in my opinion, their most proper & dignified course." He explained to another Portsmouth lawyer more clearly what he meant: "If the *negligence* of the judge required their notice, the House ought either to impeach, or the two houses unite & address the Executive to remove him from office." He did not quite say so, but Plumer had to be telling Mason that Livermore should have been removed by one process or the other. "And as to the Judge, his letter is reproachful & insolent," he concluded. "No legislative body ought to suffer it to lie on their table."[30]

Plumer did not mean what he said. He would never have wished any judge addressed from office.[31] Despite turning against Livermore and eventually becoming unhappy with Smith's work as chief justice, he was too concerned about what he called the "encroachments" of addressing and impeaching. The exercise of either power could erode whatever independence the Superior Court still possessed. In 1794 Governor Gilman had urged the General Court to investigate why the judges had not held court during the fall circuit, and for the governor's message just to mention that fact was improper, Plumer believed. Should the two houses address him to remove the judges, he would be on record saying that they had missed their circuit. In other words, he might have said they were guilty. If the House of Representatives did not address him to remove the judges but rather impeached all or some of them, "'tis more improper for him to address the House who are the accusers, & the Senate who are the Judges of the accused. It has a tendency to create a bias & prepossession ag[ains]t the Judiciary, who have neither numbers or power to withstand the encroachments of the more popular branches of the government." In 1806, with Livermore still sitting as a judge on the Superior Court, Plumer was so grateful that Governor Langdon had kept silent during the controversy and had not asked the two houses to investigate judicial "negligence" that he wrote the governor what could be called a thank-you letter. "'Tis certain that a people had better submit to some inconvenience, & even to partial evils, than encounter the more substantial ones that necessarily follow innovation," he assured Langdon. "Not that I think our Courts, or system of laws perfect; but great & material changes ought not to be made but from necessity, & with great caution."[32] Chief Justice Smith would have agreed.

Conclusion

Historians of judicial dependency must be grateful to Arthur Livermore. We may never find another state judge of such impetuous personality during the era of the early republic who so frequently irritated the members of a state's house of representatives and senate. Simply unable to restrain himself when dilatory lawyers triggered his temper or he felt the urge to complain in public about some perceived insult, he upset legislators of both parties enough that they willingly took the trouble to investigate his intentions, almost yearly calling on him to explain something he had done, failed to do, or said. As a result, the General Court manifested an active and publicly visible supremacy, the import of which eventually would be forgotten by lawyers as the principle of judicial independence became dominant in American constitutional law.

True to form, Livermore was not finished when, unhappy about salaries, he stayed home and did not travel his circuits. He continued to commit indiscretions that aroused the ire of the lawmakers. After Jeremiah Smith was elected governor of the state in 1809, he resigned as chief justice, leaving Livermore on the court. Livermore not only remained a judge; he actually moved up in judicial rank, becoming chief justice of New Hampshire. It was a consummation of his career that deeply disturbed several of the state's leading lawyers. When elected chief executive, Smith did not resign from the bench until the morning he was sworn into office. Hoping to make certain he could appoint his own successor, he tried to avoid creating a vacancy that the Republicans could fill. To his surprise and bitter disappointment, the outgoing governor, John Langdon, outmaneuvered him by selecting a Republican judge during what was practically his last hour in office. The appointment infuriated Smith both because the opportunity to make the choice had been vitally and professionally important to him, and because Langdon's appointee was a nonlawyer. Nothing else, Smith feared, could do so much damage to the high court. It was an absolutely devastating turn of events, particularly crushing to Smith as one of the main reasons he had agreed to be a candidate for governor was the expectation of using that office to strengthen the judiciary, especially by putting strong, educated, and competent lawyers on the bench. Instead, he now found it even more difficult to interest a suitable nominee, for along with the problem of low salaries, there was the reluctance among competent attorneys to serve with a nonlawyer. Having a nonlawyer for an associate meant much extra work for a law-trained judge. The nonlawyer could likely learn to write opinions (though few were written) and decide some questions of substance but could not preside at jury trials and might be mystified by technical matters such as motions for demurrer, certiorari, or to reserve questions.

Before Langdon's lame-duck appointment, Smith had expected to fill two judgeships. A small number we might think, but a brace of judges were two-thirds of the court's membership, giving Smith the chance to strengthen the bench considerably if he could find competent candidates. Arthur Livermore let him know he intended to remain a judge, so, after Langdon made his appointment, Smith had only his own former office to fill, which, if he could persuade an outstanding lawyer to accept, could still make a difference for the court's success and prestige. After all, his tenure on the bench had demonstrated the impact that an outstanding chief justice could assert.

The governor knew who should be appointed, and, at the same time, undoubtedly knew he would not be able to persuade the man to become chief justice. He asked Jeremiah Mason. It would have been a stunning appointment, instantly returning to the chief justiceship the prestige lost when Smith resigned. Even Republicans would have applauded. But Mason would not accept; the compensation was too low. Unable to persuade Mason, Smith confronted the dynamics of New Hampshire constitutionalism whenever the two political parties shared power. In New Hampshire the governor, together with his appointees, was not the entire executive department as was the case in most states. He was not even the only executive official who was elected by the people. There were five others, the members of the Council, who collectively had as much authority as the governor to make judicial appointments. In the election of 1809, the Federalists had won the governorship and small majorities in both houses of the General Court. But the Republicans had captured the Council, three Republicans to two Federalists, and Smith was outvoted. The mechanics of Council appointments were not complicated. Neither the governor nor the Council was exclusively vested with authority to nominate candidates for office. The governor could suggest names and so, also, could each individual councillor. As Plumer would later explain, "no nomination is of any avail, unless the governor and a majority of the council agree to it: nor can any appointments be made without the consent of the governor and three of the council." As the law operated regarding both nominations and appointments, it is accurate to think of the governor and the Council having a veto on each other.[1]

Smith faced two problems. The most important was dealing with the Republican majority on the Council, which not only was uninterested in appointing a lawyer of quality but seems to have been opposed. Second, it was difficult to convene the Council. It was able to convene only if sessions were scheduled with much notice. He arranged two meetings, but both ended in stalemate even though at the second he nominated two members of the Council itself, both of whom were excellent candidates. One was a Federalist and the other Republican, but neither would serve. Nor would other lawyers whom Smith approached. When the state had been without a chief justice for almost half a year, Smith realized he had run out of time. Reluctantly, but necessarily, he nominated Arthur Livermore to head the court. The Council concurred.[2]

It was surely a bitter disappointment to Smith that he had no choice; he had to accept Livermore as chief justice. There was simply no one better who would then accept the office or who would have been approved by the Council. Besides, Livermore was competent and experienced: he was the only judge who had served on the high court longer than Smith himself. It was his personality, his impetuous nature, that gave everyone pause. Livermore was, quite frankly, nonjudicial and very much disliked by influential members of both houses of the General Court—serious detriments for the leader of a court that had little public respect and was subject to constant legislative supervision.

Livermore and his two associates cannot be blamed for all the damage to New Hampshire's judiciary. Other jurists contributed their mite. Low as the judges had sunk when Livermore assumed the chief justiceship, their reputation was driven even lower by others on New Hampshire's courts— others such as Nahum Parker. By June 1810 he was well into his third year serving both as U.S. senator and as chief justice of the Common Pleas, openly in violation of law. "The clamors against him is [sic] loud," Plumer wrote of Parker. "If he does not resign his Senatorship I think it probable they will remove him from that of Judge." He meant that the two houses of the General Court would vote to address Parker from his judicial office. Parker, who does not come through the historical record as very intelligent, replied that he should not resign from the court because if he did he would be opening the position for a Federalist appointee: "this I supposed my friends would not wish." He did not resign from the senate, he claimed, for that would create too much work for the legislators who would have difficulty agreeing on a successor. "[T]here is one Senator and five Representatives to elect without filling my place," he told Plumer, referring to contested elections in the two houses of the General Court. "I am not fully determined what to do." He was soon told, however, that members of both parties had lost patience. He was forced to resign from the senate, and because his conduct had received little publicity, he caused less harm than otherwise might have been expected. But with those who knew how willing he had been to disregard the law, the reputation of the judiciary suffered a bit.[3]

The judiciary's image was further damaged by Smith's only appointment of an associate justice, Jonathan Steele, who was named to Livermore's former seat when he became chief. Upset at something that he had read in a Republican newspaper, Steele wrote "an angry insolent letter" to the printer of the *Gazette* demanding that the paper no longer be sent to him. The printer knew how to handle saucy lawyers. He printed Steele's letter in full, with a reply of his own, "which excites some indignation against the judge." It was a small, unimportant incident, yet the court's reputation suffered a bit more.[4]

By October 1811 even Federalists were sending articles to the press criticizing the Superior Court, and the *New-Hampshire Patriot* printed those from Republicans, at least if they also faulted lawyers. "The administration of this department of government," JUSTUS reported of the judiciary, "is both weak and wicked. The confidence of the people is withdrawn from it." He had a particular complaint about the recent September term at Exeter, which had lasted a week. "It is possible, that the business of the Court at this place can be ordinarily performed in that time," he supposed. "At the last term of the Superior Court in that town, there were three or four hundred cases upon the dockets for trial; but they were not noticed, the court not having arrived at them. . . . [I]s this justice? *Short* terms and *unfinished* business suit the lawyers, but they do not suit the people."[5]

One reason the *Patriot* found JUSTUS suitable for publication was what the writer had to say about Arthur Livermore. The chief justice was a Republican, but because he had been appointed by Federalist governors, many people thought him Federalist, and any one associated with Federalism was fair game for attack in the *Patriot*. "I speak now of the Judges of the Superior Court, one of whom has, for years, been the subject of the people's animadversion," JUSTUS complained of Livermore. "[H]is constant endeavor to display an utter contempt for the people, will not be forgotten—will not go unpunished. The people are not *blind*! They have seen, and with the sensibility of freemen, that the business of our Superior Court is often directed by *petulance* and *acrimony*—often directed by injustice and inhumanity. A *continuance*, a *new trial*, a *dismission of the juries*, is decreed with as little ceremony as that with which a man would put on his glove."[6]

It is a telling and unfortunate commentary on the status of the judiciary, but it appears that the chief justice was more unpopular among lawyers than he was with members of the general public like JUSTUS. There were members of the bar who actually discussed having him addressed from

office, and they included Federalists as well as Republicans. Even after being appointed head of the Superior Court, Livermore was unable to control
his sarcasm or his tetchiness. During trials he would be annoyed by quite
minor occurrences, by the tardiness of counsel, for example, and without
warning declare a continuance, order a postponement, or dismiss the jurors
sitting on the case at bar and also the panel waiting to be called. The Republican press, including the *Patriot,* was not certain how to explain Livermore to the public. It could not tar him with the brush it had used on
Smith, for he was not of the same caliber, the same originality, and, certainly, not of the same reforming zeal. There was one litigation, however,
the *Hillsborough Bank Case,* in which he dared to enforce a procedural rule
much as Smith would have done, giving Republicans a chance to question
his judicial restraint.

Like many Republican theorists of the era, Isaac Hill, publisher of the *Patriot,* detested banks. They were, he contended, "instruments of public suffering." Just before the 1810 election, he accused them of what was to him
a most serious offense. "It may be fairly said that the influence of the
Banks"—meaning the Hillsborough and Cheshire banks, two engines of
Federalist politics, have—"placed Jeremiah Smith in the chair of State."[7]

It made political sense for the *Patriot* to blame banks for the ills of New
Hampshire if, as that newspaper claimed, "almost all banks are under the
control of federalists." The Republican press had a problem, however, dealing with the Hillsborough Bank, the most notorious and scandalous failure
in the state. It was headed by Samuel Bell, one of the most promising
younger Republicans of New Hampshire. But no matter, the *Patriot* decided,
Bell was only an incidental factor. "[A]lthough its President, Mr. Bell, was a
republican," the bank itself "was in the hands of federalists and had a majority of federalists for its directors."[8]

During August 1809, unable to redeem its bills, and sued by their holders, the Hillsborough Bank closed. Bell advertised in Boston newspapers
that debts owed to the bank were more than sufficient to discharge all demands, and the *Patriot* urged those holding bills to trust Bell's promises of
solvency. But the lawsuit, which was based on a statute making stockhold-
ers of banks individually liable "for the redemption of bills issued from
these banks," was pressed forward.[9]

When the case was finally adjudicated in April 1811, Livermore did not
rule on the merits. To the surprise and annoyance of most New Hampshirites, he dismissed the action because it sought relief through an improper form of action. In other words, he reached a decision by applying
the technical jurisprudence Smith had been introducing into the adjective
law of New Hampshire. The ruling unexpectedly served Republican purposes for it allowed the *Patriot* to focus attention away from Samuel Bell
and against the lawyers and what Hill misrepresented as Livermore's readiness to employ technicalities to deny justice.

The causes pending against the Hillsborough Bank were decided in favor of the ex-stockholders—not on the ground that the ex-stockholders were not bound by the terms of the charter—*that* remains to be settled when those who have already been deprived for years of their bona fide property, shall have the temerity to prosecute their actions in a different form, which after lying years in Court may, equally with the other, be decided to be brought wrong; but because a plea of *assumpsit* would not lie in this case! We believe it has been the custom in all former cases, when an action has been brought wrong, that it should in no wise ultimately affect the merits of the final question, but that the plaintiff should have the privilege of a plea in abatement. In *this* case the action has been in a course of law upwards of two years, and costs accumulated to a great amount; and what was least of all thought of, when the time for a decision on the *merits* of the question was expected, the action was decided, we believe only by one judge, to have been brought wrong![10]

No other holding could so well have served the cause of republicanist jurisprudence and Jeffersonian demagoguery. Not only Livermore and the court, but the law itself and receptionist jurisprudence could all be chastised, and it was done without mentioning Bell and his fellow directors of the defaulting Hillsborough Bank. The plaintiffs had alleged fraud, misrepresentation, and stockholder statutory liability. The action of *assumpsit* was based on the contractual liabilities of a promise not performed, and all Livermore had ruled was that he was not empowered to grant relief as the plaintiffs had not sued on a promise unperformed but on the statutory liability. Had the plaintiffs moved a plea in abatement, they might have been allowed to amend the action from *assumpsit* to *case*. The issue for the Republican press was not the merits but the technicality and the legal theory. The *Patriot* even made an argument for returning to New Hampshire common-sense jurisprudence. "We profess to know but little of the forms and technical meaning of law, as interpreted by our courts," Hill confessed. But there was not need to know the forms of action or technicalities when you knew what the law ought to be. "We had ever conceived that common reason and justice ought to be the guides by which decisions were to be made."[11]

Criticism of particular legal decisions such as *Hillsborough Bank* were mainly raised by Republican newspapers. Members of the General Court complained about cancelled court sessions and sometimes about delays, not about specific judicial holdings. They found fault not with the judiciary's rulings but with the judiciary itself, especially with Arthur Livermore. By 1813 he was becoming weary of the legislative investigations, tired of the sniping from the bar, and, most of all, overburdened by his two associates, undoubtedly the worst pair of high-court judges to serve together on a three-member New Hampshire tribunal. One was Richard Evans, the nonlawyer Republican to whom Governor Langdon had given the last-minute, lame-duck appointment, to the disgust and anger of Jeremiah Smith. He not only was a nonlawyer; he was also almost chronically sick, more often than not notifying Livermore that he would not be attending court. For well over two years he missed all the court sessions, although, the *Farmer's Cabinet* reported, "it is believed he never failed to claim his salary." That meant Livermore had to preside at trials with only one associate, Clifton Claggett, a new judge. The Republican Council had insisted on appointing Claggett to the bench as a reward for party services. He was an attorney, but that was about all that could be said for his credentials to be a judge. It is not a guess or an exaggeration to say that he was undoubtedly the most incompetent jurist ever to sit on New Hampshire's highest court, at least the most incompetent who was admitted to the bar. Even when Claggett was on the bench beside him, Livermore had to clear most dockets as if he were sitting alone. He complained to William Plumer, who then was governor, that he must be given abler associates and told his brother "that he intended to resign as he felt himself inadequate to the task of doing the whole [judicial] business of the State."[12] As usual, Livermore was complaining, but this time he was not exaggerating. He did do the whole business because he was the whole court.

As the government of New Hampshire gathered in Concord for the opening of the legislative session in June 1812, there was a general consensus that some actions had to be taken to remedy the many and obvious defects of the judiciary system. For the first time in the state's history, there was some discussion about legislating the entire high court from office. Again, what is telling is that much of the dissatisfaction was among lawyers, Federalists as well as Republicans. The talk was in contrast with the legislative sessions of the year before. Then, at both the June and November terms, discussion had not been on legislating the Superior Court out but of either impeaching or addressing from office individual justices. The targets that most lawmakers had in mind were either Chief Justice Livermore, whom some attorneys wanted addressed out, or Richard Evans, the nonlawyer appointed by Langdon. Because he was largely an absentee judge, many legislators, especially those representing counties in which court sessions were sometimes cancelled, wanted him off the court.

"Complaints against the Justices of that court, particularly the C[hief] Justice, are numerous," William Plumer informed Congressman John Adams Harper three months before the legislature met; "they do not proceed from one party only, but many of both parties [are] dissatisfied." Complaints against the chief justice had been multiplying. We cannot know all the causes today or measure their intensity, but it seems Livermore became more arbitrary as the burdens of the office bore on him more and more. With Evans staying at home, and his other associate, Clifton Claggett, too inept to be of help, Livermore undertook to conduct trials alone. The practice was not authorized by statute, and it does not seem to have been frequent. Nothing is known of the process. The best guess is that desperate litigants, anxious to have their legal disputes resolved, willingly waived their rights to be tried by two or more judges and asked Livermore to preside alone, whether such trials were statutory or not. One reason Livermore did not often sit alone is that he had Claggett, but that did little to relieve the burdens. From everything that contemporaries have told us of Claggett, we know that the chief had to make the rulings and formulate the decisions.[13]

For litigants there were some risks in asking Livermore to preside alone if Claggett were not available. His impatience and short temper made his trials both unpredictable and unnerving. There were, however, two sides to his contentious personality. On the negative side he could be arbitrary, but on the positive he could be quite decisive. THE VOICE OF NEW-HAMPSHIRE claimed that when Evans took sick and stopped coming to court, Livermore ordered the clerk of the Superior Court not to pay his salary.[14]

Almost all the complaints about Livermore's conduct in court were private, voiced to friends and acquaintances by unhappy or abused attorneys but not brought against him as formal charges. As a result, with the exception of what can be read in extant private correspondence, they are lost to history. As far as research has uncovered, only one incident that did not become the subject of public complaint was ever detailed in a newspaper, and it does not show Livermore out of control, only being egocentric. THE VOICE OF NEW-HAMPSHIRE, addressing the chief justice in the second person, told how Livermore, while conducting a trial in Grafton County with judges Steele and Evans as his associates, stopped the proceedings and abruptly announced that he was going home. "When the judge on your right hand expressed his astonishment at your proposal to return home," VOICE recalled, "and observed that you knew that there were many great questions pending, upon which a decision was expected, you replied, 'I HAVE MEN AT MY HOUSE DIGGING A WELL, AND YOU KNOW HOW IT IS WHEN YOU HAVE HANDS TO WORK, AND ARE NOT THERE WITH THEM.'" And with that announcement, according to VOICE, Livermore left the courtroom and was absent from the circuit for three weeks.[15]

Although there is no direct evidence, there is reason to suggest that lawyers, angered by incidents like this, or who in court had experienced the blunt of Livermore's sharp tongue, were talked out of filing complaints with either house of the legislature. After all, if the complainant proved his case and Livermore was disciplined by being addressed from office, what lawyer of his caliber would be willing to make the financial sacrifice and take his place? Then, at the June 1812 meeting of the General Court, Peyton R. Freeman presented a memorial and remonstrance against the chief justice, and no one persuaded him to withdraw it. Freeman was a Hanover lawyer who had removed to Portsmouth in 1803 where he built a somewhat successful practice, for he was well trained and had a reputation for hard work. Plumer would think enough of him to appoint him Deputy Secretary of State in 1816, and a year later he became clerk of the United States District Court.[16]

It is not necessary to examine all the details. It is enough to know that, while presiding at a court session in Haverhill, Livermore became upset with Freeman and suspended him from practicing at the bar of the Superior Court. Reporting Freeman's petition to the legislature, the *New-Hampshire Patriot* published one of the very few compliments paid Livermore by the press. Saying it could not comment on the facts of Freeman's suspension, the *Patriot* did want to praise the chief justice for charges recently delivered at various grand jury sessions. "[W]herein he inculcated the duty of the citizens to acquiescence in the measures of rulers chosen by, and from ourselves," the newspaper explained. "That charge undoubtedly has had an excellent effect on our State, and however we may have formerly disapproved of some official conduct of Judge Livermore, we cannot but approbate him in this thing."[17]

The war of 1812 had just begun. The *Patriot,* a loyal Republican paper, supported the Madison administration, but most New Hampshirites were strongly opposed to the war. In his charges that the *Patriot* praised, the chief justice, speaking beyond the grand jurors to the general public, said every citizen had a legal duty to aid the national government. When Livermore next arrived in Concord, Plumer asked him if he was changing his politics. "[H]e frankly said he had not changed his opinion upon politics." But he supported "the laws of Congress. That on the last circuit—had recommended it [obedience] to the grand jurors in his charges to them, '& for that some portion of the federalists were offended with him.'"[18]

When the Freeman memorial was being debated by the two houses of the General Court, Livermore surprised the state by arriving in Concord and announcing that he would defend himself at the legislative hearing. Perhaps people should have expected he might do so, considering both his impulsiveness and the seriousness of Freeman's accusations. Not only had the chief justice suspended him "from practising at the bar of the Superior Court" but, Freeman asserted, Livermore did so "without any formal accusation being preferred against him;" that the chief justice's conduct was "arbitrary and unjust, and without a precedent—destructive to the memorialist in his means of living and of his rights as a citizen."[19] Plumer, who was then governor, recorded what he was told had touched off Livermore's anger. At that court term at Haverhill, the chief justice accused Freeman of uttering "at a public tavern . . . in the presence of many people, such accusations against the court, in particular against the Chief Justice respecting the court, as were not true." They were, from what Livermore heard, such "that they tended to destroy the reputation of the Court, & impair public confidence in them—& that until he explained his conduct to their satisfaction, he as an officer of that court must consider himself suspended from the practise of law in that court."[20]

Freeman had not answered these charges when they were made nor did he apologize. He went to his lodging and sent Livermore a note asking for a copy of the order. The chief justice readily sent one to him. After the memorial that recited these facts was read at one of its daily sessions, the House of Representatives referred it to a committee. The committee took testimony from Freeman and then prepared a report recommending that he be advised he had liberty to withdraw his memorial. Before the report could be considered by the full membership of the house, Livermore arrived in Concord and presented a memorial of his own, justifying his conduct. The house referred this memorial to the same committee, and the committee replied that both parties should be heard by the full house.[21]

An unfamiliar, very surprising Arthur Livermore was in Concord that June day of 1812. He was an Arthur Livermore that most of New Hampshire had not previously seen and probably never suspected existed. The *New-Hampshire Patriot,* not given to saying anything favorable about Federalist appointees, reported that his defense before the full house "was a *masterpiece.*" "The drift of his argument was, that attornies were mere officers of, and removable at the pleasure of the Court," the newspaper told the public, "that they possessed no privileges there which were not possessed by the Clerk, the Crier, or even the humble waiter who makes and tends the fire for the Court—that as they retained no privileges as attornies by any statute of the State, so their suspension destroyed no rights which they had not in common with other citizens." Livermore then took a different tact and went off in a direction that surely astonished much of his audience. He no longer questioned the authority of the General Court to complete an unrestricted superintendence over the judiciary. Now he freely acknowledged the supremacy of the legislature. "He described himself amenable to the House of Representatives, as the Grand Inquest of the State, for all his conduct," admitting "that he was liable, not only to be removed by impeachment, but by the Governor and Council, on the address of the two branches of the Legislature."[22]

Livermore's surprising defense also impressed the governor, although Plumer was more interested in what the judge told him about some of the leading Federalist lawyers. Livermore probably stretched the truth, but he asserted that he had treated Freeman no differently than he did the best practitioners in Rockingham County, and he suspected they retaliated by urging Freeman to file his memorial. "He observed that what was done in relation to Freeman was not done by himself only, but was the act of the court." That theory of judicial discipline was a bit of a stretch, but it served Livermore's purpose, and Plumer had no reason to quarrel with it. "He observed the court had authority not only to suspend, but to expel lawyers from practice, that it was a power incidental & necessary to all courts of record," Plumer recorded in his daily *Register,* again not questioning Livermore's law. "That he knew that in discharging his official duties, he had made some of the Bar his personal enemies. That he had never been obliged to order but two lawyers to sit down, & those were Jeremiah Mason & John C. Chamberlain, & that in consequence of that they were inimical to him. . . . He made allusions which conveyed the *idea* that Freeman was induced to make this a complaint, to gratify the resentment of Mason, Chamberlain, & Daniel Webster, & they urged him to this course."[23]

In his reply to Livermore's impressive argument, Plumer thought Freeman "not only short, but cold, formal, & feeble. . . . The result was that he had liberty by a unanimous vote of the House to *withdraw* his memorial." The Federalists were surprised as well as delighted by the unanimous vote. "After the foul abuse we have heard lavished by the democrats on Judge Livermore," the *Constitutionalist* exclaimed, "we cannot consistently account for the impunity with which he escaped—but we congratulate the Judge upon the honorable nature of his acquit[t]al."[24]

Stubbornly, Freeman drafted a second memorial, which he presented at the November session of the General Court that same year. It was described by the *Democratic-Republican* as "a re-petition" of the original complaint. In addition it charged that Livermore, "at the last term of the Court at Exeter refused to hear the said Freeman as council in a case where he had a written power of attorney from one of the parties. It complains of the proceedings of the Chief Justice as violent, oppressive and extra-judicial—as destructive to the rights of the citizens, and as making the *bar* the mere automatons and machines of the *Court*."[25]

Again the General Court had an opportunity to assert its supremacy over the judiciary and, at the same time, discipline an unpopular judge. But attitudes and constitutional perceptions were changing, and again the legislature did not act. Freeman's new memorial was, as usual, submitted to a committee that dismissed it summarily. There was, the committee reported, no need for further hearings. The charges had been thoroughly investigated, and no new evidence had been uncovered mandating a different outcome. The question was then put to the House of Representatives: "Do the facts reported by the committee . . . warrant the impeachment of the chief justice of the Superior Court of Judicature?" Overwhelmingly, 141 to 22, the house answered no.[26]

At the same session of the General Court a motion was made in the House of Representatives to address the governor and Council to remove Judge Evans from office. The vote, reported to the *Patriot* by Plumer, writing as CATO, "was ayes 28, nays 142—every federal member, I believe, voted in the negative."[27] Once again the Republicans of New Hampshire spurned the leadership set by Thomas Jefferson and the national party. They declined to use the authority of the legislature to strip a judge serving at good behavior of his tenure in office. At the next session of the General Court the Federalists would not hesitate to do so.

That next session—June 1813—was the greatest turning point, the most pregnant legislative meeting in New Hampshire judicial history. The War of 1812 had been declared by the Republican Congress, and opposition in New Hampshire was so contentious, it produced a political revolution. At the next election, that of 1813, the Republicans were swept from power, and, with a complete turnaround of fortunes, the Federalists captured all three branches of government. Not counting Arthur Livermore, the Superior Court consisted of two Republicans, Evans and Claggett. By exercising the ultimate legislative authority over the judicial branch, the newly elected Federalist majority voted all three judges from office. The Superior Court was legislated out of existence by repealing the statute that had created it. In its place, the two houses created a new high tribunal, the Supreme Judicial Court.[28] Governor John Taylor Gilman and the Federalist Executive Council made Jeremiah Smith chief justice. Then, in 1816, with the war ended, there was a second reversal in politics and a second exercise of the ultimate legislative dominance over the judiciary. Led by William Plumer, who was reelected governor, the Republicans returned to power. They legislated out of existence the Supreme Judicial Court and created another high court named the Superior Court of Judicature. Smith was removed as chief justice, legislated off the bench for a second time in his career; he had been legislated out once before by Thomas Jefferson and Congress as a midnight judge in 1802. He would never hold judicial office again.

To the surprise of most Republicans, as well as to the annoyance of many, Plumer indulged in one further legislative-executive exercise of domination over the judiciary. Since 1813, when they were first legislated from office, the old court—particularly Evans and Claggett—had been mounting a very public and vocal campaign, insisting that their removal had been unconstitutional, and, therefore, they argued that they were still judges entitled to be reinstated in their former offices. Publicly Plumer treated the contention with contempt, as did the Federalists, rejecting all contentions that the two men were still judges, that their tribunal had not been constitutionally terminated, and that it remained New Hampshire's only high court. But there was one legal contingency that caused the governor considerable concern. There was always the possibility that an appellate court, whether New Hampshire or federal, that was competent to decide constitutional disputes might rule it unconstitutional for the other two branches of the government to legislate from office a bench of legitimate judges serving at the tenure of good behavior. It would have been difficult for Plumer to have questioned the ruling or to have refused to obey it. After all, on behalf of preserving the judicial tenure of his former friend Jeremiah Smith, he had publicly and loudly argued in 1802 that the congressional act legislating out of existence the federal circuit court of midnight judges had been unconstitutional.

Plumer was not being overly fearful. He was not concerned that if legislating out good-behavior judges was declared unconstitutional, Evans and Claggett could reclaim their seats on the bench. Their tribunal, the Superior Court, no longer existed. The Superior Court of Judicature created by the act of that year, 1816, was a different institution than the one on which they had sat. What troubled him was that if the legislating-out process was ruled unconstitutional, Evans and Claggett might be owed their salaries, both their back pay when they had been removed from office in 1813 and their future pay, which by the tenure of good behavior meant until they died or reached the mandatory retirement age of seventy years. Plumer knew that Jeremiah Smith and other midnight judges, whether they were serious or not, said they still should be paid their salaries as members of the defunct federal circuit court. The possibility of the question being ruled on was not remote. Any person who had lost a litigation in Smith's Supreme Judicial Court might refuse to pay the judgment and if sued by the winning party, defend on the ground that the award had been unconstitutional as Smith's court had been unconstitutional. In the alternative, if the losing litigant had already paid the judgment, he or she could sue in detinue, alleging the money should not have been demanded as it had not been constitutionally owed.

Plumer was a cautious politician, especially with the public's money. He did not want to pay salaries to out-of-work judges who were not earning those salaries, and, seeking a way out of the problem, he found his solution in the legislature's authority to address judges from office. The governor requested the two houses of the General Court to address the Council and him, as governor, requesting that they dismiss from office all of the judges who, in both 1813 and 1816, had been legislated out. Addressing from office was undisputedly constitutional. No cause or offense needed to be charged or proven, and there were no substantive grounds for petitioning a court to reverse a removal from office by address. The two houses of the legislature, controlled by Plumer's party, readily obliged—that is, the legislature addressed him and the Council to remove from office judges who had already been legislated from office. The process was so incredible in constitutional law that it bears repeating: they *addressed out* the judges of the Superior Court who had been *legislated out* in 1813 as well as the judges of the Supreme Judicial Court *legislated out* earlier that very same legislative session.[29]

There has been no other judicial moment to equal it, the most spectacular instance of legislative domination over courts of law, not just in New Hampshire but in all U.S. history. Jefferson's legislating out of office the midnight judges is, of course, far better remembered, but it was not so constitutionally, legally, and politically anomalous or so nonimitative. In that one short legislative session of 1816, the New Hampshire state assembly addressed from office all the judges of two separate highest courts, both of which had been legislatively abolished and all the members legislated out of office. To appreciate the uniqueness of the event, consider the fact that the legislature and the executive not only addressed judges from office but also addressed them from offices that did not exist. It was surely a day to be marked in American judicial history but certainly not a day of credit to American constitutional law.

Had he been asked when reelected governor, William Plumer would have said he was committed to Jeffersonian political theory. At that same legislative session of 1816, he demonstrated how willingly he had adopted Jeffersonian political theoretics when asking the General Court to nullify the charter of the trustees of Dartmouth College. Turning away from receptionist principles of rule of law and vested rights of property, he wanted the two houses to assert sheer legislative power—that is, by the authority of mere statute alone to recharter Dartmouth as a public institution belonging to the people, converting the private college into a state university. The legal tactics that he adopted were not what they would have been a decade earlier; they were not what his former friends and colleagues at the Rockingham County bar—Jeremiah Smith, Daniel Webster, and Jeremiah Mason —thought prerequisite legal procedure. He did not ask the legislators to instruct the attorney general, in their name, to sue the college trustees on the grounds that they had forfeited their charter rights when arbitrarily removing the long-serving president, heir of the founder, and restructuring the governance, purpose, and direction of Dartmouth. More specifically, the constitutional principle, as Smith, Webster, and Mason were to argue, was that the charter and the property of the college were "rights" that had been vested in the trustees, and vested rights can be constitutionally divested only by judicial, not by legislative, authority.[30] Instead, Plumer urged the two houses of the General Court to adopt the Jeffersonian doctrine that the world belongs to the living generation, not to the "dead hand" of "lawyers," "priests," or "aristocrats," and that the legislative branch of the government, as it speaks for a majority of the people, need pay no heed to legalistic concepts such as the rule of law or principles of immutable vested rights, because the "law of the land," or due process of law, is whatever a majority of legislators say it is.[31] Plumer was successful. The lawmakers enacted his bill, and Dartmouth College became a state institution, Dartmouth University.

We should give heed to the Dartmouth University litigation. It may not bear on our story of legislating the courts, but it reveals much about how Governor Plumer refashioned the New Hampshire judiciary, bringing a new professional respect to the high court, setting a new foundation on which it could begin to resist legislative interference. It is a matter of comparing the governor's political strategy in the college case with his jurisprudence. Plumer may or may not have thought through his disregard for the immutability of vested rights or his espousal of the Jeffersonian disregard for the rule of law, but he wanted his courts to have trained, competent, even outstanding judges just as he had worked to bring about during his first decade as a lawyer when he mounted political campaigns for the appointments of Arthur Livermore and Jeremiah Smith. He may have yielded some legal principles to Jeffersonian politics, as the Dartmouth litigation indicates, but he would never become committed to Jeffersonian jurisprudence. When it came to unadulterated issues of law—not clouded by political questions such as stopping the trustees of the state's only college from returning their institution to Congregational control—he did not change his legal philosophy. The demise of the Federalist Supreme Judicial Court and the creation of the Republican Superior Court of Judicature provided him the unique opportunity to appoint the state's highest tribunal from scratch, to place on it his kind of judge, and it was then that he remained consistent to the judicial standards of his Federalist past. There was a cost, and he was willing to pay it. In fact, from what we know today, he did not hesitate. He ignored the political pressures of the majority of his own party who demanded he either reappoint the court of Livermore, Evans, and Claggett or appoint judges of the same undistinguished caliber, whether they were Republican lawyers needing a job, nonlawyers, or men whom the party should reward for political services. The one criterion that his fellow Republicans did not urge on Plumer was professional competency.

Adhering to his receptionist common-law origins, the governor angered and even shocked many of his Republican supporters. He may have no longer been a friend or admirer of Jeremiah Smith, but in 1816 he was determined to create a court in Smith's image, a court of professional lawyers, who understood the rules of pleadings, the concept of judicial precedents, and the common-law methodology. He wanted, in other words, a court of talented advocates, who, while they had been practitioners, had been capable of appearing as attorneys in a jury trial before Chief Justice Smith, knowing what to argue, what to answer, and what to expect. And that is what he got, after much searching for a high level of competency and intense resistence to fellow Republicans who had no idea what legal competency was, how to recognize it, or why it was needed. Against the odds, he appointed one of the finest courts in New Hampshire history—with William Merchant Richardson as chief justice and Samuel Bell and Levi Woodbury as associates. It was a court worthy to succeed Jeremiah Smith.

Smith's coming to the high court as chief justice in 1802 marked the demise in New Hampshire of common-sense jurisprudence. So the coming of the Richardson court meant that Jeffersonian judicial theory would never dominate New Hampshire law despite a continuous series, over thirty-nine years, of uninterrupted election victories for the Jeffersonian-Jacksonian Democratic party. The removal of Smith as chief justice had not meant the defeat of Smith's legal legacy. Even the era of jury dominance, which he struggled hard to curtail, was about to end. To the complete surprise of American legal theorists, New Hampshire was one of the first jurisdictions to rule that not just civil but even criminal juries no longer were the judges of law as well as fact and that they must accept and apply the law as laid down in the court's charge.[32]

There is another ruling by the Republican court even more important for this study. Just at the time William Plumer retired from the governorship and left public life, the judges he had appointed to the Superior Court of Judicature handed down a judgment challenging what was then the most pronounced exercise of legislative supremacy over the judiciary. It was a decision that may not mark the end of the era of legislative supremacy, but once acquiesced in by the General Court was surely a signal that the end had begun. It questioned and—by the metamorphosis by which dispensable judicial rulings, propelled by time and legal mythology, are converted into potent constitutional precedents—overruled the legislature's authority to restore litigants to their law. The decision, the first important judicial opinion issued by the new court of Richardson, Bell, and Woodbury, challenged the legislative practice that Plumer had very much opposed when he was a young lawyer and, most likely, still did: the General Court's authority to enact legislation restoring litigants, defeated in a jury trial, to their "law" by ordering a new jury trial—that is, a new trial in a cause that had been fully adjudicated and declared completed.

The legality of the process had been challenged several times in court and had been declared unconstitutional by Superior Court judges more than once. But the legislators had paid no attention to what the judges held.[33] In fact, the two houses might have given little heed to the ruling being considered had they not, at their June 1818 session, passed a joint resolution asking the Superior Court for an opinion on whether they, as legislators, had the constitutional authority to restore private citizens to their law. "Resolved," it was voted, "by the Senate and House of Representatives in General Court convened, That the Justices of the Superior Court of Judicature be requested to express to the Legislature at their next session, an opinion in writing on the following question, viz: —Has the Legislature a right to grant new trials or restoration to law in any case; and if so, in what case or cases?"[34]

The suggestion is merely conjecture, but perhaps we should not take the resolution at its face value. It appears to be a straightforward, unencumbered order for an *Opinion of the Justices,* a procedure of the New Hampshire Constitution authorizing "[e]ach branch of the legislature as well as the governor and council . . . to require the opinions of the justices of the superior court, upon important questions of law, upon solemn occasions."[35]

If the request was for an *Opinion of the Justices,* it could be a grave mistake to interpret the resolution from the perspective of twenty-first century law. Today for the General Court or the executive branch to request an *Opinion of the Justices* is to ask an opinion on the constitutionality or legality of contemplated legislation or a state action. It is doubtful if legislators in 1818 were questioning the court about constitutionality. They might not have considered themselves as competent experts as were the judges about issues of private law, but they did feel themselves as able to interpret the constitution and knew that they were as authorized to make constitutional rulings as were the justices. Most likely they had reached the limits of their tolerance of the time-consuming procedures that the demands of due process forced upon them when they restored litigants to their law. Petitions praying to be restored to law simply took up too much legislative time. In both that year, 1816, and the year of the high court's decision, 1818, the House of Representatives and the Senate had each appointed a "standing committee on new trials or restoration to law." As recently as the previous June session, the General Court had granted a "new trial" and "relief" to two litigants seeking restoration.[36] And, it should be noted, these enactments were two legislative bills that Governor Plumer, long vocal against restoring legislation, signed into law![37]

There is some indication that legislators in both houses were feeling burdened by extraneous business such as restoring petitions. At that same session of the General Court, a house committee reported a bill "on the expediency of proving by law that names be altered by the Courts of Common Pleas" and not any longer by the two houses. The bill was rejected, but the very fact that it had been drafted and favorably reported shows that some representatives believed their time was being wasted by reading petitions to allow suppliants to change their names.[38] True, petitioners did not have to say why they sought a name change, just that they no longer wanted to be known as "Hogg" or preferred "Washington" to "Davis" and, as a result, did not take up the amount of time that restoring-to-law petitions took. Yet the time that was consumed must have been annoying to some lawmakers.[39]

Why ask the judges at all? Why not just announce that the General Court would no longer restore disappointed litigants to their law by nullifying judgments and granting rights to second trials? One obvious answer is the moral persuasion of a ruling by the Superior Court. An *Opinion of the Justices,* holding that restorations to law were either illegal or unconstitutional, certainly could be expected to strengthen the arguments of legislative leaders seeking to dissuade members from introducing legislation to restore constituents to their law. Legislators pressured by voters for acts relieving them from judicial judgments and granting them new trials could tell their constituents that the judges would not allow retrials, that even if the two houses passed bills restoring them to their law and the governor signed the bills into acts, the judges would not obey. They would, instead, quash the legislative order for a new trial.

The judges did not answer the legislature directly, as they had been expected to, with a specially drafted and issue-specific *Opinion of the Justices.* At the time they received the official notice from Governor Plumer that the General Court sought their opinion, the judges explained, "an action was pending before us, which appeared to involve most of the questions proposed in the resolve. That action has since been decided, and the report of it hereto annexed, forms a part of our reply to those questions."[40] That is to say, they submitted to the Senate and House of Representatives a decision of an actual litigation: the legal issue in dispute was a motion on which they passed judgment, the opinion for which they drafted in the regular course of their docket. As with most judicial decisions, it dealt with the facts of the case, with the legal issue presented by the motion, explained how they resolved the controversy, and gave their reasoning why.

It is a matter of some historical regret that the court chose to file the decision in *Merrill* v. *Sherburne* rather than preparing an *Opinion of the Justices.* Richardson had been of counsel in the case and therefore "did not sit." That meant he did not write the document, as he, the chief justice, most likely would have done had a separate *Opinion* been drafted. Only the other two judges participated in the decision, and the writing was assigned to Woodbury. Although one of his earliest attempts at judicial composition, it is very much an example of the opinions he would become known for: overlong, filled with simplicities,[41] irrelevancies,[42] and even sloppy work.[43] Samuel Bell was the second judge, joining Woodbury in the decision, but he was not responsible for its writing. By the time *Merrill* v. *Sherburne* was submitted to the General Court, he had become governor, thus signing the opinion as an associate justice and signing as governor the communication sending it to the two houses.[44]

Merrill v. *Sherburne* was a fact-simple case of restoring a litigant to law. Benjamin Merrill had lost a will contest in Rockingham County's probate court. He died, and the administratrix, his widow, petitioned to be restored to his law. The two houses voted to restore her,[45] empowering her "to enter the cause anew at the superior court," directing "that said cause have a day in said court, and shall be heard, tried and determined in said court upon pleadings had in the former trial," and authorizing the Superior Court "to affirm or reverse the former judgment or decree, . . . as the said trial may terminate for or against either party."[46] Joseph Sherburne, one of the plaintiffs in the original lawsuit, served with a copy of the restoring legislation and ordered to appear in the Superior Court for a new trial, moved to quash "on the ground that the act of the legislature was unconstitutional." It was that motion to quash that Woodbury and Bell ruled on, and it was their opinion explaining why they ordered "the proceedings in this case to be quashed," that they submitted to the legislature.[47]

Twenty-seven years earlier, William Plumer had convinced Chief Justice John Pickering that legislation, restoring a losing litigant to her law, was unconstitutional on the grounds that it deprived the plaintiff of his right to trial by jury.[48] The argument was striking. It is possible that Plumer thought it his only argument; it is even possible that he did not think of contending that restoring the defendant to her law violated either the principle of judicial independence or the doctrine of separation of powers. But it is also possible that he argued that restoring to law deprived the plaintiff of his right to a trial by jury because that argument was quite persuasive at that time and the one best calculated not to irritate New Hampshire legislators. Woodbury, less an original thinker than Plumer, spun no new theories and announced no dramatic breakthrough in constitutional principle. His reasoning rested squarely on the doctrine of separation of powers, introduced into New Hampshire law by the Constitution of 1784, the constitution written by Pickering. By reversing an adjudicated probate-court judgment, and restoring Merrill to her husband's law, the legislature, Woodbury contended, was exercising a judicial power beyond the bounds of its constitutional legislative authority, violating the doctrine of separation of powers.[49]

As a legal scholar Woodbury may not have been on a par with Plumer, but his argument was more calculated to impress lawyers, at least lawyers of the next several generations and of the twentieth century. As time went on, and the principle of trial by jury as the chief guardian of liberty lost much of its constitutional vogue, the separation-of-powers theory became the one that impressed that new breed of lawyers, the graduates of law schools. The sequence is by no means certain, but from what existing research tells us, it does seem that the decision did not take on constitutional luster until lawyers in the twentieth century elevated it as one of New Hampshire's great opinions, establishing, in state law, the power in the courts of judicial review.[50] That interpretation is pure legal anachronism. Woodbury certainly had judicial review in mind, though it is doubtful that he foresaw any of its twentieth- and twenty-first-century nuances when he wrote of separation of powers. Consider what he in fact said:

> That clause, which confers upon the "general court" the authority "to make laws," provides at the same time, that they must not be "repugnant or contrary to the constitution." One prominent reason for creating the judicial, distinct from the legislative department, was, that the former might determine when laws were thus "repugnant," and so operate as a check upon the latter, as a safeguard to the people against its mistakes or encroachments. But the judiciary would in every respect cease to be a check on the legislature, if the legislature could at pleasure revise or alter any of the judgments of the judiciary. The legislature too would thus become the court of last resort, "the superior court," or "supreme judicial" tribunal of the state; and those expressions so often applied to this court in the constitution would become gross mis-nomers.[51]

It is true that Woodbury was not quite saying that the Supreme Court of Judicature had the authority to review the constitutionality of legislation. New Hampshire jurisprudence had undoubtedly accepted that concept, but it was not yet wise for the judiciary to proclaim it too loudly. He was claiming that as long as the General Court could interfere in the judicial process by restoring litigants to their law, the Superior Court could not effectively question the constitutionality of enacted legislation. But no matter. Lawyers being so expert at reading into the past the contemporary law with which they are familiar, his words were readily spun into a broader ruling. Lawyers of a later era, an era of judicial supremacy, could convert his opinion into an assertion of judicial review. Even history students writing for outstanding mentors could say that "Woodbury claimed in *Merrill* the 'unquestionable' power to void clearly unconstitutional laws," which he did, because looking back we know that is the way the law developed, so that must have been what he meant.[52]

What usually goes unnoticed by twentieth- and twenty-first-century observers is, as Timothy Lawrie noted, that Woodbury "refused to offer an absolute statement of the legislature's authority." It is not surprising that he made none. It was better not to antagonize certain members of the General Court. And besides, a ruling on the legislative authority was not relevant to the constitutional principles he established in the *Merrill* holding. It was a holding for his law, not for another, later law, such as the law of today. Members of the legislature were not sure what he intended about their authority, and they likely did not care. As Plumer wrote five years later, after *Merrill* "the legislature continued to hear petitions and pass bills directing new trials, without vacating the former judgments; but the courts of law decided these were also unconstitutional and dismissed the process." Eventually the legislators realized that they no longer were absolutely supreme over the judiciary and ceased ordering new trials. In fact, they gave that power to the judiciary, vesting the judges of the Superior Court with authority "to grant new trials in such cases as in their opinion justice and equity required." And so, Plumer concluded in 1823, "it now appears to be settled that the legislature have no authority to interfere in the trial of *suits between* individuals."[53]

It is not historically material that, for a few years, New Hampshire lawmakers continued to restore litigants to their law. The *Merrill* decision, like many judicial decisions, had a life separate from factual history. Woodbury's holding was a clear signal that the era of legislative supremacy was coming to an end. *Merrill v. Sherburne* may not have ruled specifically that the judiciary was an independent branch of the government, but law is not just archaic; it is anachronistic. *Magna Carta,* when promulgated, had nothing to do with the rights of villeins and other common people of England. By the eighteenth century, *Magna Carta* was one of the main instruments of English liberty. So, also, did *Merrill* take on new meaning and, in time, help change constitutionalism in New Hampshire. Thinking as lawyers, we may continue to say that Woodbury, in *Merrill v. Sherburne,* wrote into New Hampshire law the doctrine of judicial review. But thinking as historians, it would be better to say that the legacy of *Merrill* is that it created a "new relationship between New Hampshire's judiciary and the legislature." With Woodbury's decision, the principle of legislative supremacy began to pass from New Hampshire constitutional law. "Woodbury's theory," Lawrie has pointed out, "did not establish the court 'supreme' arbiter of the constitution, as some have suggested. Rather, it provided judges an independent part in the political functions of government."[54] Although judiciary supremacy lay decades in the future, legislative supremacy was beginning to recede into the past.

Jeremiah Smith may have been driven from office in 1816. He was no longer chief justice and no longer could promulgate New Hampshire law. Yet he had won. His life's work was for the ages. His law was the law of New Hampshire's future.

Notes

Introductory Note

1. *Tucker's Blackstone* 1:135.
2. Burbank, "Architecture of Independence," p. 319.
3. *Authority of Law*, pp. 163–73.
4. John Adams, "Autobiography," *Works of Adams* 3:20; [Madison,] "Federalist" #39, *Federalist*, p. 251; Proclamation of the Great and General Court of Massachusetts-Bay, January 1776, *American Archives* 4:833.
5. Jurisprudential dichotomy: *Controlling the Law*, pp. 33–55; Rakove, *Original Meanings*, p. 290; Wood, "Origins of Judicial Review," pp. 1304–305.
6. Turner, *Ninth State*, p. 102.
7. *New Hampshire Constitution*, p. 5.
8. *Controlling the Law*, pp. 53–55.
9. *Rule of Law*, pp. 33–51.
10. Wood, "Origins of Judicial Review," p. 1301; Nelson, *Marbury v. Madison*, p. 14.
11. Gay, *Accomplished Judge*, p. 20.
12. Sullivan to Meshech Weare, 12 December 1775, *Letters of Sullivan*, p. 143.
13. Selsam, *Pennsylvania Constitution*, p. 173. Paine's constitutional theory had enough support among intellectuals that Adams wrote his most important book to refute it. Thompson, "Adams and the Science of Politics," p. 238.
14. Patrick Henry, Speech of 5 June 1788, printed in *Founders' Constitution*, p. 289.
15. For the concept of "arbitrary" as then defined in constitutional theory, see *Authority to Legislate*, pp. 134–41.
16. Sullivan to Meshech Weare, 12 December 1775, *Letters of Sullivan*, p. 143.
17. *Gould* v. *Raymond*, 56 N.H. 260, 272–73 (1879).
18. The main exception is the extensive attempts by Pennsylvania Republicans to restrict, by legislation, the authority of the courts and the influence of common lawyers. As all of the more radical enacted bills were either vetoed, ineffective, or ignored, Pennsylvania anticourt radicalism did not have the impact on the remainder of the nation that otherwise could have been expected.
19. Carpenter, *Judicial Tenure*, pp. 156–59; Selsam, "History of Judicial Tenure"; Webster, "Comparative Study of Constitutions," p. 86.
20. Good behavior: Wootton, "Introduction," p. xxvi; Prerevolutionary: Bailyn, *Pamphlets*, pp. 249–55; "Essays of Brutus," #5, 20 March 1788, reprinted in *Essential Federalist*, p. 93.
21. Even in Federalist Massachusetts there had been preconstitution demands that tenure be limited for one to five years. *One year:* Returns of Sandisfield, August 1779; *Three years:* Returns of Belchertown, 22 May 1780; *Five years:* Returns of Wren-

tham, 26 May 1780, *Popular Sources of Political Authority,* pp. 421, 540, 803. Tenure for good behavior, one town complained, made judges "Independant [*sic*] *of the people.*" *Returns of Shrewsbury, 6 June 1780,* ibid., p. 868.

22. Quoted in Selsam, "History of Judicial Tenure," p. 174 n40. Also, see Eastman, *Courts and Lawyers of Pennsylvania,* p. 304; Loyd, *Early Courts of Pennsylvania,* pp. 149–50; Loyd, "Courts from Revolution to Revision," pp. 11–12; Chroust, *Rise of Legal Profession* 2:67.

23. *Controlling the Law,* pp. 157–79; Utter, "Ohio and Common Law," pp. 323–24.

24. Desan, "Legislative Adjudication," pp. 1384, 1386.

25. Desan, "Remaking Constitutional Tradition," p. 258. Standing committees were used in most colonies to report on accounts. Shimomura, "History of Claims," pp. 629–30. New Hampshire, however, employed special committees. Harlow, *History of Legislative Methods,* pp. 65–68, 78.

26. Desan, "Contesting Political Economy," pp. 178, 181, 229, 202.

27. Shimomura, "History of Claims," pp. 627, 648.

28. "There is no doubt that legislative adjudication was a routine part of the constitutional regimes of South Carolina, Virginia, and North Carolina." Desan, "Legislative Adjudication," p. 1496 [*sic*].

29. In New York, legislative adjudication seems to have been less extensive. Ibid., p. 1495 [*sic*]. The practice was terminated there earlier than in New England. Desan, "Remaking Constitutional Tradition," p. 315 (also, see p. 257).

30. For Massachusetts: Hammond, "Great and General Court," p. 62; Grinnell, "Brief History of Court," p. 9. For Rhode Island: Kaminski, "Democracy Run Rampant," p. 259.

31. *Calder* v. *Bull,* 3 *U.S.* 386, 395 (1798) (Paterson, J. concurring); Reno, *Memoirs of the Judiciary* I:20.

32. Swift, *System of Laws,* p. 39.

33. For Connecticut, see Baldwin, *American Judiciary,* pp. 20–21. For Rhode Island, see Durfee, "Judicial History of Rhode Island," pp. 2380–84. For New Hampshire: see Chapter Three of this book.

34. "At the close of the Revolution . . . it was the most common form of legislation" in New Hampshire. Lawrie, "Interpretation and Authority," p. 312. Restoring to law is the topic of Chapter Three.

35. Wood, *Creation of Republic,* p. 226.

36. Shankman, "Malcontents and Tertium Quids," pp. 56, 59.

37. Brunhouse, *Counter-Revolution in Pennsylvania,* p. 226; Eastman, *Courts and Lawyers of Pennsylvania,* pp. 343, 345–51; Ferejohn and Kramer, "Independent Judges," p. 979.

38. Peeling, "Governor McKean," p. 341. For common-sense jurisprudence, see *Controlling the Law,* pp. 18–32.

39. In Kentucky, to take one jurisdiction, address was used to clear the bench of some or all judges. Carpenter, *Judicial Tenure,* pp. 128–30; Carrington, "Judicial Independence," p. 89.

40. Mays, *Edmund Pendelton,* p. 274; Anon., *Friend to Constitution,* p. 31; Nelson, "Cases of the Judges," pp. 256–57. The judges apparently felt that they had to explain to the legislature why they should be independent. "The propriety and necessity of the independence of the judges is evident in reason and the nature of their office," they pointed out, "since they are to decide between government and the people." Mays, *Edmund Pendelton,* p. 396n2 (reprinting the judges' "Remonstrance").

41. Cases of the Judges of the Court of Appeals, 8 *Virginia* (4 *Call*) 135, 149 (1788); Nelson, "Cases of the Judges," p. 245.

42. Cases of the Judges of the Court of Appeals, 8 *Virginia* (4 *Call*) 135, 149, 150 (1788).

43. Mays, *Edmund Pendleton,* p. 273; Cullen, *St. George Tucker,* p. 76.

44. Cases of the Judges of the Court of Appeals, 8 *Virginia* (4 *Call*) 135, 145–46 (1788). For a summary, see Nelson, "Cases of the Judges"; Geyh and Van Tassel, "Independence of Judicial," p. 39.

45. Anon., *Friend to Constitution*, pp. 28–29. Also, see Miller, *Juries and Judges*, pp. 64, 72.

46. Almand, "Supreme Court of Georgia," p. 1.

47. *Chisholm* v. *Georgia*, 2 *U.S.* 419 (1793).

48. Hicks, *Joseph Henry Lumpkin*, p. 87.

49. "Resolution of 29 November 1815," pp. 132–33. Also, see Baldwin, *American Judiciary*, pp. 112–13; Haines, *Judicial Supremacy*, p. 260; Almand, "Supreme Court of Georgia," p. 3.

50. Constitution of 1789, Art. III, § 5, and Constitution of 1798, Art. III, § 1, *Sources and Documents* 2:454, 463.

51. Almand, "Supreme Court of Georgia," pp. 4, 5.

52. Constitution of 1798, Art. III, § 4, and Amendments of 1812. *Sources and Documents* 2:463, 468.

53. *Controlling the Law*, pp. 37–55.

54. This explanation is not the view of most Georgia constitutional historians. *Controlling the Law*, p. 7. They agree with William F. Swindler that anger against the United States Supreme Court "contributed to an antipathy for judicial power generally and perpetuated the decentralized court system . . . for half a century." *Sources and Documents* 2:467. Similarly, see Coulter, *Georgia*, pp. 294–95; Cleveland, "Establishment of Georgia Court," pp. 418, 419; Huebner, *Southern Judicial Tradition*, p. 72; Lamar, "History of Establishment of Court," pp. 92–93; Almand, "Supreme Court of Georgia," p. 5; Hicks, *Joseph Henry Lumpkin*, p. 87.

55. Amendments of 1835, Art III, § 1, *Sources and Documents* 2:471.

56. Tribute of Respect, Supreme Court of Georgia, Talbotton, January Term, 6 *Georgia*, 115, 116–17 (1849).

1—The Legislative Constitution

.1. An Elector, *Osborne's Spy*, 8 December 1790, p. 50, cols. 1–2.

2. An Elector, *Osborne's Spy*, 8 December 1790, p. 50, col. 2; A Citizen of Portsmouth, *Osborne's Spy*, 11 December 1790, p. 54, col. 3.

3. Jeremiah Smith to Eliza Ross, 18 November 1796, Morison, *Life of Smith*, pp. 124–25.

4. A Citizen of Portsmouth, *Osborne's Spy*, 11 December 1790, p. 54, col. 3; A Voter, *Osborne's Spy*, 25 August 1790, p. 141, col. 2.

5. The next election Smith received "the vote of nearly every elector in the three western counties." Turner, *Ninth State*, p. 124.

6. *Controlling the Law*, pp. 11–12; Resch, "Transformation of Peterborough," p. 229; Resch, *Suffering Soldiers*, p. 33. Smith studied law in Barnstable, Andover, and Salem.

7. "Notice of Oliver Peabody," p. 303.

8. Smith to Plumer, 31 October 1787, First Plumer Letterbook.

9. Smith to Plumer, 31 October 1787, Morison, *Life of Smith*, pp. 26–28; Turner, *Plumer*, p. 29.

10. Plumer to Smith, 10 December 1791, First Plumer Letterbook, #68.

11. Smith to Plumer, 31 October 1787 and 31 January 1797, First Plumer Letterbook, #58, #109.

12. Plumer to William Coleman, 31 May 1786, Turner, *Plumer*, pp. 34–35 (Coleman became famous as editor of New York's *Evening Post*); [William Plumer,] Cincinnatus #123, *Grafton Journal*, 10 October 1825, p. 158, col. 3. "There is no department in

government more useful and necessary to the people than that of the Judiciary—none that requires more talent, skill, and unbending integrity." [William Plumer,] CINCINNATUS #130, *Portsmouth Journal,* 13 May 1826, p. 2, col. 5.

13. Smith to Plumer, 28 January 1795 and 5 March 1796, *Plumer Documents.*

14. For a detailed discussion of common-sense jurisprudence, see *Controlling the Law,* pp. 18–32.

15. Turner, *Ninth State,* pp. 105–6. For an outline of the development of Common Pleas, see [William Plumer,] CINCINNATUS #124, *Grafton Journal,* 22 October 1829, p. 170, col. 4.

16. In New England "an appeal from one jury to another is familiar both in language and practice, and is even a matter of course, until there have been two verdicts on one side. The word 'appellate' therefore will not be understood in the same sense in New-England as in New-York. . . ." [Alexander Hamilton,] *Federalist* #81, p. 550.

17. Page, "Judicial Practice," p. 199. Plumer believed the figure was one less than four: "there may be three Verdicts given in each cause." Plumer to Calvin Goddard, 12 October 1805, Fourth Plumer Letterbook, p. 453. "There is an appeal *of course* from one jury to another till there have been two verdicts out of three on one side." [Alexander Hamilton,] *Federalist* #83, p. 566.

18. Report of Committee, 9 February 1792, Plumer, *Repository IV* (Frame 313). Some contemporaries thought this process "of defaults" "so burthensome to the people in Massachusetts, that it was one of the principal causes" of Shays's Rebellion in that state five years before Plumer wrote. BRUTUS, Letter XIV, 6 March 1788, *Anti-Federalist,* p. 179.

19. Page, "Judicial Practice," pp. 199–201.

20. "This defect has long been seen with regret by the most intelligent men in this state, and our sister state Massachusetts." Anon., *Observations Occasioned By,* pp. 4–5. Massachusetts had a similar "defect." Nelson, *Americanization,* pp. 72–73; Ellis, *Jeffersonian Crisis,* pp. 184–85.

21. Message of Governor William Plumer to the General Court, 4 June 1818, *Concord Gazette,* 9 June 1818, p. 2, col. 4. Even at the rare times when there was a trial, "cases really are not tried at the inferior court. The parties do not want to show their strengths." Anon., *Observations Occasioned By,* p. 5.

22. In Massachusetts, appeal from Common Pleas "provided the debtor an invaluable commodity at no immediate cost: time. . . . Defaulting and appealing meant postponing the reckoning beyond the day of judgment to the point when the creditor secured the return on his writ of execution." Chu, "Debt Litigation," p. 91.

23. Turner, *Plumer,* p. 44; Plumer, "Constitution of New Hampshire," pp. 173–74; Jameson, *Constitutional Convention,* pp. 119–20. The only indication in the Constitution of 1776 that a judiciary might be contemplated is a provision that "the two houses" would not appoint "clerks of Court." Constitution of 1776, *Sources and Documents* 6:343.

24. Turner, *Ninth State,* p. 15; Plumer, "Constitution of New Hampshire," p. 180. In the Inferior Courts, 5 of the 20 justices were members of the Council; 4 were members of the house. Of the 5 chief justices, 3 were members of the house. Nicholas, *History of Nonjudicial Functions,* p. 45.

25. Lettieri and Wetherell, "Committees of Safety," pp. 259–61, 271–72, 274; Dodd, "Constitutional History of New Hampshire," pp. 388–89.

26. PHILOTEKNON, *New-Hampshire Gazette,* 17 August 1779, quoted in Turner, *Ninth State,* p. 20.

27. Turner, *Ninth State,* pp. 13, 18; *New Hampshire Constitution,* p. 7.

28. *Address of the Convention,* pp. 7–8.

29. Wood, "New Hampshire Constitution," p. 12; Article 15, *Declaration of Rights and Plan of Government;* Dodd, "Constitutional History of New Hampshire," pp. 390–93.

30. Turner, *Plumer,* p. 44; *Address of the Convention,* p. 7. Proposed Bill of Rights, Article 37: "In the government of this State, the three essential powers thereof, to wit,

the LEGISLATIVE, EXECUTIVE, and JUDICIAL, ought to be kept as separate from, and independent of each other, as the nature of a free government will admit. . . ." (p. 27).

31. *Second Address of the Convention,* pp. 7–8. Also, see Lettieri and Wetherell, "Committees of Safety," p. 280.

32. Lawrie, "Interpretation and Authority," p. 317; *Address of the Convention,* p. 14.

33. Constitution of 1784, Part II, "The General Court," *Sources and Documents* 6:348; Lambert, *Ten Pound Act,* p. 6; [William Plumer,] Cincinnatus #92, *Portsmouth Journal,* 23 August 1823, p. 2, col. 2.

34. For the contention that this "is among the weakest statements of the [separation] principle to be found in the constitutions of the states," see Nicholas, *History of Nonjudicial Functions,* pp. 11–12 (also 13, 68). Also, Webster, "Comparative Study of Constitutions," pp. 73–74. For a contrary view, see [James Madison,] *Federalist* #47, p. 327.

35. Corwin, "Progress of Theory," p. 59.

36. Anderson, *To This Day,* pp. 101–2; Solon, *New-Hampshire Gazette,* 11 December 1790, p. 3, col. 1.

37. Ellis, *Jeffersonian Crisis,* p. 9. Also, see Corwin, "Progress of Constitutional Theory," pp. 516–17; Currie, "Separating Judicial Power," pp. 9–10.

38. E.g., "a special Court of General Sessions . . . to consider the situation of Josiah Kenny now a prisoner in the Goal at Amherst and remit or take security from him for the fine imposed on him by the Superior Court of Judicature holden at said Amherst in October last." Minutes for 16 June 1790, *Senate Journal* (June 1790), p. 37; special justices: Wingate, *Wingate,* p. 472.

39. Minutes for 18 and 15 June 1790, *Senate Journal* (June 1790), pp. 41, 30–31. As the would-be plaintiff in the second instance was British, it is likely that the Superior Court was being ordered to obey the Act of 11 June 1787, repealing all statutes and resolves repugnant to the Treaty of Paris ending the Revolution.

40. Plumer, *Plumer,* p. 120.

41. Act: Lambert, *Ten Pound Act,* p. 42; Protest: Plumer, *Plumer,* p. 59. The printed record of Plumer's protest did not raise the issue of constitutionality. The record states: "Mr. William Plummer entered his protest against the Act passed this day entitled An Act for the recovery of small debts in an expeditious way and manner, which protest is on file." Minutes of 9 November 1785, *House Journal* (October 1785), *State Papers* 20:450.

42. Crosskey, *Politics and the Constitution* 2:969.

43. Minutes for 25 December 1786, *House Journal* (December 1786), in *State Papers* 20:759; Turner, *Ninth State,* p. 121; Lambert, *Ten Pound Act,* p. 107.

44. In fact, Rockingham County's Inferior Courts ruled the "Ten Pound Act" unconstitutional on at least six occasions. Lambert, *Ten Pound Act,* pp. 78, 101 (also 90–91, 98).

45. Plumer to William Coleman, 31 May 1786, in Lambert, *Ten Pound Act,* p. 103; Minutes for 26 and 27 June 1787, *House Journal* (June 1787), in *State Papers* 21:72–73; Crosskey, *Politics and the Constitution* 2:970; Prakash and Yoo, "Origins of Judicial Review," pp. 936–37.

46. Crosskey, *Politics and the Constitution* 2:970. Instead the house voted to repeal the "Ten Pound Act." Minutes for 28 June 1787, *House Journal* (June 1787), in *State Papers* 21:83.

47. See Opinion of Attorney General Levi Lincoln, Friedman, "History of Countermajoritarian," p. 375. Contrary, [Alexander Hamilton,] *Federalist* #78, pp. 524–25. A Kentucky senator reportedly said "that our courts had no right to declare a law unconstitutional and that the legislature themselves were the only power competent to decide upon the constitutionality of a law, and when they had decided the judges were bound by it." *Newhampshire Sentinel,* 6 March 1802, p. 3. col. 3.

48. Constitution of 1784, Part II, "Senate," *Sources and Documents* 6:350.

49. "[W]e can never hope to see realised in practice the complete separation of the judicial from the legislative power, in any system, which leaves the former dependent for pecuniary resources on the occasional grants of the latter." [Alexander Hamilton,] *Federalist #79*, p. 531.

50. *Address of the Convention*, p. 14.

51. Constitution of 1784, Part I, Article XXXV, and Part II, *Sources and Documents* 6:347, 353.

52. Minutes for 28 November 1792, *House Journal* (November 1792), p. 645; Minutes for 14 June 1790, *Senate Journal* (June 1790), p. 29.

53. Minutes for 12 December 1792, *House Journal* (November 1792), p. 679; Minutes for 13 December 1792, *Senate Journal*, (November 1792), p. 618; Act of 20 June 1797.

54. Minutes for 8 January, 1 February, 10 February, and 15 February 1791, *House Journal* (January 1791), pp. 147, 197–98, 216, 228–29. On at least one occasion the House of Representatives voted the justices "the sum of *four hundred dollars*" in addition to their regular salary but only "for one year." Minutes for 14 December 1796, *House Journal* (November 1796), p. 126.

55. *New-Hampshire Gazette*, 19 February 1791, p. 3, col. 3; Minutes for 10 and 22 December 1791, *House Journal* (November 1791), pp. 427, 442–43; Minutes for 30 December 1791, *Senate Journal* (November 1791), p. 392. The General Court of Massachusetts also made annual grants to the state judges even though the constitution required "permanent and honourable salaries." Address of Governor Caleb Strong, 31 May 1803, *Farmer's Museum*, 7 June 1803, p. 3, col. 3.

56. Minutes for 17 and 19 June 1789, *Senate Journal* (June 1789), pp. 32, 41. Plumer, "Samuel Livermore," pp. 21–22.

57. *Osborne's Spy*, 13 January 1790, p. 91, col. 1; and (dissent) 23 January 1790, p. 103, cols. 1–2. Also, see WATCHMAN, *Concord Herald*, 3 February 1790, p. 1, col. 1; WATCHMAN, *Osborne's Spy*, 10 February 1790, p. 121, col. 1. While still serving as state president, Sullivan not only held court as federal district judge, but also as circuit judge, sitting with Chief Justice John Jay. *Osborne's Spy*, 22 May 1790, p. 30, col. 2.

58. Sullivan to Senate and House, n.d., *Concord Herald*, 13 January 1790, p. 3, cols. 2–3; Sullivan to General Court, 4 June 1790, *House Journal* (June 1790), p. 47. On the same day the lower house voted "that it is the Opinion of this House that an Attorney for the District of New Hampshire is constitutionally Eligible to a seat in this House." Ibid., p. 48.

59. Plumer, "Woodbury Langdon," pp. 812–13; Turner, *Ninth State*, pp. 121–22.

60. Plumer to Smith, 10 January 1795, Mayo, *John Langdon*, p. 252.

61. Plumer, "Woodbury Langdon," pp. 813, 815. Also, Plumer, *Autobiography*, pp. 42–43.

62. Plumer, "Woodbury Langdon," p. 815; Page, *Rider for Freedom*, pp. 499, 531; Smith to Plumer, 12 April 1796, *Plumer Documents*; Anderson, *To This Day*, p. 100.

63. Copy of letter from Bartlett and Dudley to House Committee, 17 September 1789, *Plumer Documents* (Reel 13, Frame 261); Mayo, *John Langdon*, p. 253.

64. Copy of letter from Langdon to the General Court, 23 December 1789, *Plumer Documents* (Reel 13, Frames 262–63). Also, see Turner, *Ninth State*, p. 122.

65. Minutes of 16 and 17 June 1790, *House Journal* (June 1790), pp. 76–77, 81–82.

66. Articles of Impeachment, 18 June 1790, *House Journal* (June 1790), pp. 89–90, 91.

67. Turner, *Plumer*, p. 41. "I thot his negligence did not require it . . . tho I thot his inattention improper, yet not being wilful or corrupt, did not appear to me expedient to subject him to such a process." Plumer, *Autobiography*, pp. 41–42.

68. Turner, *Ninth State*, p. 124; *Papers of Josiah Bartlett*, p. 331; Page, *Rider for Freedom*, p. 529.

69. Plumer to Smith, 6 July 1790, First Plumer Letterbook, #64. To draw the articles of impeachment, Smith had to make a long trip to Worcester, Massachusetts, to obtain forms. Morison, *Life of Smith*, p. 38.

70. *Impeachment of Langdon,* p. 754; Turner, *Ninth State,* p. 122; Plumer, "Woodbury Langdon," p. 814. At the next constitutional convention, Plumer and Smith wrote an article authorizing the Senate: "whenever they shall sit on the trial of any impeachment, they may adjourn to such time and place as they think proper, although the Legislature be not assembled." *Articles in Addition,* p. 12. It was adopted 2,946 to 813. Jeffries and Hazelton, *New Hampshire Conventions,* p. 18.

71. Page, *Rider for Freedom,* p. 530.

72. Morison, *Life of Smith,* pp. 39–40. For Smith's efforts to rid the courts of lay judges, see *Controlling the Law,* pp. 131–42.

73. Plumer, "Woodbury Langdon," p. 814.

74. Copy of letter from Langdon to State Senate, n.d., *Plumer Documents* (Reel 13, Frames 265–66).

75. Turner, *Ninth State,* pp. 122–23. The full letter is in Plumer, *Repository IV* (Frames 245–49).

76. Copy of letter from Langdon to State Senate, n.d., *Plumer Documents* (Reel 13, Frame 265).

77. Plumer, "Woodbury Langdon," p. 814.

78. Copy of House Resolutions, 20 January 1791, *Plumer Documents* (Reel 13, Frame 268).

79. Minutes for 22 January and 17 February 1791 (quoting the Senate's message), *House Journal* (January 1791), pp. 171, 172–73, 241–42. Also, see Minutes for 26 January 1791; *Impeachment of Langdon,* p. 756.

80. Minutes for 26 January 1791, *House Journal* (January 1791), p. 177; Minutes for 28 January 1791, *Senate Journal* (January 1791), p. 117.

81. Plumer to Langdon, 26 March 1791, First Plumer Letterbook #66.

2—Plumer's Constitution

1. *New-Hampshire Gazette,* 24 June 1790, p. 71, col. 4, and 11 December 1799, p. 3, col. 5.

2. Turner, *Plumer,* pp. 20–25; Plumer to Smith, 2 January 1792, quoted in Lawrie, "Interpretation and Authority," p. 319.

3. Proceedings of House, 24 December 1789, *Osborne's Spy,* 25 December 1789, p. 3, col. 1; Minutes for 25 January 1790, *House Journal* (December 1789), p. 65. Another difficult committee was "to draught a Resolve expressive of the Sentiment of the Legislature of this State on the Subject of the Assumption of the debts of the Several states by the Congress." New Hampshire had paid her Revolution debts and was strongly opposed to assumption, as was Smith. Minutes for 19 June 1790, *House Journal* (June 1790), pp. 92–93.

4. Minutes for 25 January 1790, *House Journal* (December 1789), p. 90; Minutes for 19 June 1790, *Senate Journal* (June 1790), pp. 50–51; Morison, *Life of Smith,* p. 38; Turner, *Ninth State,* pp. 110–11. For a discussion of New Hampshire's earlier efforts to compile colonial and state laws, see Shirley, *Early Jurisprudence,* pp. 69–73.

5. Minutes for 17 February 1791, *House Journal* (January 1791), p. 242; Minutes for 17 February 1791, *Senate Journal* (January 1791), p. 136. After Smith left the state for Congress, the clerk of court was appointed "to superintend the press and examine the proof sheets while the new edition of the laws are printing [and] also prepare an index for said Book." Minutes for 5 January 1792, *House Journal* (November 1791), p. 477.

6. Minutes for 16 February 1791, *House Journal* (January 1791), p. 217; Minutes for 16 February 1791, *Senate Journal* (January 1791), p. 134. Smith was also paid £32 "as one of the Com[mit]tee on revision of the laws." Minutes for 14 June 1791, *Senate Journal* (June 1791), p. 296.

7. Minutes for 20 January 1791, *House Journal* (January 1791), pp. 164–65.

8. Temporary clerk: *House Journal* (June 1790), p. 35 n1; elected clerk: Minutes for 2 June 1790, ibid., p. 40; speaker: *Osborne's Spy,* 8 June 1791, p. 51, col. 3; *New-Hampshire Gazette,* 9 June 1791, p. 3, col. 4. Also, see Turner, *Ninth State,* p. 114.

9. A CITIZEN, *Concord Herald,* 3 August 1791, p. 1, col. 1; *Osborne's Spy,* 22 June 1791, p. 3, col. 2.

10. Turner, *Plumer,* pp. 10–11 (also, pp. 34, 46, 47); Wait, "William Plumer," p. 123; Plumer, *Autobiography,* p. 74.

11. Smith, *Legal Manuscripts,* p. 528. Speaking of John Phillips, the founder of Exeter Academy, Smith said: "In the constitution of the Academy he opened the door wide, embracing all sects of Protestants. He should have gone one step further, and embraced Catholics, as needing it most." Smith, *Exeter Address,* p. 203.

12. [William Plumer,] CINCINNATUS #94, *Collections Historical II,* p. 313.

13. Plumer to Smith, 5 February 1793, quoted in Lawrie, "Interpretation and Authority," p. 312n14; Smith to Plumer, 6 January 1792, *Plumer Documents.*

14. Ellis, *Jeffersonian Crisis,* pp. 5–6; Smith to Plumer, 20 December 1791, *Plumer Documents.* Also, see Nelson, *Marbury v. Madison,* p. 13.

15. *Cummings* v. *White Mountain Railroad,* 43 N.H. 114 (1861); Upton, "Independence of Judiciary." It is not clear from the evidence whether Smith and Plumer wanted the Superior Court entrenched to enhance its independence only or hoped an entrenched court would attract better judges.

16. Minutes for 7 September 1791, *Journal of Convention,* p. 38 (for list of delegates and biographical sketches, see pp. 24–29, 30–37); handwriting: Wait, "William Plumer," p. 128; reelection: *New-Hampshire Gazette,* 7 November 1792, p. 3, col. 4; Smith active: *Journal of Convention,* p. 35. Smith's biographer claimed, "The records, though he was not the clerk, are mostly in his handwriting." Morison, *Life of Smith,* p. 42.

17. Letter from a Member of the Convention, *Political Repository,* 21 September 1791, p. 2, col. 2; Jeffries and Hazelton, *New Hampshire Conventions,* p. 10.

18. Minutes for 10 September 1791, *Journal of Convention,* p. 46; Plumer, "Constitution of New Hampshire," p. 182 n; Thompson, *Thompson,* pp. 45–46. Plumer also failed to eliminate the tax supporting Congregationalism. But he did succeed in having it modified. Wood, "New Hampshire Constitution," p. 114; Turner, *Ninth State,* p. 129.

19. *Journal of Convention,* pp. 48–49; Turner, *Ninth State,* p. 129; Turner, *Plumer,* p. 47. For Plumer's support for the separation doctrine, see [William Plumer,] "Government," CINCINNATUS, No. 92, *Portsmouth Journal,* 23 August 1823, p. 2, col. 1.

20. Turner, *Ninth State,* p. 132; Letter to the Editor from a member of the Convention, *Political Repository,* 21 September 1791, p. 2, col. 3; Smith to Plumer, 20 January 1792, *Plumer Documents.*

21. Entry for 15 September 1791, *Journal of Convention,* p. 57; [William Plumer,] CINCINNATUS #123, *Grafton Journal,* 1 October 1825, p. 158, col. 4; Turner, *Ninth State,* p. 105. Also, see [William Plumer,] CINCINNATUS #126, *Grafton Journal,* 25 November 1825, p. 191, col. 1; CINCINNATUS #102, *Collections Historical,* 3:244.

22. Minutes for 15 September 1791, *Journal of Convention,* p. 57; Turner, *Plumer,* pp. 48–49; Turner, *Ninth State,* p. 133 (also, see p. 132). Minutes for 30 December 1791, *House Journal* (November 1791), p. 461 (resolution opening records to Plumer). It was claimed that the "sum total" of the costs of the court in Strafford County "exceeds the amount of the sum total of the debts for which judgments have been rendered," Anon., *Observations Occasioned By,* p. 19.

23. Anon., *Observations Occasioned By,* p. 5.

24. Minutes for 15 September 1791, *Journal of Convention,* pp. 56–57; "Questions in the Convention held at Concord, Sept. 1791," *Plumer Documents* (Reel 13, Frame 319).

25. Minutes for 15 September 1791, *Journal of Convention,* pp. 56–57. Something that Smith wrote to Plumer suggests judicial tenure was an issue: "The idea of electing judicial officers for 7 years only reminds me of returning back to the savage state, there is nothing that experience has better evinced than the doctrine that Judges should hold their offices during good behaviour." Smith to Plumer, 20 December 1791, *Plumer Documents.*

26. Plumer to Smith, 10 December 1791, First Plumer Letterbook #68. The law term was a "hidden" item, slipped into the section by Plumer and Smith. Smith would expend much effort during both his terms as chief justice trying to create law terms. *Controlling the Law*, pp. 143–56.

27. Minutes for 13 and 16 September 1791, *Journal of Convention*, pp. 53, 55.

28. *Journal of Convention*, pp. 69, 87. For one of the few contemporary discussions of the two names in the two constitutions, see Claggett, *Speech in House*, pp. 16–17. "That the terms, The Superior Court of Judicature, and The Supreme Court, are indiscriminately used in the Constitution as synonymous . . . is too evident to be disputed." "Portsmouth Memorial" to the General Court, *New-Hampshire Patriot*, 23 November 1813, p. 2, col. 3. In Massachusetts, Horace Gray said the two names meant "the highest court . . . whatever its name may be." [Gray,] *Power to Abolish Courts*, p. 8.

29. *Journal of Convention*, p. 67.

30. Anon., *Strictures upon the Observations*, pp. 9–10.

31. Freeman: Anon., *Strictures upon the Observations*, p. 13; Anon., *Observations Occasioned By*, p. 10; trial lawyer: *Chief Justice*, p. 45. Also, see Observator, *Concord Herald*, 15 February 1792, p. 1, col. 1; Turner, *Ninth State*, p. 134.

32. "For the Recorder," *Political Repository*, 23 November 1791, p. 3, col. 2; Anon., *Observations Occasioned By*, p. 5; A Freeman, "The Constitutionist #II," *Political Repository*, 26 October 1791, p. 1, col. 3; A Freeman, "The Constitutionalist #I," *Political Repository*, 19 October 1791, p. 2, col. 2.

33. Quoted in Turner, *Plumer*, p. 49. For Cogswell, see Plumer, "Thomas Cogswell," pp. 539–40; Turner, *Ninth State*, p. 134; *Journal of Convention*, p. 34.

34. Turner, *Plumer*, p. 50; Smith to Plumer, 20 December 1791, *Plumer Documents*.

35. Minutes of 16 February 1792, *Journal of Convention*, p. 99.

36. Turner, *Ninth State*, p. 133, citing *Some Remarks on the Proceedings of the Late Convention* (n.i., 1791), p. 10. Livermore was a zealous advocate, Plumer wrote, "but, as usual, in some instances, has been imprudent." Plumer to Smith, 8 February 1792, First Plumer Letterbook.

37. Minutes for 16 February 1792, *Journal of Convention*, pp. 98–99. Another section of the draft was rewritten to grant the General Court discretionary power "to make such regulations as will prevent parties from having as many trials by jury, in the same suit or action, as hath been heretofore allowed." *Articles in Addition*, p. 5.

38. Minutes for 16 February 1792, *Journal of Convention*, p. 99. For the text of the five rejected judiciary amendments, see Batchellor, "Development of Courts," p. 2304.

39. Dodd, "Constitutional History of New Hampshire," p. 400; Turner, *Plumer*, pp. 51–52; Turner, *Ninth State*, p. 137. For the popular vote, amendment by amendment, see Jeffries and Hazelton, *New Hampshire Constitutions*. For a brief summary of the argument against equity, see Lawrie, "Interpretation and Authority," p. 320.

40. Turner, *Ninth State*, pp. 138–39, 135; Turner, *Plumer*, p. 50.

41. Anderson, *To This Day*, p. 107.

42. Wait, "William Plumer," pp. 127–28. Similarly, see Johnson, "Dartmouth College Case," p. 48. "His influence was so marked that people who disliked the result of the convention's labor called it 'Plumer's Constitution.' But it was far from being Plumer's ideal." Turner, *Plumer*, p. 46.

43. Wood, "New Hampshire Constitution," pp. 113–14; Jeffries and Hazelton, *New Hampshire Constitutions*, p. 10.

44. Plumer, *Autobiography*, p. 50; Smith to Plumer, 15 March 1792, *Plumer Documents*.

3—Restoring to Law

1. Address of Governor John Taylor Gilman, 5 December 1799, *Senate Journal* (December 1799), p. 10; *New-Hampshire Gazette*, 11 December 1799, p. 3, col. 4.

2. Abolish: Minutes for 17, 19, and 20 February 1794, *House Journal* (December 1793), pp. 187, 194, 204; Minutes for 20 February 1794, *Senate Journal* (December 1793), p. 87; Tax: Minutes for 14 June 1799, *House Journal* (June 1799), p. 60; Smith to Plumer, 4 April 1794, *Plumer Documents*. Also, see Turner, *Ninth State,* p. 105; [William Plumer,] Cincinnatus, #124, *Grafton Journal,* 22 October 1825, p. 170, col. 4.

3. E.g., Minutes for 4 February 1794, *Senate Journal* (December 1793), p. 67; Minutes for 19 February 1794, *House Journal* (December 1793), pp. 196–98.

4. Mostly dealing with procedural matters. *Session Laws,* (June 1797), p. 493.

5. Minutes for 20 June 1793, *House Journal* (June 1793), p. 92; Minutes for 21 June 1793, *Senate Journal* (June 1793), p. 53.

6. Turner, *Ninth State,* p. 160; [William Plumer,] Cincinnatus #125, *Grafton Journal,* 13 November 1825, p. 183, col. 1; Minutes for 8 February 1794, *House Journal* (December 1793), p. 153.

7. *Osborne's Spy,* 3 March 1792, p. 147, col. 2.

8. Minutes for 12 December 1792, *House Journal* (November 1792), p. 71; Answer of the General Court to the Governor, 5 December 1795, *Courier of New Hampshire,* 12 December 1795, p. 3, col. 1.

9. Minutes for 14 and 18 June 1793, *House Journal* (June 1793), pp. 54, 57, 69–73; [William Plumer,] Cincinnatus #123, *Grafton Journal,* 1 October 1825, p. 158, col. 4.

10. Minutes for 13 and 15 December 1796, *Senate Journal* (November 1796), pp. 75, 84.

11. Act of 16 December 1797, *Laws of New Hampshire,* p. 458; Address of Governor J. T. Gilman, 17 December 1794, *House Journal* (December 1794), p. 9; Answer of the Senate and House, 17 December 1794, *Senate Journal* (December 1794), p. 8.

12. Minutes for 17 June 1789, *Senate Journal* (June 1789), pp. 32–33; Minutes for 1 and 31 December 1791, *House Journal* (November 1791), pp. 405, 464.

13. Turner, *Ninth State,* p. 148; Minutes for 19 and 22 December 1794, *House Journal* (December 1794), pp. 22, 29.

14. Minutes for 6 January 1795, *House Journal* (December 1794), pp. 80, 83, 85.

15. Turner, *Ninth State,* p. 107 (quoting Bell); Lawrie, "Interpretation and Authority," p. 313 (quoting Pickering). For Livermore and common-sense jurisprudence, see *Controlling the Law,* pp. 21–22.

16. Plumer, "Biographical Sketches, vol. 22," p. 842.

17. Minutes for 8 January 1795, *House Journal* (December 1794), p. 90; Plumer to Smith, 27 January 1795, First Plumer Letterbook.

18. Minutes for 23 December 1794, *House Journal* (December 1794), pp. 30–32; Smith to John Smith, 31 January 1795, Morison, *Life of Smith,* p. 73.

19. Shipton, "Pickering," p. 94.

20. *Controlling the Law,* p. 60; Smith to Plumer, 10 February 1795, *Plumer Documents.*

21. Turner, *Ninth State,* p. 149; Turner, *Plumer,* p. 62; Smith to James Sheafe, n.d., Morison, *Life of Smith,* p. 74.

22. Minutes of 13 January 1795, *House Journal* (December 1794), p. 111.

23. Minutes for 14 December 1796, *Senate Journal* (November 1796), p. 77; Minutes for 14 and 9 December 1796, *House Journal* (November 1796) pp. 124, 126, 78–80. Plumer had no doubt of the law: "Dudley ought to be removed." Plumer to Smith, 21 December 1796 and 12 January 1797, First Plumer Letterbook #105, #107, also, see Smith to Plumer, 7 January 1797, *Plumer Documents*; Plumer, "Biographical Sketches, vol. 21," p. 797.

24. "Age not impeachable": Evans, *Appeal to People,* p. 20; "early constitutions": Smith, "Impeachment, Address, and Removal," p. 257.

25. Evans, *Appeal to People,* p. 13; Frothingham, "Removal of Judges by Address," pp. 217–18. Some state constitutions require "reasonable cause" be specified. Smith, "Impeachment, Address, and Removal," pp. 257–58.

26. Evans, *Appeal to People*, p. 18; A FRIEND TO TRUTH, "On the Judicial Act—No. V," *New-Hampshire Gazette*, 24 August 1813, p. 2, col. 4.

27. Black, "Massachusetts Judges," pp. 105–7, 135; Grinnell, "Constitutional History of Court," pp. 508–11; Frothingham, "Removal of Judges by Address," p. 221.

28. Geyh and Van Tassel, "Independence of Judicial," p. 41; Note, "Judicial Disability," pp. 714–15; Frothingham, "Removal of Judges by Address," pp. 217–18. Also, see Currie, "Separating Judicial Power," p. 11; Berger, "Chilling Independence," pp. 835–36. The best known attacks on the judiciary at that time occurred in Pennsylvania, but by impeachment, not address. *Newhampshire Sentinel*, 12 February 1803, p. 3, cols. 2–3; Peeling, "Governor McKean," p. 336; Henderson, "Attack on Judiciary," p. 119.

29. They also unanimously resolved: "That if the Legislature of New-Hampshire for mere speculative purposes were to express an opinion on the acts of the General Government commonly called 'the Alien and sedition bills,' that opinion would unreservedly be, that those acts are constitutional and in the present critical situation of our country highly expedient." Minutes for 14 June 1799, *House Journal* (June 1799), pp. 60–61.

30. *New-Hampshire Gazette*, 26 May 1795, reprinted in *Documentary History of the Supreme Court*, p. 493; Remonstrance of the New Hampshire General Court, 20 February 1794, ibid., p. 402.

31. *New-Hampshire Gazette*, 26 May 1795, quoted in *Documentary History of the Supreme Court*, p. 492; Address of Governor John Taylor Gilman, 17 December 1794, *House Journal* (December 1794), p. 8; Remonstrance to Congress, 19 February 1794, *House Journal* (December 1793), pp. 198–203; Memorial to Congress, 14 January 1795, *House Journal* (December 1794), p. 119.

32. Smith to Plumer, 6 December 1794, *Plumer Documents*. Smith had been certain he knew how the case would be resolved yet had been "anxious" to hear the arguments. Smith to Plumer, 28 January 1795, *Documentary History of the Supreme Court*, p. 417. The opinions met his expectations, which may explain why he did not present the petition. "Patterson delivered one of the most elegant correct perspicuous & convincing arguments I ever heard delivered in a Court of law." Smith to Plumer, 24 February 1795, Turner, *Ninth State*, p. 148.

33. *Documentary History of the Supreme Court*, p. 417n7; Smith to Plumer, 7 February 1795, *Plumer Documents*; "New Hampshire Memorial," 27 February 1795, *Papers of James Madison* 15:483.

34. Lawrie, "Interpretation and Authority," p. 312; Kaufman, "Judicial Independence," p. 688; Hamilton, *Federalist* #81, in *Federalist*, p. 545; SOLON, *Osborne's Spy*, 11 December 1790, p. 53, cols. 1–2. For discussion of other jurisdictions, see Corwin, "Progress of Theory," pp. 64, 77.

35. *New-Hampshire Gazette*, 29 February 1792, p. 1, col. 2 (reporting on December 1791 General Court session—see cols. 2–3 for two acts lengthening the time to receive claims); House of Representatives, 3 December 1795, *Courier of New Hampshire*, 12 December 1795, p. 2, col. 3.

36. "[G]ranting the prayer of Josiah Sanborn, for liberty to enter a certain action at the next Superior Court." Minutes for 14 June 1798, *Senate Journal* (June 1798), p. 30.

37. Minutes of 6 January 1792, *Senate Journal* (November 1792), p. 398. Also, "An Act to enable Thomas Parker, Esquire, to review an Action commenced against him in the Inferior Court of Common Pleas." Minutes for 18 June 1789, *Senate Journal* (June 1789), pp. 33–34. Similarly, see three acts of January 1792 reported in *New-Hampshire Gazette*, 29 February 1792, p. 1, col. 2 and cols. 3–4; Minutes for 13 June 1792, *Senate Journal* (June 1792), p. 524. At that same June session both houses "impowered" Phinehas Parker "to review a certain action," and, later, at the November session, the Senate enacted "An Act in addition to and in Amendment to an Act intitled an Act empowering Phinehas Parker to review a certain action." Minutes for 17 December 1792, *Senate Journal* (November 1792), p. 620.

38. Minutes of 19 June 1797, *House Journal* (June 1797), p. 68.

39. Minutes of 16 June 1797, *House Journal* (June 1797), p. 58.

40. Minutes for 14 December 1791, *House Journal* (November 1791), p. 433.

41. Minutes of 23 January 1794, *House Journal* (December 1793), p. 104.

42. Minutes of 11 December 1792, *Senate Journal* (November 1792), p. 616.

43. Minutes for 13 December 1791, *Senate Journal* (November 1791), p. 379.

44. Perhaps because Jay, C.J., had declared a Rhode Island extension unconstitutional in violation of the contract clause of the United States constitution. Marcus, "Judicial Review," pp. 27–28.

45. "A bill entitled an act to give a new trial to Josiah Sanborn in a certain action, commenced against him by Samuel Holland, which hath been tried and judgment entered therein, by action of Review at the Superior Court . . . was enacted." Minutes for 14 June 1798, *Senate Journal* (June 1798), p. 30. Similarly, see Minutes for 16 December 1797, *House Journal* (November 1797), p. 101; Minutes for 9 December 1796, *Senate Journal* (November 1796), p. 40.

46. "An Act to restore Richard Tripe to his Law." Minutes for 18 June 1789, *Senate Journal* (June 1789), p. 34.

47. "An Act for restoring Stephen Evans to his law." Minutes for 20 June 1792, *Senate Journal* (June 1792), p. 531.

48. Copy of Report of the Committee, 9 February 1792, *Plumer Documents* (Reel 13, Frames 315–16). Also, see Bilder, "Origin of the Appeal," p. 925.

49. *New-Hampshire Gazette*, 29 February 1792, p. 1, cols. 1–4; Minutes for 1 December 1797, *House Journal* (November 1797), p. 34. For discussion of the increase of restoring acts, see Turner, *Ninth State*, pp. 104–5.

50. Minutes for 14 June 1790, *House Journal* (June 1790), pp. 67–68; Minutes for 16 June 1790, *Senate Journal* (June 1790), p. 22; Minutes for 14 and 25 January 1791, *Senate Journal* (January 1791), pp. 104, 113; Minutes for 14 and 21 January 1791, *House Journal* (January 1791), pp. 156, 168. For a full text of the act, see Copy of Act Restoring Elizabeth McClary to her Law, 25 January 1791, *Plumer Documents* (Reel 13, Frame 291); An act . . ., 24 January 1791, Plumer, *Repository IV* (Frames 291–92).

51. Plumer, *Plumer*, pp. 170–71.

52. Dodd, "Gilman v. McClary," pp. 349–50; Dodd, "Constitutional History of New Hampshire," pp. 399–400.

53. Plumer, *Plumer*, p. 171; Minutes of 18 June 1789, *Senate Journal* (June 1789), p. 36. There was an earlier finding of unconstitutionality in a petition for a new trial. Lawrie, "Interpretation and Authority," pp. 324–25. Also, see Reno, *Memoirs of the Judiciary* I:19.

54. Minutes for 18 December 1797, *House Journal* (November 1797), pp. 110–11.

55. Veto by the Governor, 18 December 1797, ibid., p. 112; Minutes of 19 December 1797, *Senate Journal* (November 1797), pp. 70–71.

56. Minutes for 14 June 1798, *Senate Journal* (June 1798), p. 30. A variation was to grant "leave to bring in a bill at this or the next Session." Minutes for 21 June 1792, *Senate Journal* (June 1792), p. 538.

57. "Voted that [3 members] be a committee on the part of the House, to join such of the honorable Senate . . . to consider the petition of Benjamin Pierce praying to be restored to his law in a certain action, and report thereon." Minutes for 27 January 1794, *House Journal* (December 1793), p. 122. For similar votes at the same session, see Minutes for 1 and 7 January and 15 February 1794, pp. 33, 52–53, 184.

58. Minutes for 9 December 1797, *House Journal* (November 1797), p. 70. Similarly, see Minutes of 9 June 1791, *House Journal* (June 1791), pp. 334–35.

59. Minutes for 13 June 1792, *House Journal* (June 1792), p. 567; Minutes for 26 November 1792, *Senate Journal* (November 1792), p. 605.

60. Minutes for 1 January 1795, *House Journal* (December 1794), p. 62.

61. Minutes for 22 June 1792, *House Journal* (June 1792), p. 597; Minutes for 23

December 1791, *House Journal* (November 1791), p. 447.

62. Minutes for 19 and 23 December 1794, 1, 2, 8, 9, and 12 January 1795, *House Journal* (December 1794), pp. 23, 32, 64–65, 67, 69, 89–90, 93, 94, 101; Minutes for 18 June 1795, *Senate Journal* (June 1795), p. 52.

63. Minutes for 29 January 1794, *House Journal* (December 1793), p. 133.

64. Douglas, "Judicial Review," p. 262; Lawrie, "Interpretation and Authority," p. 315; *Courier of New Hampshire,* 12 December 1795, p. 3, col. 1 (reporting on the House of Representatives, 8 December 1795).

65. Minutes for 17 and 24 December 1794, *House Journal* (December 1794), pp. 7, 36. "A bill for making entries at the Superior Court next to be holden at Charlestown . . . which should have been made at former sessions of said court." Minutes for 6 January 1795, ibid., p. 80.

66. Minutes for 13 June 1794, *House Journal* (June 1794), pp. 56, 57; Minutes for 13 December 1791, *House Journal* (November 1791), p. 430. At the same session a special act permitted Mary Tufton Mason to take an appeal from a certain decree of the Court of Probate. Minutes for 19 December 1791, *Senate Journal* (November 1791), p. 382.

67. Lawrie, "Interpretation and Authority," p. 315. Also, see the case filed by Jeremiah Mason, p. 318.

68. Petition of Mary Tufton Mason, 7 December 1791, *Legislative Papers* (Frames 338–39).

69. *Controlling the Law,* pp. 107–30.

70. Dodd, "Constitutional History of New Hampshire," p. 398; Minutes for 7 February 1794, *House Journal* (December 1793), pp. 147–48; Act of 12 February 1794, *Laws of New Hampshire,* pp. 141–42. At the Constitutional Convention, Plumer reported that "nearly one half as great parts of their [General Court's] business consists in hearing private Petitions." Report of Committee, 9 February 1792, Plumer, *Repository IV* (Frame 316).

71. *New-Hampshire Gazette,* 7 June 1792, p. 1, col. 1; *New-Hampshire Patriot,* 30 April 1811, p. 3, col. 2. The legislators had explained that they had restored the plaintiff to his law "only because unusual circumstances rendered the Superior Court deadlocked on granting a new trial in this case." Lawrie, "Interpretation and Authority," p. 325. Also, see Wood, "Origins of Vested Rights," p. 1432.

72. SOLON, *New-Hampshire Gazette,* 11 December 1790, p. 3, col. 2.

73. CINCINNATUS [Plumer], No. 92, *Portsmouth Journal,* 23 August 1823, p. 2, col. 2.

74. Plumer in 1787: Lawrie, "Interpretation and Authority," p. 318; Plumer to Smith, ibid., p. 319n63. Also, see Wood, "Origins of Vested Rights," p. 1439. The most detailed argument against legislative interference with the judicial process was by Zephaniah Swift of Connecticut, a state that had no constitution. Swift, *Vindication,* pp. 3, 37, 41–43.

4—A Midnight Judge

1. Smith to Plumer, 20 December 1791, 4 April 1796, 12 April 1796, *Plumer Documents.*

2. He wrote of Congress: "This would indeed be a pleasing thing were that cursed foul fiend called party banished [from] the Walls of this House. You have no idea my dear Friend of the mischievous influence of this demon. I have withstood it for a long time but I fancy I must at last yield." He became a Federalist, "because in the main their Views are more favourable to the welfare of the public than that of the other party who appear to me to be Enemies of good government public faith public Credit public Honesty." Smith to Plumer, 20 February 1793, *Plumer Documents.* Later he wrote: "Congress are divided into two parties. Those who support, & those who *clamour against every* measure of Government." Smith to Plumer, 12 February 1794, ibid.

3. Smith to Plumer, 12 April 1796, 12 February 1794, and 27 April 1796, ibid.

4. Smith to Plumer, 18 February 1797, *Plumer Documents*; Smith to Ames, 6 February 1796, in Morison, *Life of Smith*, p. 91 (also, see p. 73). "I have attended the Supreme Ct. when I could conveniently leave our House and have been edified." Smith to Plumer, 12 February 1794, *Plumer Documents*.

5. *Farmer's Museum*, 29 June 1802, p. 3, col. 3; Smith to Plumer, 31 January 1803, and Plumer to Smith, 14 February 1803, *Plumer Documents*; Alfange, "Marbury v. Madison," p. 329.

6. Plumer to Smith, 14 February 1803, and Smith to Plumer, 20 February 1803, *Plumer Documents*. Logan was Senator George Logan of Pennsylvania, a physician. Jackson was Senator James Jackson of Georgia, who had practiced law.

7. Rakove, "Origins of Judicial Review," p. 1038.

8. *Controlling the Law*, pp. 34–35.

9. Plumer to Thomas Thompson, 13 July 1802, *Plumer Documents*.

10. For the economic and political importance of Exeter and of the Exeter Junto, of which Smith soon was a leading member, see Opal, "Politics of Industry"; Turner, *Ninth State*, pp. 172–73.

11. Morison, *Life of Smith*, p. 142. In 1879 Smith's probate treatise was published. *Smith's Reports*, pp. 447–520.

12. *United States Statutes at Large* 2:156 (1802).

13. Nelson, *Marbury v. Madison*, p. 56; Turner, "Judiciary Act of 1801," p. 4; Surrency, "Judiciary Act of 1801," p. 56.

14. Turner, "Midnight Judges," pp. 494–95; Turner, "Judiciary Act of 1801," pp. 5–6, 21, 32; Surrency, "Judiciary Act of 1801," pp. 58, 63.

15. *Judicial Independence at Crossroads*, p. 170; Miller, *Juries and Judges*, p. 59; Alfange, "Marbury v. Madison," p. 351.

16. Carpenter, *Judicial Tenure*, p. 57; Alfange, "Marbury v. Madison," pp. 351–52.

17. Turner, "Federalist Policy and Judiciary," pp. 27–28.

18. Ibid., p. 28; Turner, "Judiciary Act of 1801," p. 31; Adams, *Administration of Jefferson* 1:297.

19. For a brief account of the dichotomy, see *Controlling the Law*, pp. 33–55.

20. Plumer to Thatcher, 16 February 1801, *Plumer Papers*.

21. Turner, "Midnight Judges," p. 497; Ames to Smith, 16 February 1801, *Works of Ames* 1:291–92.

22. Turner, "Midnight Judges," pp. 496–98.

23. Smith to Marshall, 11 March 1801, printed in Morison, *Life of Smith*, pp. 143–44.

24. Ibid., p. 144; Stockton to Adams, 2 February 1801, quoted in Turner, "Midnight Judges," p. 511.

25. Newmyer, *John Marshall*, p. 153; Griswold: Simon, *What Kind of Nation*, p. 167; Giles: Carpenter, *Judicial Tenure*, p. 73; Ross: O'Fallon, "Marbury," p. 225.

26. Ellis, *Jeffersonian Crisis*, p. 46; Speech of Mason, 8 January 1802, *New-Hampshire Gazette*, 2 February 1802, p. 1, col. 3; *Newhampshire Sentinel*, 20 March 1802, p. 3, col. 2.

27. Giles to Jefferson, 16 March 1801, Anderson, *William Branch Giles*, pp. 77–78; Speech of Tracy, 12 January 1802, *New-Hampshire Gazette*, 9 February 1802, p. 2, col. 1; *Newhampshire Sentinel*, 23 January 1802, p. 3, col. 1.

28. Speech of Mason, n.d., *Newhampshire Sentinel*, 27 February 1802, p. 1, col. 4; Speech of Tracy, 12 January 1802, ibid., 13 February 1802, p. 4, col. 2; Speech of Giles, 18 February 1802, *New-Hampshire Gazette*, 6 April 1802, p. 1, col. 3 (also *Newhampshire Sentinel*, 3 April 1802, p. 2, col. 2).

29. Speech of Mason, n.d., *Newhampshire Sentinel*, 13 February 1802, p. 1, cols. 2–3.

30. Speech of Mason, 8 January 1802, *New-Hampshire Gazette*, 2 February 1802, p. 1, col. 3 (*Newhampshire Sentinel*, 6 February 1802, p. 2, col. 3).

31. Speech of Bayard, n.d., *Newhampshire Sentinel,* 29 May 1802, p. 1, col. 2.

32. Speech of Mason, 13 January 1802, *New-Hampshire Gazette,* 16 February 1802, Supplement, cols. 3–4, 1. Also, see Currie, *Constitution in Jeffersonian Congress,* p. 16.

33. Speech of Senator Stevens Mason, 13 January 1802, *Senate Debates on Judiciary,* pp. 235–36 (printed in New Hampshire in *New-Hampshire Gazette,* 16 February 1802, Supplement, col. 1; *Newhampshire Sentinel,* 20 February 1802, p. 2, col. 3).

34. HAMPDEN—No. VI, *Farmer's Museum,* 7 April 1804, p. 1, col. 4, p. 4, col. 1.

35. Speech of Bayard, n.d., *Newhampshire Sentinel,* 8 May 1802, p. 1, cols. 2–3; Speech of Giles, 18 February 1802, *New-Hampshire Gazette,* 6 April 1802, p. 2, col. 1. Also, see Adams, *Administration of Jefferson* 1:293.

36. Speech of Senator William Hill Wells, *Senate Debates on Judiciary,* pp. 235–36.

37. O'Fallon, "Case of Benjamin More," p. 52. Senator Brackenridge of Kentucky thought either of the second two alternatives would violate republican principles. "It is a principle of our constitution . . . that no man shall receive public money, but in consideration of public services. Sinecure offices therefore are not permitted by our laws or constitution." Speech of Brackenridge, n.d., *Newhampshire Sentinel,* 6 February 1802, p. 2, col. 1.

38. Protest of Richard Bassett, 14 August 1802, *Newhampshire Sentinel,* 11 September 1802, p. 2, col. 2; Whittington, "Reconstructing the Judiciary," p. 70 (quoting Jefferson); Speech of Mason, n.d., *Newhampshire Sentinel,* 27 February 1802, p. 2, col. 1; Speech of Morris, n.d., *Newhampshire Sentinel,* 27 March 1802, p. 1, col. 3. "[I]f the office is to be considered as a property, it is a property held in trust for the benefit of the people, and must therefore be held, subject to the condition of which Congress is the constitutional judge." Speech of Giles, 18 February 1802, *New-Hampshire Gazette,* 6 April 1802, p. 1, col. 5.

39. Speech of Brackenridge, 8 January 1802, *New-Hampshire Gazette,* 26 January 1802, p. 2, col. 3; Speech of Bayard, n.d., *Newhampshire Sentinel,* 8 May 1802, p. 1, col. 2.

40. Speech of Senator Gouverneur Morris, *Senate Debates on Judiciary,* p. 39. For the jurisprudential dichotomy, see *Controlling the Law,* pp. 33–55.

41. [Webster,] *Appeal to Old Whigs,* p. 9.

42. [Plumer,] *Address to Electors,* p. 7; Plumer to John Park, 7 January 1804, *Plumer Papers.*

43. Woodman, *Election Sermon,* pp. 9–10. Similarly, see Moore, *Fast Day Discourse at Milford,* pp. 5–6; Church, *Oration at Pelham,* p. 16.

44. Anon., *Republican Address to New-Hampshire,* pp. 8–9; *American Patriot,* 25 October 1808, p. 3, col. 1. In 1802 the New Hampshire chief justice's salary was $850. *Controlling the Law,* p. 61.

45. Morison, *Life of Smith,* pp. 146, 144–45.

46. Smith to Dexter, 7 June 1802, ibid., pp. 152–53.

47. Tilghman to Smith, 22 May 1802, and Smith to Tilghman, 7 June 1802, ibid., pp. 148–50.

48. Any lawsuit would have been difficult. See Justice Samuel Chase to John Marshall, 24 April 1802, *Papers of Marshall* 6:109–16; O'Fallon, "Case of Benjamin More," p. 54; Whittington, "Reconstructing the Judiciary," p. 62; Haskins, "Law Versus Politics," pp. 11–12; Graber, "Federalist or Friends," p. 251.

49. *Stuart v. Laird,* 5 *U.S.* 299, 308–9 (1803). For brief discussions, see Nelson, *Marbury v. Madison,* p. 68; Nelson, "Eighteenth-Century Background," p. 941; O'Fallon, "Case of Benjamin More," pp. 54–55; Geyh and Van Tassel, "Independence of Judicial," pp. 84–85.

50. *Newhampshire Sentinel,* 9 October 1802, p. 2, col. 4.

51. Entry for 7 January 1804, Plumer, *Memorandum,* p. 103.

52. "Memorial of the Judges," *Courier of New Hampshire,* 24 March 1803, p. 2, cols. 2, 1.

53. Plumer to Smith, 27 January 1803, *Plumer Papers*.

54. Morison, *Life of Smith*, p. 146.

55. "Sketches for the Biographer," *People's Advocate*, 15 October 1816, p. 4, col. 2. The circuit judges "it is said are making regular charges against the United States for their salaries, on the assurance that they will all be paid, as well as reinstated in office, when Mr. Jefferson is turned out." *New-Hampshire Gazette*, 26 October 1802, p. 3, col. 2. For XYZ, who pretended to be a Federalist, predicting that when the Federalists returned to power, the court would be resurrected and the midnight judges paid all their arrears in salary, see *New-Hampshire Gazette*, 1 November 1808, p. 2, col. 2.

5—A Hydrophobic Judge

1. Smith to Plumer, 20 February 1803, *Plumer Documents*; Entry for 7 January 1804, Plumer, *Memorandum*, p. 101.

2. Jefferson to Dickinson, 19 December 1801, Jefferson, *Memoir* 3:495.

3. Entry for 7 January 1804, Plumer, *Memorandum*, p. 102; Turner, *Plumer*, pp. 122–23.

4. Plumer, "Biographical Sketches, vol. 22," p. 840; Plumer, "Biographical Notes on John Pickering," *Biography Papers* (Frame 974). Also, see True, *Committees of Correspondence*, p. 60.

5. Plumer to John Hale, 18 September 1786, First Plumer Letterbook #38; Plumer, "Biographical Sketches, vol. 22," p. 840. Also, see Parker, "Heroic Age of the New Hampshire Bar," pp. 26–27.

6. "[T]he Honourable John Pickering had 1500 votes . . . more than the gentleman elected!" *Osborne's Spy*, 26 June 1790, p. 71, col. 3.

7. "I am at no loss to account for Pickering's opposition to the amendments proposed to the Constitution. What is all the business of amendments but a declaration that the original (a favourite Child of his own begetting) is very imperfect?" Smith to Plumer, 15 March 1792, *Plumer Documents*.

8. Shipton, "Pickering," p. 92; Richard F. Upton, "Drafting the Constitution," in *New Hampshire the State*, pp. 23–24; Plumer, "Biographical Sketches, vol. 22," p. 841. Together with John Sullivan and John Langdon, he was a leader in the adoption of the U.S. Constitution by New Hampshire.

9. *Osborne's Spy*, 14 July 1790, p. 92, col. 3; Plumer, "Biographical Sketches, vol. 22," p. 843; Turner, *Plumer*, pp. 123–24.

10. "Premature senility": Richard F. Upton, "John Langdon and John Sullivan," in *New Hampshire the State*, p. 222; Currie, *Constitution in Federalist Congress*, pp. 198–99; Currie, "Separating Judicial Power," p. 11; Act of 3 April 1794, *United States Statues at Large* 1:352–53.

11. Turner, *Ninth State*, p. 211; Ellis, *Jeffersonian Crisis*, p. 70; Turner, "Impeachment of Pickering," pp. 488–89; Entry for 6 March 1804, "Trial of Pickering," p. 337 (printing order authorizing Smith to act as district judge); Morison, *Life of Smith*, pp. 146–47.

12. Turner, *Ninth State*, pp. 211–13; Turner, "Impeachment of Pickering," pp. 489–90. The story is most fully told in the articles of impeachment. Minutes for 4 January 1804, "Trial of Pickering," pp. 319–22.

13. Ellis, *Jeffersonian Crisis*, p. 70; Turner, "Impeachment of Pickering," p. 490.

14. Bushnell, *Crimes, Follies, and Misfortunes*, pp. 44–45; Turner, "Jefferson Through Plumer," pp. 207–8.

15. Turner, "Impeachment of Pickering," pp. 490–91; Adams, *Administration of Jefferson* 2:143–44.

16. Smith to Plumer, 20 February 1803, and Plumer to Sheafe, 12 February 1803, *Plumer Documents*.

17. Ellis, *Jeffersonian Crisis*, p. 71; Turner, "Impeachment of Pickering," p. 487.

18. Plumer to James Sheafe, 13 December 1802, quoted in Turner, "Impeachment of Pickering," p. 491; Plumer to Bradbury Cilley, 20 February 1803, and Plumer to James Sheafe, 12 February 1803, *Plumer Documents*.

19. Plumer, "John Samuel Sherburne," pp. 492, 493, 490.

20. Turner, *Plumer*, p. 29; Turner, "Impeachment of Pickering," p. 491n15; Smith to Plumer, 10 January 1795 and 7 February 1795, *Plumer Documents*. Plumer's son wrote that Smith reversed "the apostolic injunction." Plumer, *Plumer*, p. 114n. When in Congress, Sherburne had been a Federalist.

21. Ellis, *Jeffersonian Crisis*, p. 71; Sheafe to Plumer, 30 December 1802, *Plumer Documents*.

22. Turner, "Impeachment of Pickering," p. 496; Turner, *Plumer*, pp. 126–27.

23. Turner, *Plumer*, p. 125; Turner, *Ninth State*, p. 213.

24. Mason to Plumer, 28 January 1804, *Historical Society Correspondence* (Frames 30–31).

25. "The four articles of impeachment all but proclaimed in writing that Pickering was to be sacrificed to political expediency." Turner, "Impeachment of Pickering," p. 495.

26. Ibid., p. 496; Brown, "Impeachment of Federal Judiciary," p. 700; Currie, *Constitution in Jeffersonian Congress*, p. 24; Brown, "Impeachment of Federal Judiciary," p. 704.

27. Minutes of 30 December 1803, *Annals of Congress*, House of Reps., 8th Cong., 1st Sess., pp. 794–95. "Nicholson responded that, if Pickering was mad, it was because of his drinking; his theory seems to be that it was a crime to drink oneself insane." Currie, *Constitution in Jeffersonian Congress*, p. 24.

28. Entry for 5 January 1804, Plumer, *Memorandum*, p. 100; [William Plumer,] Cincinnatus No. 126, *Grafton Journal*, 25 November 1825, p. 191, col. 1; Plumer, *Autobiography*, p. 130.

29. [William Plumer,] "Judiciary of the United States," Cincinnatus No. 130, *Portsmouth Journal*, 13 May 1826, p. 2, col. 5.

30. *Supra*, p. 60.

31. Currie, *Constitution in Jeffersonian Congress*, p. 30 (quoting Madison); Turner, *Plumer*, p. 125 (quoting Plumer). Also, see Turner, "Impeachment of Pickering," pp. 493–94.

32. Hamilton, Federalist #79, *Federalist*, p. 514.

33. Entry for 10 March 1804, Plumer, *Memorandum*, p. 176 (quoting Wright); Speech of Senator Stone, 13 January 1802, *New-Hampshire Gazette*, 23 February 1802, Supplement, p. 1, col. 4.

34. Turner, "Impeachment of Pickering," p. 493; Whittington, "Reconstructing the Judiciary," pp. 73–74 (quoting Giles). "The national Republican party, as appears plainly from the reported conversation of senators and congressmen, regarded impeachment not as a trial for high crimes and misdemeanors, but merely as a convenient method of ousting from office anyone not otherwise to be removed." Henderson, "Attack on Judiciary," p. 118.

35. Adams, *Administration of Jefferson* 2:154.

36. Turner, *Ninth State*, pp. 213–14; Turner, *Plumer*, pp. 127–28; Petition of Jacob S. Pickering, Minutes for 12 January 1804, and Depositions of J. Brackett and Edward St. Loe Livermore, Minutes for 6 March 1804, "Trial of Pickering," pp. 328–30, 335, 340; Currie, *Constitution of Jeffersonian Congress*, pp. 25–26 (quoting Harper).

37. Entry for 3 March 1804, *Memoirs of Adams*, 1:299; Adams, *Administration of Jefferson* 2:156.

38. Turner, *Plumer*, pp. 128–30.

39. Turner, "Impeachment of Pickering," p. 501 (quoting Plumer); Ellis, *Jeffersonian Crisis*, p. 73; Plumer to Smith, 11 March 1804, quoted in Turner, *Plumer*, p. 128. For

the testimony, see entries for 6 and 9 March 1804, "Trial of Pickering," pp. 350–59, 361–62. Steele was the son-in-law of the first district judge, General John Sullivan.

40. For the senators' oaths, see Hoffer and Hull, *Impeachment,* pp. 210–11.

41. Turner, *Plumer,* p. 129; Turner, "Impeachment of Pickering," p. 502; Olcott's testimony: Entry for 9 March 1804, "Trial of Pickering," pp. 359–60.

42. Minutes for 9 March 1804, "Trial of Pickering," p. 361; Entry for 10 March 1804, Plumer, *Memorandum,* p. 175.

43. Minutes for 12 March 1804, "Trial of Pickering," pp. 363–65; Turner, "Impeachment of Pickering," p. 504 (quoting Adams); Bushnell, *Crimes, Follies, and Misfortunes,* pp. 52, 55; Currie, *Constitution in Jeffersonian Congress,* pp. 26–27.

44. Entry for 5 March 1804, Plumer, *Memorandum,* pp. 167, 163. But Ohio's John Smith concluded, "Intemperance produced his insanity, & not the latter the former." Entry for 8 & 9 March 1804, ibid., p. 171.

45. [William Plumer,] "Judiciary of the United States," Cincinnatus No. 130, *Portsmouth Journal,* 13 May 1826, p. 2, col. 6; Plumer to Smith, 11 March 1804, quoted in Turner, "Impeachment of Pickering," pp. 503–4.

46. Entries for 22, 24, and 27 March 1804, Plumer, *Memorandum,* pp. 178–79, 181; *Farmer's Museum,* 12 May 1804, p. 3, col. 1 (quoting Steele); Plumer, "Jonathan Steele," p. 12; Turner, *Plumer,* p. 131; Turner, *Ninth State,* p. 214.

47. Turner, *Ninth State,* p. 214; Turner, *Plumer,* p. 131; Plumer, "John Samuel Sherburne," pp. 493, 494. The Rockingham Probate Court appointed a guardian for Sherburne. Story acted by authority of the Act of 2 March 1809, *U.S. Statutes at Large* 2:534–35.

48. Whittington, "Reconstructing the Judiciary," p. 71; Turner, "Impeachment of Pickering," p. 505. Plumer's article was reprinted in *Portsmouth Oracle,* 7 April 1804, p. 2, col. 3.

49. Plumer to Smith, 10 January 1804, *Plumer Papers;* Smith to Plumer, 29 January 1804, Fourth Plumer Letterbook.

50. Plumer, *Plumer,* p. 325 (quoting Plumer); Plumer to Smith, 10 January 1804, *Plumer Papers;* Plumer to Mason, 14 January 1803 and Smith to Plumer, 11 February 1804, Beveridge, *Life of Marshall* 3:160, 161.

51. Plumer, *Plumer,* p. 320; Plumer to Smith, 10 January 1804, *Plumer Papers.*

52. [Webster,] *Appeal to Old Whigs,* pp. 9–10.

53. Plumer to Smith, 16 January 1804, *Plumer Papers.*

54. Beveridge, *Life of Marshall* 3:158; Entry for 21 December 1804, *Memoirs of Adams* 1:322–23.

55. Plumer, *Plumer,* pp. 320–21; Entry for 21 December 1804, *Memoirs of Adams* 1:322. Also, see Blair and Coblentz, "Trials of Chase," pp. 382–83.

56. Plumer, *Plumer,* p. 324.

57. Ibid, p. 325; Plumer to T. W. Thompson, 18 February 1803, printed in ibid., p. 253.

58. Minutes for 22 December 1808, *House Journal* (November 1808), pp. 116–20. Church, *Oration at Pelham,* pp. 22–23. Randolph and other congressmen introduced the amendment several times. *Portsmouth Oracle,* 1 March 1806, p. 1, cols. 2–3; 15 March 1806, p. 2, col. 2; 20 January 1808, p. 1, col. 2.

6—A Dependent Court

1. Claggett, *Speech in House,* p. 3; Lieber, *Manual of Political Ethics,* p. 343. For platitudes also, see Carrington, "Judicial Independence," p. 80.

2. Cases of the Judges of the Court of Appeals, 8 *Virginia* (4 *Call*) 135, 143 (1788).

3. "The Judiciary," *Farmer's Cabinet,* 18 June 1811, p. 3, col. 2; Pembroke: *Concord Gazette,* 11 July 1809, p. 3, col. 3; Londonderry: *Farmer's Cabinet,* 22 July 1815, p. 1, col.

2; Amherst: *Farmer's Cabinet*, 12 July 1808, p. 1, col. 3; Portsmouth: *Portsmouth Oracle*, 21 July 1810, p. 1, col. 3.

4. American belief: Anon., "Mistakes of Westminster Review," p. 283; Complex law: Shapiro, "Judicial Independence," pp. 614–15, 616, 624.

5. Bailyn, *Pamphlets*, pp. 249–50; Stimson, *American Revolution in Law*, pp. 25–26; Berger, "Chilling Independence," p. 834; Anon., "Independence of the Judiciary," p. 41.

6. Wood, "Launching," p. 12; Smith, "Independent Judiciary," p. 1117; Wood, *Creation of Republic*, p. 298.

7. Bailyn, *Ideological Origins*, pp. 105–6; Stimson, *American Revolution in Law*, p. 50; [Joseph Galloway,] *A Letter to the People of Pennsylvania*, reprinted in Bailyn, *Pamphlets*, pp. 257, 259.

8. Bailyn, *Ideological Origins*, pp. 106, 107–8; Bailyn, *Pamphlets*, pp. 253, 255; Bostonians: Smith, "Independent Judiciary," p. 1145.

9. Montesquieu, *Spirit of Laws* I:174.

10. Wood, "Origins of Judicial Review," pp. 1301–302. Also, Wood, "Judicial Review," p. 155. Contrary: Prakash and Yoo, "Origins of Judicial Review," p. 931.

11. Kent, *Commentaries* I:294 (see quotation cited below at note 14); Hamilton, Federalist #78, *Federalist*, p. 522. Also, see Anon., *Friend to Constitution*, p. 55; *Tucker's Blackstone* I:126, 353; Wood, *Creation of Republic*, pp. 453–54; Wood, "Launching," p. 12.

12. Burbank, "Architecture of Independence," p. 320; Stimson, *American Revolution in Law*, pp. 102, 104; by 1810s: Pasley, *Tyranny of Printers*, p. 301; Jefferson: Zuckert, "Founder of Natural Rights," p. 44. The usual explanation for the division is that it was between "Agrarian-minded people" and "commercial-minded people." Ellis, *Jeffersonian Crisis*, pp. 256–57. If, however, attention is paid to the arguments of the time, it will be evident that the dichotomy was more jurisprudential than economic. *Controlling the Law*, pp. 33–55.

13. Massachusetts Constitution of 1780, Article XXIX, Peters, *Massachusetts Constitution*, p. 54; New Hampshire Constitution of 1784, Part I—The Bill of Rights, Article XXXV, Thorpe, *Constitutions* 4:2457; New Hampshire Constitution of 1792, Part First, Article XXXV, Thorpe, *Constitutions* 4:2474–75.

14. New Hampshire Constitution of 1792, Part Second, Section LXXIII, Thorpe, *Constitutions* 4:2486; [Plumer], CINCINNATUS—No. 126, *Grafton Journal*, 25 March 1825, p. 191, col. 1. Smith thought that tenure was less important for preserving judicial independence than were the personal attributes of judges. Smith, "Hon. Caleb Ellis," *Collections Historical* 2:228.

15. New Hampshire Constitution of 1792, Part First, Article XXXV, Thorpe, *Constitutions* 4:2475; [Alexander Hamilton,] Federalist #79, *Federalist*, p. 531. Also, see Address of the Massachusetts Convention, March 1780, *Popular Sources of Political Authority*, p. 439; [James Madison,] Federalist #51, *Federalist*, pp. 348–49.

16. Kent, *Commentaries* 1:294; Stychin, "Commentaries of Kent," p. 455; Madison to Jefferson, 17 October 1788, *Madison Letters*, p. 425. Also, see Ames, "Dangers of American Liberty," p. 1304.

17. Claggett, *Speech in House*, p. 8; *Farmer's Cabinet*, 8 October 1811, p. 3, col. 2.

18. Returns of Greenwich, 5 June 1780, and Wilbraham, 7 June 1780, *Popular Sources of Political Authority*, pp. 562, 623. Also, see p. 49; [Higgins,] *Sampson Against*, p. 63; Adams, *First American Constitutions*, p. 268.

19. Graves, "Our Early Courts," p. 20; [Bowen,] "Independence of Judiciary," pp. 412–13; Chipman, *Sketches of Government*, pp. 160–61; Ellis, *Jeffersonian Crisis*, p. 7; Adams, *First American Constitutions*, pp. 268–69; Stimson, *American Revolution in Law*, p. 104.

20. MARCELLUS, "The Judiciary," *Farmer's Cabinet*, 4 October 1813, p. 1, col. 2; *Portsmouth Oracle*, 17 July 1813, p. 3, col. 3.

21. MARCELLUS, "The Judiciary," *Farmer's Cabinet*, 4 October 1813, p. 1, cols. 1, 2. Similarly, for the national government, see Ellis, *Jeffersonian Crisis*, pp. 74–75; Thomas Jefferson to James Pleasants, 26 December 1821, *Writings of Thomas Jefferson*, 10:198–99; Autobiography, reprinted in *Jeffersonian Principles*, pp. 41–42.

22. *New-Hampshire Gazette,* 19 February 1805, p. 2, col. 5 (from a "Boston paper") and 6 October 1807, p. 3, col. 1 (from the *Trenton American*).

23. *New-Hampshire Gazette,* 6 October 1807, p. 3, col. 1 (from the *Trenton American*).

24. Geyh and Van Tassel, "Independence of Judicial," p. 41 (quoting Morris); Black, "Massachusetts Judges," p. 160; Grinnell, "Brief History of Court," p. 13; Davis, *History of Judiciary,* pp. 277–83. Also, see Frothingham, "Removal of Judges by Address," pp. 218–19.

25. "The constitution does not . . . contemplate that the Judges should be entirely independent; the nature of a free government does not admit this." Report of the House Committee on the Judiciary, *New-Hampshire Patriot,* 25 June 1816, p. 2, col. 4.

26. Aristides, "The Pretensions of Gov. Smith examined," *New-Hampshire Gazette,* 20 February 1810, Supplement, p. 2, col. 3; Plumer, Governor's Address, *New-Hampshire Patriot,* 11 June 1816, p. 2, col. 2; "The Pretensions of Govr. Smith," 30 January 1810, Plumer, *Repository* II, p. 101 (published in *New-Hampshire Patriot,* 6 February 1810). Not just judges, but military officers and coroners, were addressed out by Plumer. Officers: Plumer, *Autobiography,* p. 297; Address of 12 June 1818, Gubernatorial Papers I (Frame 1045). Coroners: Address of 9 December 1816 and 19 June 1817, Gubernatorial Papers I (Frames 993, 1006); Minutes of Governor and Council, 20 June 1817, Gubernatorial Papers (Frame 164). For other addressing out, see Carpenter, *Judicial Tenure,* pp. 125–30; for texts of addresses, see Grinnell, "Constitutional History of Court," pp. 508–11.

27. Tracy: *Judicial Independence at Crossroads,* p. 170; Entirely destroy: Anon., *Friend to Constitution,* p. 19; The People, "The Administration of Gov. Gilman," *New-Hampshire Gazette,* 25 January 1814, p. 2, col. 3; Federalist: *Farmer's Cabinet,* 18 October 1813, p. 3, col. 2.

28. *Tucker's Blackstone* 1:360–61. Also, see *Gorham* v. *Robinson,* 57 R.I. 1, 21–22, 37, 61 (1936).

29. [Gray,] *Power to Abolish Courts,* p. 24. The distinction was sometimes drawn between *constitutional courts* and *legislative courts.* Also, see Geyh and Van Tassel, "Independence of Judicial," pp. 43, 80; *Judicial Independence at Crossroads,* p. 170.

30. Report of the House Committee on the Judiciary, *New-Hampshire Patriot,* 25 June 1816, p. 2, col. 4.

31. Legislated-out: *New-Hampshire Patriot,* 9 July 1816, p. 2, cols. 1–2; Addressed-out: *Farmer's Cabinet,* 6 July 1816, p. 2, col. 3; Address to the Executive from a "Committee of both Branches of the Legislature," Gubernatorial Papers (Frames 136–37).

7—A Man for One Office

1. Morison, *Life of Smith,* p. 141n1.

2. A Friend to Truth, "On the Judicial Act—No. 11," *New-Hampshire Gazette,* 20 July 1813, p. 2., col. 4. For discussion of the salary problem, see *Controlling the Law,* pp. 71–82.

3. Turner, *Ninth State,* p. 159.

4. Letter of 27 February 1798, quoted in Stearns, "Livermore," p. 445. For Smith's candidacy, see Turner, *Ninth State,* p. 162.

5. Turner, *Ninth State,* p. 161. Also, Governor Gilman was not friendly with the Livermores. Ibid., p. 162.

6. Letter of 5 April 1798, quoted in Stearns, "Livermore," p. 445; Plumer quoted in Turner, *Ninth State,* p. 161.

7. Plumer to Smith, 25 January 1797, First Plumer Letterbook #108; Turner, *Ninth State,* pp. 101–2.

8. Federalist newspapers: *Concord Gazette,* 1 November 1808, p. 3, col. 1; Querist, "A Few Plain Questions," *Farmer's Cabinet,* 23 August 1808, p. 2, col. 3; Rockingham, *New-Hampshire Gazette,* 1 November 1808, p. 3, col. 2; Rattle, "The Tory Lawyers in an Uproar," *New-Hampshire Gazette,* 6 March 1810, p. 2, col. 4.

9. *New-Hampshire Patriot,* 11 July 1809, p. 3, col. 4; *New-Hampshire Gazette,* 10 December 1805, p. 2, col. 1.

10. *New-Hampshire Patriot,* 30 July 1816, p. 2, col. 5.

11. *New-Hampshire Patriot,* 18 July 1809, p. 3, col. 3, and 12 July 1814, p. 2, col. 5.

12. DECIUS, "British Influence—Letter VII," *New-Hampshire Patriot,* 6 February 1810, p. 1, col. 3, reprinted in *New-Hampshire Gazette,* 6 March 1810, Supplement, p. 1, cols. 2–3. A Federalist newspaper asserted: "Two articles in the Jefferson creed are to denounce Lawyers and Merchants. Lawyers because they read English law-books, and merchants because they trade with England." *Portsmouth Oracle,* 24 February 1810, p. 3, col. 3.

13. *New-Hampshire Gazette,* 1 November 1808, p. 3, col. 2.

14. A DOVER FARMER, "Farmers of New-Hampshire," *New-Hampshire Gazette,* 1 November 1808, p. 2, col. 2; VERITAS, *Concord Gazette,* 31 July 1810, p. 4, cols. 3–4.

15. *People's Advocate,* 28 December 1816, p. 2, col. 3.

16. *Concord Gazette,* 31 July 1810, p. 2, col. 1; *New-Hampshire Gazette,* 14 September 1802, p. 2, col. 1; LUCIUS, "To the Independent Electors of New-Hampshire," *New-Hampshire Gazette,* 2 March 1802, p. 2, col. 3.

17. CIRCULAR, "Legislative and State Concerns," *New-Hampshire Gazette,* 10 December 1805, p. 2, col. 1.

18. *American Patriot,* 25 October 1808, p. 3, col. 3; "pettifogger": Robinson, *Isaac Hill,* pp. 24–25; *New-Hampshire Patriot,* 25 February 1817, p. 1, col. 3, and 11 July 1809, p. 3, col. 4.

19. A DOVER FARMER, "Farmers of New-Hampshire," *New-Hampshire Gazette,* 1 November 1808, p. 2, col. 2.

20. Ibid.

21. *New-Hampshire Patriot,* 3 May 1814, p. 1, col. 2. Also, see Lambert, *Ten Pound Act,* pp. 29–30.

22. *New-Hampshire Patriot,* 25 December 1810, p. 3, col. 3. Plumer, writing as ARISTIDES, reported that there were 130 lawyers. Ibid., 27 February 1810, p. 1, col. 4.

23. Publicola, *New Vade Mecum,* pp. 85–86; [William Plumer,] "Government," CINCINNATUS No. 87, *Portsmouth Journal,* 31 May 1823, p. 2, col. 2.

24. PHOCION, *New-Hampshire Patriot,* 1 March 1814, p. 1, col. 4.

25. ARBITRATION, *New-Hampshire Patriot,* 25 December 1810, p. 2, col. 3; Plumer to Smith, 25 January 1797, quoted in Turner, *Plumer,* p. 69; JUNIUS, *New-Hampshire Patriot,* 4 June 1811, p. 1, cols. 4–5. For efforts to regulate admission, see *General Regulations for Bar,* pp. 4–5; Report of Rockingham County Bar Committee, 20 January 1812, *Webster Legal Papers* 1:237–40.

26. *New-Hampshire Patriot,* 27 June 1809, p. 3, col. 4. For the text of Smith's address, see Morison, *Life of Smith,* pp. 246–49.

27. Webster quoted in Holmes, "Address," p. 46. For common-sense jurisprudence, the meaning of "receptionist," and Smith's reception of common law, see *Controlling the Law,* pp. 18–55, 130–70.

28. Turner, *Ninth State,* p. 160 (also 160–63); Plumer, *Autobiography,* p. 68.

29. Turner, *Ninth State,* pp. 144, 163, 167, 229.

30. Smith to Plumer, quoted in Turner, *Ninth State,* p. 145; Smith to Robert Fletcher, 3 January 1795, Morison, *Life of Smith,* pp. 67–68; Mayo, *John Langdon,* pp. 250–51.

8—An Impetuous Judge

1. Smith to Plumer, 1 January 1805, Fourth Plumer Letterbook, pp. 320–21. The judges Smith named were Justice Samuel Chase of the United States Supreme Court and three on the Pennsylvania highest court—Chief Justice Edward Shippen

and Justices Jasper Yates and Thomas Smith. They were impeached in 1804 and acquitted (by 13 to 11 vote in favor of conviction) in 1805.

2. Taishoff, "State Politics," p. 35; Plumer to Uriah Tracy, 2 May 1805, Fourth Plumer Letterbook, p. 439.

3. Entry for 15 May 1806, Plumer, *Register I*. The vote had been 15,277 for Langdon and 5,296 for a scattering of Federalists, the third highest of whom was Jeremiah Smith with 902 votes. Entry for 25 June 1806, Plumer, *Memorandum*, p. 506.

4. Plumer to Langdon, 16 December 1805, Fourth Plumer Letterbook, p. 476; *Farmer's Cabinet*, 20 December 1803, p. 2. col. 1; Entry for 5 December 1805, Plumer, *Memorandum*, p. 342; *Controlling the Law*, pp. 95–170.

5. Enlarged: Plumer to Daniel Plumer, 25 January 1807, Plumer Letters to His Brother; Mason to Plumer, 5 January 1805, Fourth Plumer Letterbook, pp. 522–23; Undigested: Plumer to Daniel Plumer, 19 January 1806, Plumer Letters to His Brother; Plumer to Thomas Cogswell, 27 January 1806, Fourth Plumer Letterbook, pp. 563–64. Also, see Plumer to Philip Carrigain, Jr., 24 January 1806, and Plumer to Mason, 27 January 1806, Fourth Plumer Letterbook, pp. 556, 567–68; Plumer to Daniel Plumer, 27 December 1805, Plumer Letters to His Brother.

6. *Controlling the Law*, pp. 110–14

7. Ibid., pp. 138–42.

8. Smith to Plumer, 22 February 1804, Fourth Plumer Letterbook.

9. MARCELLUS, "To Federal Farmers and Mechanics of New-Hampshire," *New-Hampshire Patriot*, 5 March 1816, p. 2, col. 3; *Controlling the Law*, p. 75.

10. *Controlling the Law*, pp. 61, 72–76.

11. *Controlling the Law*, pp. 78–79; Anxiety: Letter from Plumer to Daniel Plumer, 12 December 1804, and Plumer to Samuel Plumer, 14 January 1805, Plumer Letters to His Brother; Plumer to James Wilson, 7 December 1804, Fourth Plumer Letterbook, pp. 295–96.

12. Reduction: *Newhampshire Sentinel*, 15 December 1804, p. 3, col. 3; Four judges: [Plumer], CINCINNATUS—No. 125, *Grafton Journal*, 12 November 1825, p. 183, col. 1. Atkinson had been appointed in May the previous year. *Courier of New Hampshire*, 12 May 1803, p. 3, col. 3.

13. *New-Hampshire Gazette*, 18 June 1805, p. 3, col. 2 and 25 June 1805, p. 2, col. 3; Letter: Entry for 9 July 1805, Plumer, *Register I*.

14. Entry for 9 July 1805, Plumer, *Register I*, pp. 29–30.

15. Stearns, "Livermore," p. 429; Plumer, *Autobiography*, p. 74; Plumer to William Gordon, 26 June 1798, First Plumer Letterbook. Also, see Parker, *Courts and Lawyers* 3:550.

16. Plumer, *Autobiography*, p. 78; Plumer to William Gordon, 9 February 1799, Third Plumer Letterbook, pp. 25–26; Smith: Stearns, "Livermore," p. 446.

17. Colby, "Holderness and Livermores," p. 179; Samuel: Plumer, *Autobiography*, p. 77; Edward: Plumer, *Autobiography*, pp. 65–66; Plumer to Smith, 23 August 1796, First Plumer Letterbook, #104.

18. Colby, "Holderness and Livermores," p. 179; Plumer to James Sheafe, 3 January 1806, Fourth Plumer Letterbook, pp. 513–14.

19. Livermore to House Committee, 30 November 1805, Plumer, *Repository III*, pp. 155–56.

20. Livermore to House Committee, 30 November 1805, Plumer, *Repository III*, pp. 155–57; Turner, *Ninth State*, p. 222.

21. "Your reply, sir, was fraught with *contempt for the people*. You told their representatives, that *the people did not give you salary enough, and that you would give them only their money's worth of service*." THE VOICE OF NEW-HAMPSHIRE, "To Arthur Livermore, Esq.", *People's Advocate*, 29 October 1816, p. 1, col. 3.

22. *New-Hampshire Gazette*, 31 December 1805, p. 2, col. 3, and 14 January 1806, p. 2, col. 4.

23. *New-Hampshire Gazette,* 14 January 1806, p. 2, col. 4.

24. Ibid.

25. *New-Hampshire Gazette,* 14 January 1806, p. 2, col. 4.

26. *New-Hampshire Gazette,* 14 January 1806, p. 2, col. 4.

27. Turner, *Ninth State,* p. 222.

28. *Farmer's Cabinet,* 14 January 1806, p. 3, col. 3.

29. Mason to Plumer, 5 January 1806, Fourth Plumer Letterbook, p. 522.

30. Plumer to Mason, 27 January 1806, Plumer to James Sheafe, 3 January 1806, Fourth Plumer Letterbook, pp. 567, 513–14, 567.

31. At least, no judge addressed out who had not been impeached or legislated from office. In 1816, as governor, Plumer asked the General Court to address from office both Republican judges legislated out in 1813 and Federalist judges legislated out in 1816.

32. Plumer to Smith, 2 January 1795, First Plumer Letterbook; Plumer to Langdon, 18 January 1806, Fourth Plumer Letterbook, pp. 547–48 (also, Turner, *Plumer,* p. 161; *Controlling the Law,* p. 102).

Conclusion

1. [Plumer,] CINCINNATUS No. 100, *Collections Historical,* 3:163.

2. *New-Hampshire Patriot,* 26 September 1809, p. 3, col. 4; Turner, *Ninth State,* p. 256. Livermore apparently hesitated before accepting. In December Plumer wrote: "report says Arthur Livermore has not yet accepted the office of chief justice; & that Jeremiah Smith regrets that he resigned the office for one of so uncertain tenure as that of governor." Plumer to Nahum Parker, 22 December 1809, Third Plumer Letterbook, p. 68.

3. Plumer to Plumer, Jr., 9 June 1810, and Nahum Parker to Plumer, 14 April 1810, Eighth Plumer Letterbook, pp. 68, 53–54.

4. Plumer, "Jonathan Steele," p. 15.

5. JUSTUS, "To the People of New-Hampshire," *New-Hampshire Patriot,* 22 October 1811, p. 3, cols. 2, 3.

6. Ibid., col. 3.

7. *New-Hampshire Patriot,* 14 January 1817, p. 3, col. 1, and 13 February 1810, p. 3, col. 3.

8. Ibid., 9 January 1810, p. 2, col. 1, and 13 February 1810, p. 3, col. 2.

9. Ibid., 29 August 1809, p. 3, col. 2, and 5 September 1809, p. 3, col. 2; Bell, *Answer to Petition,* pp. 6–24.

10. *New-Hampshire Patriot,* 30 April 1811, p. 3, col. 2.

11. Ibid.

12. *Farmer's Cabinet,* 25 October 1813, p. 1, col. 2 (from the *Portsmouth Oracle*); Plumer, *Plumer,* p. 396; Edward St. Loe Livermore to Edward Cutts, 13 September 1813, Edward St. Loe Livermore Papers (file 2), New Hampshire Historical Society.

13. Plumer to John Adams Harper, 2 March 1812, Eighth Plumer Letterbook, p. 198.

14. THE VOICE OF NEW-HAMPSHIRE, "To Arthur Livermore, Esq.," *People's Advocate,* 29 October 1816, p. 1, col. 4.

15. Ibid., col. 3.

16. Bell, *Bench and Bar,* p. 380; *Farmer's Cabinet,* 22 June 1816, p. 3, col. 3.

17. *New-Hampshire Patriot,* 16 June 1812, p. 2, col. 2.

18. Entry for 18 June 1812, Plumer, *Register II.* Livermore was also complimented that year at the Republican Fourth of July celebration in Portsmouth with the toast: "Hon. Arthur Livermore, chief justice of N. Hampshire, maintaining the dignity and independence of the Judiciary, he will not fear to do right, though assailed by the shafts of faction." *New-Hampshire Gazette,* 7 July 1812, p. 3, col. 1.

19. *New-Hampshire Patriot,* 23 June 1812, p. 3, col. 2; *Farmer's Cabinet,* 6 July 1812, p. 2, col. 3.

20. Entry for 18 June 1812, Plumer, *Register II.*

21. Ibid.

22. *New-Hampshire Patriot,* 23 June 1812, p. 3, col. 3; *Farmer's Cabinet,* 6 July 1812, p. 2, col. 3.

23. Entry for 18 June 1812, Plumer, *Register II.*

24. Ibid.; *Constitutionalist,* 30 June 1812, p. 1, col. 2.

25. *Democratic Republican,* 21 December 1812, p. 2, col. 1; *Portsmouth Oracle,* 12 December 1812, p. 1, cols. 3–4.

26. Minutes of 17 December 1812, *House Journal* (November 1812), pp. 157–58.

27. Cato, *New-Hampshire Patriot,* 22 February 1814, p. 1, col. 1.

28. *Constitutionalist,* 6 July 1813, p. 1, col. 1.

29. Act of 28 June 1816, Gubernatorial Papers (Frames 936–37); Message from House of Representatives to Governor Plumer, 25 June 1816, Gubernatorial Papers (Frames 138–39). See *Concord Gazette,* 9 July 1816, p. 3. col. 2; *New-Hampshire Gazette,* 9 July 1816, p. 2, col. 4.

30. The arguments of Smith, Webster, and Mason are in *Dartmouth College* v. *Woodward,* 65 *N.H.* 473–624 (1817).

31. And so the Superior Court of Judicature ruled that enacted statutes, "if not repugnant to any other constitutional provision, are 'the law of the land,' within the true sense of the constitution." *Dartmouth College* v. *Woodward,* 1 *N.H.* 111, 132 (1817) (per Richardson, C.J.) (the quotation is at page 639 in 65 *N.H.*).

32. "Common-sense jurisprudence": *Controlling the Law,* pp. 18–32; "instructing jurors": ibid., pp. 197–98.

33. See, *supra,* pp. 63–64.

34. Minutes of 24 June 1818, *House Journal* (June 1818), p. 239.

35. New Hampshire Constitution, Article 74. For Plumer's interpretation of and his objections to this authority, see [Plumer,] Cincinnatus—No, 125, *Grafton Journal,* 12 November 1825, p. 185, col. 2.

36. Minutes of 27 November 1816, *Senate Journal* (November 1816), p. 42; Committee "On Petitions for new trials and restoration to law." *New-Hampshire Gazette,* 16 June 1818, p. 2, col. 2; *New-Hampshire Gazette,* 8 July 1817, p. 2, col. 1 (new trial for Dolly Merrill) and col. 2 (relief for Isaac Hodadon).

37. Lawrie, "Interpretation and Authority," p. 326.

38. Minutes of 20 June 1818, *House Journal* (June 1818), p. 239.

39. "An act to empower John Davis and his several sons and daughters to assume and bear the name of Washington." Minutes of 23 June 1818, *House Journal* (June 1818), p. 327.

40. Superior Court to Senate and House, 31 May 1819, *Communication from Governor,* p. 5. The opinion did not form "part," but rather, it was the judges' complete reply to the legislative request. The justices had nothing else to say.

41. E.g., "[T]he very nature and effect of a new law is a rule for future cases. They must, too, in general, be rules prescribed for civil conduct to the whole community, and not a 'transient, sudden order from a superior to, or concerning a particular person.[']" *Merrill* v. *Sherburne,* 1 *N.H.* 199, 212 (1818).

42. E.g., "The legislative power is surely one of the most honorable and useful in all governments." Ibid.

43. E.g., the House of Representatives "are the tribunal to try impeachments." Ibid., p. 210.

44. Bell to Senate and House, 24 June 1819, *Communication from Governor,* p. 4.

45. *New-Hampshire Gazette,* 8 July 1817, p. 2, col. 1.

46. *Merrill* v. *Sherburne,* 1 *N.H.* 199, 202 (1818).

47. Ibid., p. 217.

48. *Supra,* p. 64.

49. *Merrill* v. *Sherburne,* 1 *N.H.* 199, 206–11 (1818); Hesse, "Legislature, Court and Constitution," p. 43; Murphy and Van Oot, "Judicial Independence," p. 12; McNamara, "Separation of Powers," pp. 71, 84.

50. Douglas, "Judicial Review," pp. 262–63; Carpenter, *Judicial Tenure,* pp. 159–60; Lawrie, "Interpretation and Authority," pp. 327, 310.

51. *Merrill* v. *Sherburne,* 1 *N.H.* 199, 210 (1818).

52. Lawrie, "Interpretation and Authority," p. 327.

53. Ibid., p. 326; [Plumer,] CINCINNATUS No. 92, *Portsmouth Journal,* 23 August 1823, p. 2, col. 2.

54. Lawrie, "Interpretation and Authority," p. 326.

Short Titles

Adams, *Administration of Jefferson*
> Henry Adams, *History of the United States of America During the First Administration of Thomas Jefferson*. Vols. 1 and 2. New York: Charles Scribner's Sons, 1903.

Adams, *First American Constitutions*
> Willi Paul Adams, *The First American Constitutions: Republican Ideology and the Making of the State Constitutions in the Revolutionary Era*. Chapel Hill: University of North Carolina Press, 1980.

Address of the Convention
> *An Address of the Convention for Framing a New Constitution of Government for the State of New-Hampshire, to the Inhabitants of said State*. Portsmouth and Exeter, N.H., 1781.

Alfange, "Marbury v. Madison"
> Dean Alfange, Jr., "Marbury v. Madison and Original Understanding of Judicial Review: In Defense of Traditional Wisdom," *Supreme Court Review* (1993): 329–446.

Almand, "Supreme Court of Georgia"
> Bond Almand, "The Supreme Court of Georgia: An Account of its Delayed Birth," in *A History of the Supreme Court of Georgia: A Centennial Volume*. Edited by John B. Harris. Macon, Georgia: J. W. Burke, 1948, pp. 1–18.

American Archives
> *American Archives. Fourth Series. Containing a Documentary History of the English Colonies in North America From the King's Message to Parliament, of March 7, 1774, to the Declaration of Independence by the United States*. Vols. 1 and 2. Washington, D.C., 1837.

American Patriot
> *The American Patriot*. Weekly newspaper published in Concord, N.H. (became the *New-Hampshire Patriot*).

Ames, "Dangers of American Liberty"
> Fisher Ames, "The Dangers of American Liberty," in *American Political Writing during the Founding Era 1760–1805*. Volume 2. Edited by Charles S. Hyneman and Donald S. Lutz. Indianapolis, Indiana: Liberty Press, 1983, pp. 1299–1348.

Anderson, *To This Day*
> Leon W. Anderson, *To This Day: The 300 Years of the New Hampshire Legislature*. Canaan, N.H.: Phoenix Publishing, 1981.

Anderson, *William Branch Giles*
> Dice Robins Anderson, *William Branch Giles: A Study in the Politics of Virginia and the Nation from 1790 to 1830*. Gloucester, Mass.: Peter Smith, 1965.

Annals of Congress
> *The Debates and Proceedings in the Congress of the United States*. 42 volumes. Washington, D.C.: Gales and Seaton, 1834–1856.

Anon., *Friend to Constitution*
  Anonymous, *A Friend to the Constitution.* n.p., 1801.
Anon., "Independence of the Judiciary"
  Anonymous, "The Independence of the Judiciary," *The United States Democratic Review* 23 (July 1848): 37–44.
Anon., "Mistakes of Westminster Review"
  Anonymous, "Mistakes of the Westminster Review on the Subject of American Jurisprudence," *American Jurist and Law Magazine* 8 (July and October 1832): 275–83.
Anon., *Observations Occasioned By*
  Anonymous, *Observations Occasioned by Writings against Alterations, Proposed in the Convention, to be Made in the Judiciary System.* Portsmouth, N.H.: George and John Osborne, 1792.
Anon., *Republican Address to New-Hampshire*
  Anonymous, *Republican Address to the Electors of New-Hampshire, on the Choice of Electors of President and Vice-President.* Walpole, N.H., 1804.
Anon., "Review of Collection of Cases"
  Anonymous [Theron Metcalf], Book Review, *North American Review* 15 (July 1822): 65–72 (reviewing Simon Greenleaf, *A Collection of Cases Overruled, or Limited in their Application. Taken from American and English Reports* (1821)).
Anon., *Strictures Upon the Observations*
  Anonymous, *Strictures Upon the Observations of a Member of Convention: In Answer to the "Author of Some Remarks, &c."* [Dover, N.H.], 1792.
Anti-Federalist
  The Anti-Federalist: An Abridgment, by Murray Day, of The Complete Anti-Federalist. Edited by Herbert J. Storing. Chicago: University of Chicago Press, 1981.
"Arena of the Giants"
  John Reid, "The Arena of the Giants: Rockingham County, New Hampshire," *American Bar Association Journal* 46 (January 1960): 163–66, 214–16.
Articles in Addition
  Articles in Addition to and Amendment of the Constitution of the State of New-Hampshire, Agreed to by the Convention of said State, and Submitted to the People thereof for their Approbation. Exeter, N.H.: Henry Ranlet, 1792.
Authority of Law
  John Phillip Reid, *Constitutional History of the American Revolution: The Authority of Law.* Madison: University of Wisconsin Press, 1993.
Authority to Legislate
  John Phillip Reid, *Constitutional History of the American Revolution: The Authority to Legislate.* Madison: University of Wisconsin Press, 1991.
Bader and Mersky, "Justice Woodbury"
  William D. Bader and Roy M. Mersky, "Justice Levi Woodbury: A Reputational Study," *Journal of Supreme Court History* 2 (1998): 129–42.
Bailyn. *Ideological Origins*
  Bernard Bailyn, *The Ideological Origins of the American Revolution.* Enlarged Edition. Cambridge, Mass.: Harvard University Press, 1992.
Bailyn, *Pamphlets*
  Pamphlets of the American Revolution, 1750–1776. Edited by Bernard Bailyn. Cambridge, Mass.: Harvard University Press, 1965.
Baldwin, *American Judiciary*
  Simeon E. Baldwin, *The American Judiciary.* New York: The Century Co., 1905.
Batchelder, "Independence of Judiciary"
  William F. Batchelder, "The Independence of the Judiciary in New Hampshire Revisited," *New Hampshire Bar Journal* 39 (June 1998): 62–70.

Batchellor, "Development of Courts"
    Albert Stillman Batchellor, "The Development of the Courts of New Hampshire," in *The New England States: Their Constitutional, Judicial, Educational, Commercial, Professional and Industrial History*. Edited by William T. Davis. Volume 4. Boston: D. H. Hurd & Co., 1897, pp. 2295–315.
Batchellor, "Tenure of Judges"
    Albert S. Batchellor, "President's Address: The Tenure of Office of the Judges of the Supreme Court of the State Under the Constitution," *Proceedings of the Bar Association of the State of New Hampshire*. Volume One—Old Series, Volume Six (1900–1903), pp. 523–56.
Bell, *Answer to Petition*
    Samuel Bell, *An Answer to the Petition of Eli Brown, Complaining of Misconduct, &c. &c. of the Directors and Agents of the Hillsborough Bank*. Amherst, N.H.: R. Boylston, [1811].
Bell, *Bench and Bar*
    Charles H. Bell, *The Bench and Bar of New Hampshire*. Boston: Houghton, Mifflin and Company, 1894.
[Bell,] *Life of Richardson*
    [Charles Henry Bell,] *The Life of William M. Richardson, LL.D., Late Chief Justice of the Superior Court in New Hampshire*. Concord, N.H.: 1839.
Bentham, *Codification Proposal*
    Jeremy Bentham, *Codification Proposal, Addressed by Jeremy Bentham to All Nations Professing Liberal Opinions; or Idea of a Proposed all-comprehensible Body of Law, with an Accompaniment of Reasons, Applying all along to the Several Proposed Arrangements*. London: J. M'Creery, 1822.
Bentham, *Papers*
    Jeremy Bentham, *Papers Relative to Codification and Public Instruction: Including Correspondence with the Russian Emperor, and Divers Constitutional Authorities in the American United States*. London: J. M'Creery, 1817.
Berger, "Chilling Independence"
    Raoul Berger, "Chilling Judicial Independence: A Scarecrow," *Cornell Law Review* 64 (1979): 822–54.
Beveridge, *Life of Marshall*
    Albert J. Beveridge, *The Life of John Marshall*. 4 volumes. Boston: Houghton Mifflin, 1916.
Bilder, "Origin of the Appeal"
    Mary Sarah Bilder, "The Origin of the Appeal in America," *Hastings Law Journal* 48 (July 1997): 913–68.
Black, "Massachusetts Judges"
    Barbara Aronstein Black, "Massachusetts and the Judges: Judicial Independence in Perspective," *Law and History Review* 3 (Spring 1985): 101–62.
Blair and Coblentz, "Trials of Chase"
    Richard R. Blair and Robin D. Coblentz, "The Trials of Mr. Justice Samuel Chase," *Maryland Law Review* 5 (1967): 365–86.
[Bowen,] "Independence of Judiciary"
    [F. Bowen,] "The Independence of the Judiciary," *North American Review* 57 (October 1843): 400–32.
Breyer, "Cherokees and Supreme Court"
    Stephen Breyer, "The Cherokee Indians and the Supreme Court," *Georgia Historical Quarterly* 87 (Fall & Winter 2003): 408–26.
Brown, "Impeachment of Federal Judiciary"
    Wrisley Brown, "The Impeachment of the Federal Judiciary," *Harvard Law Review* 26 (June 1913): 684–706.

Brunhouse, *Counter-Revolution in Pennsylvania*
    Robert L. Brunhouse, *The Counter-Revolution in Pennsylvania, 1776–1790*. Harrisburg, Pennsylvania: Pennsylvania Historical Commission, 1942.
Burbank, "Architecture of Independence"
    Stephen B. Burbank, "The Architecture of Judicial Independence," *Southern California Law Review* 72 (1999): 315–35.
Bushnell, *Crimes, Follies, and Misfortunes*
    Eleanore Bushnell, *Crimes, Follies, and Misfortunes: The Federal Impeachment Trials*. Urbana: University of Illinois Press, 1992.
Capowski, "Era of Good Feelings"
    Vincent J. Capowski, "The Era of Good Feelings in New Hampshire: The Gubernatorial Campaigns of Levi Woodbury, 1823, 1824," *Historical New Hampshire* 21 (Winter 1966): 3–30.
Capowski, *Making of Democrat*
    Vincent Julian Capowski, *The Making of a Jacksonian Democrat: Levi Woodbury, 1789–1831* (Ph.D. Dissertation, Fordham University, 1966).
Carpenter, *Judicial Tenure*
    William S. Carpenter, *Judicial Tenure in the United States With Especial Reference to the Tenure of Federal Judges*. New Haven, Connecticut: Yale University Press, 1918.
Carrington, "Judicial Independence"
    Paul D. Carrington, "Judicial Independence and Democratic Accountability in Highest State Courts," *Law and Contemporary Problems* 61 (Summer 1998): 79–126.
Chief Justice
    John Phillip Reid, *Chief Justice: The Judicial World of Charles Doe*. Cambridge, Mass.: Harvard University Press, 1967.
Chipman, *Sketches of Government*
    Nathaniel Chipman, *Sketches of the Principles of Government*. Rutland, Vt.; Press of J. Lyon, 1793.
Chroust, *Rise of Legal Profession*
    Anton Hermann Chroust, *The Rise of the Legal Profession in America*. 2 volumes. Norman: University of Oklahoma Press, 1965.
Chu, "Debt Litigation"
    Jonathan M. Chu, "Debt Litigation and Shays's Rebellion," in *In Debt to Shays: The Bicentennial of an Agrarian Rebellion*. Edited by Robert A. Gross. Charlottesville: University Press of Virginia, 1993, pp. 81–99.
Church, *Oration at Pelham*
    John Hubbard Church, *An Oration, Pronounced at Pelham, New-Hampshire, July 4th, 1805, the Anniversary of the Declaration of Independence*. Haverhill, Mass.: Francis Gould, 1805.
Claggett, *Speech in House*
    William Claggett, *Speech of William Claggett, Esq. in the House of Representatives of N. H. June Session, 1814*. Concord, N.H.: Isaac & W. R. Hill, 1814.
Clark, *Memoirs of Mason*
    G. J. Clark, *Memoirs of Jeremiah Mason: Reproduction of Privately printed Edition of 1873 Illustrated and Annotated, with Enlarged Index*. Boston: Boston Book Co., 1917.
Clement, *Discourse on Richardson*
    Jonathan Clement, *Discourse Delivered at the Funeral of Hon. William M. Richardson, on the 26th Day of March, A.D., 1838*. Concord, N.H., 1838.
Cleveland, "Establishment of Georgia Supreme Court"
    Len G. Cleveland, "The Establishment of the Georgia Supreme Court," *Georgia State Bar Journal* 9 (May 1973): 417–23.
Colby, "Holderness and Livermores"
    Fred Myron Colby, "Holderness and the Livermores," *The Granite Monthly: A New Hampshire Magazine* 4 (February 1881): 175–81.

Cole, *Jacksonian Democracy*
  Donald B. Cole, *Jacksonian Democracy in New Hampshire, 1800–1851.* Cambridge, Mass.: Harvard University Press, 1970.
Collections Historical
  Collections Historical and Miscellaneous; and Monthly Literary Journal. Volumes I and II. Concord, N.H.: J. B. Moore, 1824.
"Common Sense to Common Law"
  John Reid, "From Common Sense to Common Law to Charles Doe: The Evolution of Pleading in New Hampshire, *New Hampshire Bar Journal* 1 (No. 3) (April 1959): 27–43.
Communication from Governor
  Communication from his Excellency the Governor, Covering the Report of the Justices of the Superior Court, on the Question of Granting New Trials. n.i., [1819].
Concord Gazette
  Concord Gazette. A weekly newspaper published in Concord, N.H.
Concord Herald
  Concord Herald. A weekly newspaper published in Concord, N.H.
Constitutionalist
  The Constitutionalist and Weekly Magazine. A weekly newspaper published in Exeter, N.H.
Cook, "Politics and the Judiciary"
  Frank Gaylord Cook, "Politics and the Judiciary," *Atlantic Monthly* 83 (June 1899): 743–49.
Cooke, *Oration at Keene*
  Phinehas Cooke, *An Oration, Delivered at Keene, N. H. Before the Washington Benevolent Society, on the 5th Day of July, 1813, Being the Anniversary of American Independence.* Keene, N.H.: John Prentiss, 1813.
Controlling the Law
  John Phillip Reid, *Controlling the Law: Legal Politics in Early National New Hampshire.* DeKalb: Northern Illinois University Press, 2004.
Corwin, "Progress of Constitutional Theory"
  Edward S. Corwin, "The Progress of Constitutional Theory Between the Declaration of Independence and the Meeting of the Philadelphia Convention," *American Historical Review* 30 (April 1925): 511–36.
Corwin, "Progress of Theory"
  Edward S. Corwin, "The Progress of Constitutional Theory Between the Declaration of Independence and the Meeting of the Philadelphia Convention," in *Corwin on the Constitution: The Foundations of American Constitutional and Political Thought, the Powers of Congress, and the President's Power of Removal.* Edited by Richard Loss. Ithaca, N.Y.: Cornell University Press, 1981, pp. 56–78.
Coulter, *Georgia*
  E. Merton Coulter, *Georgia: A Short History.* Chapel Hill: University of North Carolina Press, 1947.
Courier of New Hampshire
  Courier of New Hampshire. A weekly newspaper published at Concord, N.H.
Crosskey, *Politics and the Constitution*
  William Winslow Crosskey, *Politics and the Constitution in the History of the United States.* Volume 2. Chicago: University of Chicago Press, 1953.
Cullen, *St. George Tucker*
  Charles T. Cullen, *St. George Tucker and Law in Virginia 1772–1804.* New York: Garland Publishing, 1987.
Currie, *Constitution in Federalist Congress*
  David P. Currie, *The Constitution in Congress: The Federalist Period 1789–1801.* Chicago: University of Chicago Press, 1997.

Currie, *Constitution in Jeffersonian Congress*
David P. Currie, *The Constitution in Congress: The Jeffersonians 1801–1829*. Chicago: University of Chicago Press, 2001.

Currie, "Separating Judicial Power"
David P. Currie, "Separating Judicial Power," *Law and Contemporary Problems* 61 (Summer 1998): 7–14.

Davis, *History of Judiciary*
William T. Davis, *History of the Judiciary of Massachusetts*. Boston: Boston Book Company, 1900.

Declaration of Rights and Plan of Government
A Declaration of Rights and Plan of Government for the State of New Hampshire, 5 June 1779. (Huntington Library Rare Book # 276776).

Democratic Republican
Democratic Republican. A weekly newspaper published in Walpole, N.H.

Desan, "Contesting Political Economy"
Christine A. Desan, "Contesting the Character of the Political Economy in the Early Republic: Rights and Remedies in Chisholm v. Georgia," in *The House and Senate in the 1790s: Petitioning, Lobbying, and Institutional Development*. Edited by Kenneth R. Bowling and Donald R. Kennon. Athens: Ohio University Press, 2002, pp. 178–232.

Desan, "Legislative Adjudication"
Christine A. Desan, "The Constitutional Commitment to Legislative Adjudication in the Early American Tradition," *Harvard Law Review* 111 (April 1998): 1381–1503.

Desan, "Remaking Constitutional Tradition"
Christine A. Desan, "Remaking Constitutional Tradition at the Margin of the Empire: The Creation of Legislative Adjudication in Colonial New York," *Law and History Review* 16 (Summer 1998): 257–317.

Documentary History of the Supreme Court
The Documentary History of the Supreme Court of the United States, 1789–1800. Volume Six. Cases: 1790–1795. Edited by Maeva Marcus. New York: Columbia University Press, 1998.

Dodd, "Constitutional History of New Hampshire"
W. F. Dodd, "The Constitutional History of New Hampshire, 1772–92," *Proceedings of the Bar Association of the State of New Hampshire*. Volume Two (Volume Seven, Old Series). Concord, N.H., 1904–1909, pp. 379–400.

Dodd, "Gilman v. McClary"
Walter F. Dodd, "Gilman v. McClary: A New Hampshire Case of 1791." *American Historical Review* 112 (1907): 348–50

Douglas, "Judicial Review"
Charles G. Douglas III, "Judicial Review and the Separation of Powers Under the New Hampshire Constitutions of 1776 and 1784," *New Hampshire Bar Journal* 18 (1977): 250–64.

Durfee, "Judicial History of Rhode Island"
Thomas Durfee, "Judicial History of Rhode Island," in *The New England States: Their Constitutional, Judicial, Educational, Commercial, Professional and Industrial History*. Edited by William T. Davis. Volume 4. Boston: D. H. Hurd & Co., 1897, pp. 2362–97.

Eastman, *Courts and Lawyers of Pennsylvania*
Frank Marshall Eastman, *Courts and Lawyers of Pennsylvania: A History, 1623–1923*. New York: American Historical Society, 1922.

Egan, "Path to War"
Clifford L. Egan, "The Path to War in 1812 through the Eyes of a New Hampshire 'War Hawk'," *Historical New Hampshire* 30 (Fall 1975): 147–77.

Eighth Plumer Letterbook
"Letters to & from William Plumer Volume 8th. Beginning November 11. 1809, and Ending August 1. 1815." *Plumer Documents* (Library of Congress, Reel 3, Container 8).

Ellis, *Jeffersonian Crisis*
Richard E. Ellis, *The Jeffersonian Crisis: Courts and Politics in the Young Republic*. New York: Oxford University Press, 1971.

Essential Federalist
The Essential Federalist and Anti-Federalist Papers. Edited by David Wootton. Indianapolis: Hackett Publishing Company, 2003.

Evans, *Appeal to People*
Estwick Evans, *An Appeal to the People of New-Hampshire*. Exeter, N.H.: Henry A. Ranlet, 1817.

Farmer's Cabinet
The Farmer's Cabinet. A weekly newspaper published at Amherst, N.H.

Farmer's Museum
Farmer's Museum, or Literary Gazette. A weekly newspaper published in Walpole, N.H.

Federalist
The Federalist: A Commentary on the Constitution of the United States. Being a Collection of Essays written in Support of the Constitution agreed upon September 17, 1787 by the Federal Convention. Edited by Edward Mead Earle. New York: The Modern Library, [1937].

First Plumer Letterbook
"A Collection of Letters written to and by William Plumer, and transcribed for his Amusement & Instruction. Many to Jere[miah] Smith, MC. Volume I. From January 18, 1781 to January 14, 1804. Contains 177 Letters." *Plumer Documents* (Library of Congress, Reel 2, Container 4).

Founders' Constitution
The Founders' Constitution. Volume Five: Amendments I-XII. Edited by Philip B. Kurland and Ralph Lerner. Chicago: University of Chicago Press, 1987.

Fourth Plumer Letterbook
"Letters to & from William Plumer from January 25, 1804 to February 6th 1807. Volume 4th." *Plumer Documents* (Library of Congress, Reel 3, Container 7).

Friedman, "History of Countermajoritarian"
Barry Friedman, "The History of Countermajoritarian Difficulty, Part One: The Road to Judicial Supremacy," *New York University Law Review* 73 (May 1998): 333–433.

Frost, *Oration at Durham*
John Frost, *An Oration Delivered at the Request of the Citizens of Durham, New Hampshire. On the Fourth of July, 1805*. Portsmouth, N.H.: Pierce & Gardner, 1805.

Frothingham, "Removal of Judges by Address"
Louis A. Frothingham, "The Removal of Judges by Legislative Address in Massachusetts," *American Political Science Review* 8 (May 1914): 216–21.

Gannon, "Escaping Jefferson's Plan"
Kevin M. Gannon, "Escaping 'Mr. Jefferson's Plan of Destruction': New England Federalists and the Idea of a Northern Confederacy, 1803–1804," *Journal of the Early Republic* 21 (Fall 2001): 413–43.

Gates, *Oration at Bedford*
Isaac Gates, *An Oration Pronounced Publicly at Bedford, New-Hampshire. Before the Washington Benevolent Society in that Place, July 4th, 1814*. Concord, N.H.: George Hough, 1814.

Gay, *Accomplished Judge*
Bunker Gay, *The Accomplished Judge; or, A Compleat Dress for Magistrates. A Sermon Preached at Keene, at the first Opening of the Inferior Court, in the County of Cheshire. October 8. 1771*. Portsmouth, N.H.: D. Fowle, 1773.

General Regulations for Bar
    General Regulations for the Gentlemen of the Bar in the State of New Hampshire.
    Portsmouth, N.H.: J. Melcher, 1805.
Geyh and Van Tassel, "Independence of Judicial"
    Charles Gardner Geyh and Emily Field Van Tassel, "The Independence of the Judi-
    cial Branch in the New Republic," *Chicago-Kent Law Review* 74 (1998): 31–89.
Graber, "Federalist or Friends"
    Mark A. Graber, "Federalist or Friends of Adams: The Marshall Court and Party Pol-
    itics," *Studies in American Political Development* 12 (Fall 1998): 229–66.
Grafton Journal
    Grafton Journal. A weekly newspaper published in Plymouth, N.H.
Graves, "Our Early Courts"
    Collins M. Graves, "Our Early Courts," *Report of Proceedings of the Vermont Bar Asso-
    ciation* 29 (1935): 15–22.
[Gray,] *Power to Abolish Courts*
    [Horace Gray,] *The Power of the Legislature to Create and Abolish Courts of Justice.*
    Boston: Geo. C. Rand & Avery, 1858.
Grinnell, "Brief History of Court"
    Frank W. Grinnell, "A Brief History of the Supreme Judicial Court of Massachu-
    setts," *Massachusetts Law Quarterly* 16 (1930): 1–16.
Grinnell, "Constitutional History of Court"
    Frank W. Grinnell, "Constitutional History of the Supreme Judicial Court from the
    Revolution to 1813," *Massachusetts Law Quarterly* 2 (May 1917): 359–552.
Gubernatorial Papers
    Original Manuscript Acts Signed by William Plumer: Partial Representation of
    Original Acts found at New Hampshire State Archives. *Plumer Documents* (Reel 21,
    Frames 1–305).
Haines, *Judicial Supremacy*
    Charles Grove Haines, *The American Doctrine of Judicial Supremacy.* Second edition.
    Berkeley: University of California Press, 1932 (Publications of the University of
    California at Los Angeles in Social Sciences, Volume 1).
Hamburger, "Law and Judicial Duty"
    Philip Hamburger, "Law and Judicial Duty," *George Washington Law Review* 72
    (2003): 1–41.
Hammond, "Great and General Court"
    John C. Hammond, "The Great and General Court of Massachusetts Bay Colony,"
    *Fourth Annual Report of the Massachusetts Bar Association Containing the Charter and
    By-Laws, A List of Officers and Members and the Proceedings of the Fourth Annual Meet-
    ing.* Boston: The Rockwell & Churchill Press, 1914, pp. 42–63.
Harlow, *History of Legislative Methods*
    Ralph Volney Harlow, *The History of Legislative Methods in the Period Before 1825.*
    New Haven, Conn.: Yale University Press, 1917.
Haskins, "Law Versus Politics"
    George L. Haskins, "Law Versus Politics in the Early Years of the Marshall Court,"
    University of Pennsylvania Law Review 130 (November 1981): 1–27.
Henderson, "Attack on Judiciary"
    Elizabeth K. Henderson, "The Attack on the Judiciary in Pennsylvania, 1800–1810,"
    Pennsylvania Magazine of History and Biography 61 (April 1937): 113–36.
Hesse, "Legislature, Court and Constitution"
    Richard Hesse, "The Legislature, the Court and the Constitution," *New Hampshire
    Bar Journal* 41 (March 2000): 38–45.
Hicks, *Joseph Henry Lumpkin*
    Paul DeForest Hicks, *Joseph Henry Lumpkin: Georgia's First Chief Justice.* Athens: Uni-
    versity of Georgia Press, 2002.

[Higgins,] *Sampson Against*
>[Jesse Higgins,] *Sampson Against the Philistines, or the Reformation of Lawsuits; and Justice made Cheap, Speedy, and Brought Home to Every Man's Door: Agreeably to the Principles of the Ancient Trial by Jury, Before the same was Innovated by Judges and Lawyers. Compiled for the Use of the Honest Citizens of the United States.* 2d edition. Philadelphia: B. Graves, 1805.

Historical Society Correspondence
>Correspondence of William Plumer, New Hampshire Historical Society, *Plumer Documents* (Reel 8).

Hoffer and Hull, *Impeachment*
>Peter Charles Hoffer and N. E. H. Hull, *Impeachment in America, 1635–1805.* New Haven, Conn.: Yale University Press, 1984.

Holmes, "Address"
>Nathaniel Holmes, "An Address Delivered at the 150th Anniversary of the town of Peterborough, N. H., October 24, 1889," in *Proceedings of the Sesqui-Centennial Celebration Held at Peterborough, N.H. Thursday, Oct. 24, 1889.* "Peterboro," N.H.: Peterboro' Transcript Office, 1890, pp. 16–56.

[Hopkinson,] *Considerations on Common Law*
>[Joseph Hopkinson,] *Considerations on the Abolition of the Common Law in the United States.* Philadelphia: W.P. Farrand, 1809.

House Journal (December 1789)
>*Journal of the House of Representatives Containing the Proceedings from December 23, 1789, to January 26, 1790,* reprinted in *Early State Papers of New Hampshire Including the Journals of the Senate and House of Representatives and Records of the President and Council, from June, 1787, to June, 1790.* Volume 21. Edited by Albert Stillman Batchellor. Concord, N.H.: Ira Evans, 1892, pp. 667–737.

House Journal (June 1790)
>*Journal of the House of Representatives Containing the Proceedings from June 2 to June 19, 1790,* reprinted in *Early State Papers of New Hampshire Including the Journals of the Senate and House of Representatives and Records of the President and Council, from June, 1790, to June, 1793.* Volume 22. Edited by Albert Stillman Batchellor. Concord, N.H.: Ira C. Evans Public Printer, 1893, pp. 33–93.

House Journal (January 1791)
>*Journal of the House of Representatives Containing the Proceedings from January 5 to February 18, 1791,* reprinted in *Early State Papers of New Hampshire Including the Journals of the Senate and House of Representatives and Records of the President and Council, from June, 1790, to June, 1793.* Volume 22. Edited by Albert Stillman Batchellor. Concord, N.H.: Ira C. Evans Public Printer, 1893, pp. 139–244.

House Journal (November 1791)
>*Journal of the House of Representatives Containing the Proceedings from November 30, 1791, to January 6, 1792,* reprinted in *Early State Papers of New Hampshire Including the Journals of the Senate and House of Representatives and Records of the President and Council, from June 1790, to June 1793.* Volume 22. Edited by Albert Stillman Batchellor. Concord, N.H.: Ira C. Evans Public Printer, 1893, pp. 401–83.

House Journal (June 1792)
>*Journal of the House of Representatives Containing the Proceedings from June 6 to June 22, 1792,* reprinted in *Early State Papers of New Hampshire Including the Journals of the Senate and House of Representatives and Records of the President and Council, from June 1790, to June 1793.* Volume 22. Edited by Albert Stillman Batchellor. Concord, N.H.: Ira C. Evans Public Printer, 1893, pp. 541–99.

House Journal (November 1792)
>*Journal of the House of Representatives Containing the Proceedings from November 21 to December 28, 1792,* reprinted in *Early State Papers of New Hampshire Including the Journals of the Senate and House of Representatives and Records of the President and*

Council, from June, 1790, to June, 1793. Volume 22. Edited by Albert Stillman Batchellor. Concord, N.H.: Ira C. Evans Public Printer, 1893, pp. 635–714.

House Journal (June 1793)

A Journal of the Proceedings of the Hon. House of Representatives of the State of New-Hampshire, at their Session, Begun and Holden at Concord, on the first Wednesday of June, Anno Domini 1793. Portsmouth, N.H.: John Melcher, Printer to the Hon. General-Court, 1793.

House Journal (December 1793)

A Journal of the Proceedings of the Hon. House of Representatives of the State of New-Hampshire, At their Session, Begun and Holden at Exeter, on Wednesday, the Twenty-Fifth Day of December, Anno Domini 1793. Portsmouth, N.H.: John Melcher, 1794.

House Journal (June 1794)

A Journal of the Proceedings of the Hon. House of Representatives of the State of New-Hampshire, at their Session, Begun and Holden at Amherst, the 4th Day of June, 1794. Portsmouth, N.H.: John Melcher, 1794.

House Journal (December 1794)

A Journal of the Proceedings of the Honorable House of Representatives for said State at their Session Begun and Holden at Concord, the 16th of December, 1794. (No title page.)

House Journal (November 1796)

A Journal of the Proceedings of the Hon. House of Representatives, of the State of New-Hampshire, at their Session, Begun and Holden at Concord, the 23d November, 1796. Portsmouth, N.H.: John Melcher, 1797.

House Journal (June 1797)

A Journal of the Proceedings of the Hon. House of Representatives, of the State of New-Hampshire, at their Session, Begun and Holden at Portsmouth, June, 1797. Portsmouth, N.H.: John Melcher, 1798.

House Journal (November 1797)

A Journal of the Proceedings of the Hon. House of Representatives of the State of New-Hampshire, at their Session Begun and Holden at Portsmouth, November, 1797. Portsmouth, N.H.: John Melcher, 1798.

House Journal (June 1799)

A Journal of the Proceedings of the Hon. House of Representatives of the State of New-Hampshire, at their Session Begun and Holden at Concord, June, 1790. Portsmouth, N.H.: John Melcher, 1799.

House Journal (June 1810)

Journal of the House of Representatives of the State of New-Hampshire, at their Session Begun and Holden at Concord, on the First Wednesday of November, 1810. Concord, N.H.: Isaac Hill, 1810.

House Journal (June 1812)

Journal of the House of Representatives of the State of New Hampshire, at their Session Begun and Holden at Concord, on the First Wednesday of June, Anno Domini, 1812. Concord, N.H.: I. and W. R. Hill, 1812.

House Journal (November 1812)

Journal of the House of Representatives of the State of New-Hampshire, at their Session, Begun and Holden at Concord, on the third Wednesday of November, 1812. Concord, N.H., 1813.

House Journal (October 1813)

Journal of the Proceedings of the House of Representatives of the State of New-Hampshire, at their Special Session, Begun and Holden at Concord, on Wednesday, October 27, 1813. Concord, N.H., 1813.

House Journal (June 1817)

Journal of the House of Representatives, of the State of New-Hampshire, at their Session, Begun and Holden at Concord, on the first Wednesday of June, 1817. Concord, N.H., 1817.

House Journal (June 1818)
　　Journal of the House of Representatives, of the State of New-Hampshire, at their Session Begun and Holden at Concord, on the First Wednesday of June, Anno Domini, 1818. Concord, N.H.: Isaac Hill, 1818.

Huebner, *Southern Judicial Tradition*
　　Timothy S. Huebner, *The Southern Judicial Tradition: State Judges and Sectional Distinctiveness, 1790–1890.* Athens: University of Georgia Press, 1999.

Impeachment of Langdon
　　Journal of the Senate on the Impeachment of Woodbury Langdon: Special Sessions, printed in *Early State Papers of New Hampshire Including the Journals of the Senate and House of Representatives and Records of the President and Council, from June, 1790, to June, 1793.* Volume 22. Edited by Albert Stillman Batchellor. Concord, N.H.: Ira C. Evans Public Printer, 1893, pp. 747–56.

Jameson, *Constitutional Convention*
　　John Alexander Jameson, *The Constitutional Convention: Its History, Powers, and Modes of Proceedings.* New York: Charles Scribner and Company, 1867.

Jefferson, *Memoir*
　　Memoir, Correspondence, and Miscellanies, from the Papers of Thomas Jefferson. 4 volumes. Edited by Thomas Jefferson Randolph. Charlottesville, Virginia: F. Carr and Co., 1829.

Jeffersonian Principles
　　Jeffersonian Principles and Hamiltonian Principles: Extracts from the Writings of Thomas Jefferson and Alexander Hamilton. Edited by James Truslow Adams. One-volume edition. Boston: Little, Brown, and Company, 1932.

Jeffries and Hazelton, *New Hampshire Conventions*
　　Ruth Jeffries and Philip A. Hazelton, *New Hampshire Constitutional Conventions.* Concord, N.H.: State Library Legislative Service, 1956.

Johnson, "Dartmouth College Case"
　　Eldon L. Johnson, "The Dartmouth College Case: The Neglected Educational Meaning," *Journal of the Early Republic* 3 (Spring 1983): 45–67.

Journal of Convention
　　Journal of the Convention which Assembled in Concord, to Revise the Constitution of New Hampshire 1791–1792. Edited by Nathaniel Bouton. Concord, N.H.: Edward A. Jenks, State Printer, 1876.

Judicial Independence at Crossroads
　　Judicial Independence at the Crossroads: An Interdisciplinary Approach. Edited by Stephen B. Burbank and Barry Friedman. Thousand Oaks, California: Sage Publications, 2002.

Kaminski, "Democracy Run Rampant"
　　John P. Kaminski, "Democracy Run Rampant: Rhode Island in the Confederation," in *The Human Dimensions of Nation Making: Essays on Colonial and Revolutionary America.* Edited by James Kirby Martin. Madison: State Historical Society of Wisconsin, 1976, pp. 243–69.

Kaufman, "Judicial Independence"
　　Irving R. Kaufman, "The Essence of Judicial Independence," *Columbia Law Review* 80 (May 1980): 672–701.

Kent, *Commentaries*
　　James Kent, *Commentaries of American Law.* Volume 1. 6th edition. New York: William Kent, 1848.

Lamar, "History of Establishment of Court"
　　Joseph R. Lamar, "History of the Establishment of the Supreme Court of Georgia," *Report of the Twenty-Fourth Annual Session of the Georgia Bar Association Held at Tybee Island, GA. on May 30 and 31, 1907.* Atlanta: Franklin-Turner Company, 1907, pp. 85–103.

Lambert, *Ten Pound Act*
 Richard M. Lambert, *The "Ten Pound Act" in Cases and the Origins of Judicial Review in New Hampshire* (Master's Thesis, University of New Hampshire, 1985).
Lambert, "Ten Pound Cases"
 Richard M. Lambert, "The 'Ten Pound Act' Cases and the Origins of Judicial Review in New Hampshire," *New Hampshire Bar Journal* 43 (March 2002): 37–54.
Lawrie, "Interpretation and Authority"
 Timothy A. Lawrie, "Interpretation and Authority: Separation of Powers and the Judiciary's Battle for Independence in New Hampshire, 1786–1818," *American Journal of Legal History* 39 (1995): 310–36.
Laws of New Hampshire
 Laws of New Hampshire, including the Public and Private Acts, Resolves, Votes, Etc. Volume Six Second Constitutional Period 1792–1801. Concord, N.H.: Evans Printing Co., 1917.
Legislative Papers
 Legislative Papers of William Plumer: Partial Representation of Legislative Papers found at New Hampshire. *Plumer Documents* (Reel 21, Frames 308 to 366).
Leidtker, *Political Development*
 Frank L. Leidtker, *Political Development in New Hampshire from the Revolution to 1850* (Master's Thesis, University of New Hampshire, 1952).
Letters of Sullivan
 Letters and Papers of Major General John Sullivan Continental Army. Edited by Otis G. Hammond. Volume 1. Concord, N.H.: New Hampshire Historical Society, 1930.
Lettieri and Wetherell, "Committee of Safety"
 Ronald Lettieri and Charles Wetherell, "The New Hampshire Committees of Safety and Revolutionary Republicanism, 1775–1784," *Historical New Hampshire* 35 (Fall 1980): 241–83.
Lieber, *Manual of Political Ethics*
 Francis Lieber, *Manual of Political Ethics, Designed Chiefly for the Use of Colleges and Students at Law*. Edited by Theodore D. Woolsey. Volume 1. Second Edition, Revised. Philadelphia: J. B. Lippincott & Co., 1881.
Loyd, "Courts from Revolution to Revision"
 William H. Loyd, Jr., "The Courts from the Revolution to the Revision of the Civil Code," *University of Pennsylvania Law Review* 56 (January 1908): 88–115.
Loyd, *Early Courts of Pennsylvania*
 William H. Loyd, *The Early Courts of Pennsylvania*. Boston: Boston Book Company, 1910.
Madison Letters
 Letters and Other Writings of James Madison Fourth President of the United States. Vol. I:, 1769–1793. New York: R. Worthington, 1884.
McNamara, "Separation of Powers"
 Richard B. McNamara, "The Separation of Powers Principle and the Role of the Courts in New Hampshire," *New Hampshire Bar Journal* 42 (June 2001): 66–87.
Marcus, "Judicial Review"
 Maeva Marcus, "Judicial Review in the Early Republic," in *Launching the "Extended Republic": The Federalist Era*. Edited by Ronald Hoffman and Peter J. Albert. Charlottesville: University Press of Virginia, 1996, pp. 25–53.
Mayo, *John Langdon*
 Laurence Shaw Mayo, *John Langdon of New Hampshire*. Port Washington, N.Y.: Keinnikat Press, 1970.
Mays, *Edmund Pendleton*
 David John Mays, *Edmund Pendleton 1721–1803: A Biography*. Volume 2. Cambridge, Mass.: Harvard University Press, 1952.

Memoirs of Adams
    Memoirs of John Quincy Adams, Comprising Portions of his Diary from 1795 to 1848. Edited by Charles Francis Adams, 12 volumes. Philadelphia: J. B. Lippincott & Co., 1874–1877.

Miller, *Juries and Judges*
    F. Thornton Miller, *Juries and Judges Versus the Law: Virginia Provincial Legal Perspective, 1783–1828.* Charlottesville: University Press of Virginia, 1994.

Miller, *Life of the Mind*
    Perry Miller, *The Life of the Mind in America: From the Revolution to the Civil War.* New York: Harcourt, Brace & World, 1965.

Montesquieu, *Spirit of Laws*
    Charles de Secondat, Baron de Montesquieu, *The Spirit of Laws.* Translated by Thomas Nugent. 2 volumes. Cincinnati, Ohio: Robert Clark & Company, 1873.

Moore, *Fast Day Discourse at Milford*
    Humphrey Moore, *A Discourse Delivered at Milford, August 20th, 1812, the Day Recommended by the President, for National Humiliation.* Amherst, N.H.: Richard Boylston, 1812.

Moore, *Oration at Bedford*
    Humphrey Moore, *Oration Delivered at Bedford, New-Hampshire, February 22, 1815, at the Request of the Washington Benevolent Society.* Concord, N.H.: George Hough, 1815.

Morison, *Life and Letters of Otis*
    Samuel Eliot Morison, *The Life and Letters of Harrison Gray Otis, Federalist, 1765–1848.* 2 volumes. Boston: Houghton Mifflin Company, 1913.

Morison, *Life of Smith*
    John H. Morison, *Life of the Hon. Jeremiah Smith, LL.D.* Boston: Charles C. Little and James Brown, 1845.

Murphy and Van Oot, "Judicial Independence"
    Walter L. Murphy and Mary Van Oot, "Please be Careful with the Constitution: A Call for the Preservation of Judicial Independence," *New Hampshire Bar Journal* 42 (June 2001): 11–15.

Nelson, *Americanization*
    William E. Nelson, *The Americanization of the Common Law: The Impact of Legal Change on Massachusetts Society, 1760–1830.* Cambridge, Mass.: Harvard University Press, 1975.

Nelson, "Cases of the Judges"
    Margaret V. Nelson, "The Cases of the Judges," *Virginia Law Review* 31 (December 1944): 243–55.

Nelson, "Eighteenth-Century Background"
    William E. Nelson, "The Eighteenth-Century Background of John Marshall's Constitutional Jurisprudence," *Michigan Law Review* 76 (1978): 893–960.

Nelson, *Marbury v. Madison*
    William E. Nelson, *Marbury v. Madison: The Origins and Legacy of Judicial Review.* Lawrence: University Press of Kansas, 2000.

New Hampshire Constitution
    The New Hampshire Constitution 1784–1984: 200 Years of Constitutional Government. n.i., 1985.

New-Hampshire Gazette
    New-Hampshire Gazette. A newspaper published weekly at Portsmouth, N.H.

New-Hampshire Patriot
    New-Hampshire Patriot. A weekly newspaper published in Concord, N.H.

New Hampshire the State
    New Hampshire the State that Made Us a Nation: A Celebration of the Bicentennial of the United States Constitution. Edited by William M. Gardner, Frank C. Mevers, Richard F. Upton. Portsmouth, N.H.: Peter E. Randall, Publisher, 1989.

Newhampshire Sentinel
> *Newhampshire Sentinel.* A weekly newspaper published in Keene, N.H.

Newmyer, *John Marshall*
> R. Kent Newmyer, *John Marshall and the Heroic Age of the Supreme Court.* Baton Rouge: Louisiana State University Press, 2001.

Nichols, *History of Nonjudicial Functions*
> Maurice S. Nichols, *A History of the Nonjudicial Functions of New Hampshire Courts* (Master's Thesis, University of New Hampshire, 1948).

Ninth Plumer Letterbook
> Letters to & from William Plumer, commencing July 22, 1817 and ending August 5, 1833. Volume 9. *Plumer Documents* (Library of Congress, Reel 4, Container 9).

Note, "Judicial Disability"
> Note, "Judicial Disability and the Good Behavior Clause," *Yale Law Journal* 85 (1976): 706–20.

"Notice of Oliver Peabody"
> "Notice of the Life and Character of the late Hon. Oliver Peabody, of Exeter," *Collections of the New-Hampshire Historical Society* 3 (1832): 297–304.

O'Fallon, "Case of Benjamin More"
> James M. O'Fallon, "The Case of Benjamin More: A Lost Episode in the Struggle over Repeal of the 1801 Judiciary Act," *Law and History Review* 11 (Spring 1993): 43–57.

O'Fallon, "Marbury"
> James M. O'Fallon, "Marbury," *Stanford Law Review* 44 (January 1992): 219–60.

Opal, "Politics of Industry"
> J. M. Opal, "The Politics of 'Industry': Federalism in Concord and Exeter, New Hampshire, 1790–1805," *Journal of the Early Republic* 20 (Winter 2000): 637–71.

Opinions of Clagett and Evans
> *Opinions of the Hon. Clifton Clagett, and Hon. Richard Evans, Justices of the Superior Court of Judicature, on the Act of the Legislature of New-Hampshire, Passed June 24, A.D. 1813, Entitled "An Act establishing a Supreme Judicial Court, and Circuit Courts of Common Pleas".* n.i., n.d.

Osborne's Spy
> *Osborne's New-Hampshire Spy.* A twice-weekly newspaper published in Portsmouth, N.H.

Page, "Judicial Practice"
> Elwin L. Page, "Judicial Practice, Eighteenth Century," *New Hampshire Bar Journal* 4 (July 1962): 194–201.

Page, *Rider for Freedom*
> Elwin L. Page, *Rider for Freedom: Josiah Bartlett 1729–1795.* Typescript, New Hampshire Historical Society (Elwin L. Page Papers, Series I: Manuscripts, Box 1).

Papers of James Madison
> *The Papers of James Madison. Volume 15. 24 March 1793–20 April 1795.* Edited by Thomas A. Mason, Robert A. Rutland, and Jeanne K. Sisson. Charlottesville: University Press of Virginia, 1985.

Papers of Josiah Bartlett
> *The Papers of Josiah Bartlett.* Edited by Frank C. Mevers. Hanover, N.H.: University Press of New England, 1999.

Papers of Marshall
> *The Papers of John Marshall: Volume VI, Correspondence, Papers, and Selected Judicial Opinions November 1800–March 1807.* Edited by Charles F. Hobson. Chapel Hill: University of North Carolina Press, 1990.

Parker, *Charge to Grand Jury*
> Joel Parker, *A Charge to the Grand Jury, upon the Importance of Maintaining the Supremacy of the Laws; with a Brief Sketch of the Character of William M. Richardson, Late Chief Justice of the Superior Court of New-Hampshire.* Concord, N.H.: Marsh, Capen & Lyon, 1838.

Parker, *Courts and Lawyers*
Herbert Parker, *Courts and Lawyers of New England*. 4 volumes. New York: American Historical Society, 1934.

Parker, "Heroic Age of the New Hampshire Bar"
Herbert Parker, "An Heroic Age in the History of the New Hampshire Bar," *Proceedings of the Bar Association of the State of New Hampshire 1930–1931*. "N.S., Vol. 6, No. 3." Concord, N.H.: Bridge & Bryon, 1932, pp. 17–48.

Parker, "Inaugural Address"
"Inaugural Address delivered in the Chapel of Harvard University, by the Hon. Isaac Parker, Chief Justice of Massachusetts, and Royall Professor of Law," *The North-American Review and Miscellaneous Journal* 3 (May 1816): 11–27.

Pasley, *Tyranny of Printers*
Jeffrey L. Pasley, *"The Tyranny of Printers": Newspaper Politics in the Early Republic*. Charlottesville: University of Virginia Press, 2001.

Peeling, "Governor McKean"
James Hedley Peeling, "Governor McKean and the Pennsylvania Jacobins (1799–1801)," *Pennsylvania Magazine of History and Biography* 54 (October 1930): 320–54.

People's Advocate
The People's Advocate. A weekly newspaper, published at Portsmouth, N.H.

Peters, *Massachusetts Constitution*
Ronald M. Peters, Jr., *The Massachusetts Constitution of 1780: A Social Compact*. Amherst: University of Massachusetts Press, 1978.

[Plumer,] *Address to Electors*
[William Plumer,] *An Address to the Electors of New-Hampshire*. no imprint, 1804.

Plumer, *Autobiography*
William Plumer, Memoirs of William Plumer With some Account of the Men, Measures, & Events of the Times in which he Lived. *Plumer Documents* (Library of Congress, Reel 4, Container 12).

Plumer, Biographical Notes VII
Notes for Wm Plumer's Biography. Volume 7, *Plumer Documents* (Reel 10, Frames 190 to 324).

Plumer, "Biographical Sketches, vol. 21"
William Plumer, "Biographical Sketches of Several Persons Participating in the Government of New Hampshire in the Period from 1784 to 1793, Copied from the Manuscript of William Plumer," in *Early State Papers of New Hampshire*. Volume 21. Edited by Albert Stillman Batchellor. Concord, N.H.: Ira C. Evans Public Printer, 1892, pp. 781–830.

Plumer, "Biographical Sketches, vol. 22"
William Plumer, "Biographical Sketches of Several Persons Participating in the Government of New Hampshire in the Period from 1784 to 1793, Copied from the Manuscript of William Plumer," in *Early State Papers of New Hampshire*. Volume 22. Edited by Albert Stillman Batchellor. Concord, N.H.: Ira C. Evans Public Printer, 1893, pp. 821–64.

Plumer, *Biography Papers*
Manuscripts in the William Plumer *Documents*, New Hampshire State Library, Concord.

Plumer, "Caleb Ellis"
William Plumer, "Caleb Ellis," *Plumer Documents* (Reel 12, Volume 5, Frame 143).

Plumer, "Clifton Clagett"
William Plumer, "Clifton Clagett," *Plumer Documents* (Reel 12, Volume 5, Frames 313–14, pp. 459–61).

Plumer, "Constitution of New Hampshire"
William Plumer, [Jr.], "The Constitution of New Hampshire: A Discourse Delivered Before the New Hampshire Historical Society, June 16, 1853," *The Historical Magazine* 4 (new series) (October 1868): 172–85.

Plumer Documents
> Microfilm copies of the papers of William Plumer at the New Hampshire State Library and the Library of Congress. The first three reels contain letters in chronological order, and when cited those letters are not identified by reel.

Plumer, "John Langdon"
> William Plumer, "John Langdon," *Plumer Papers* (Reel 12, Volume 5, Frames 178–81, pp. 194–200).

Plumer, "John Pickering"
> William Plumer, "John Pickering," printed in *Early State Papers of New Hampshire.* Volume 22. Edited by Albert Stillman Batchellor. Concord, N.H.: Ira C. Evans Public Printer, 1893, pp. 839–43.

Plumer, "John Samuel Sherburne"
> William Plumer, "John Samuel Sherburne," *Plumer Documents* (Reel 12, Volume 5, pp. 490–94).

Plumer, "Jonathan Steele"
> William Plumer, "Jonathan Steele," *Plumer Documents* (Reel 12, Volume 5, Frames 244 to 247).

Plumer Letters to His Brother
> Untitled Letterbook, Containing Letters from 7 December 1802 to 11 February 1807, from William Plumer to his Brother, Daniel Plumer. *Plumer Documents* (Reel 3, Container 6).

Plumer, *Memorandum*
> *William Plumer's Memorandum of Proceedings in the United States Senate, 1803–1807.* Edited by Everett Somerville Brown. New York: The Macmillan Company, 1923.

[Plumer,] *Message from His Excellency*
> [William Plumer,] *Message from His Excellency the Governor of New-Hampshire, to the Legislature, June 4, 1818.* no imprint, n.d.

Plumer Papers
> *Plumer Papers Correspondence* (mss. New Hampshire State Library).

Plumer, *Plumer*
> William Plumer, Jr., *Life of William Plumer.* Boston: Phillips, Sampson and Company, 1857.

Plumer, *Proclamations and Writings*
> Proclamations, Political & Other Writings of William Plumer, Volume 1. *Plumer Documents* (Library of Congress, Reel 4, Container 13).

Plumer, *Register I*
> William Plumer, *Register Volume I (commencing May 2d 1805, & ending April 21, 1807), Plumer Documents* (Library of Congress, Reel 1, Containers 1 and 2).

Plumer, *Register II*
> *The Register of Opinions & Events—his Rending of so, of William Plumer From May 1, 1807 to April 2, 1836. Plumer Documents* (Library of Congress, Reel 1, Container 3).

Plumer, *Repository I*
> *The Repository; Being a collection of Charges given to the Grand Juries; sentences pronounced against criminals; rules established by courts of law; and the regulations of the bar in the State of New Hampshire. Messages & Addresses from public bodies to the public & to & from public officers. Observations & Essays on various subjects. Volume 1. Collected by William Plumer for his own eye. Plumer Documents* (Reel 13, Frames 1 to 139).

Plumer, *Repository II*
> *The Repository being a Collection of Letters, Extracts from Records, Papers, Essays &c. Volume 2d* (Reel 6, Container 18).

Plumer, *Repository III*
> *William Plumer's Repository from Records, Documents, &c. Collected for his own Private Use. Volume 3. 1805 & 1806. Plumer Documents* (Reel 6, Container 19).

Plumer, *Repository IV*
    Repository. By William Plumer. Vol. 4. Plumer Documents (Reel 13, Frames 143 to 488).
Plumer, "Richard Evans"
    William Plumer, "Richard Evans," *Plumer Documents* (Biography volume 5, Reel 12, Frames 132–33).
Plumer, "Samuel Livermore"
    William Plumer, "Samuel Livermore," *Plumer Documents* (Reel 11, Volume 4, Frames 939–40, pp. 266–69).
Plumer, "Thomas Cogswell"
    William Plumer, "Thomas Cogswell," *Plumer Documents* (Reel 12, Volume 4, Frames 19–20, pp. 539–41).
Plumer, "Woodbury Langdon"
    William Plumer, "Woodbury Langdon," in *Early State Papers of New Hampshire. Volume 21*. Edited by Albert Stillman Batchellor. Concord, N.H.: Ira C. Evans, 1891, pp. 812–15.
Political Repository
    The Political Repository, or Strafford Recorder. A weekly newspaper published in Dover, N.H. (sometimes, *Political and Sentimental Repository, or Strafford Recorder*).
Popular Sources of Political Authority
    The Popular Sources of Political Authority: Documents on the Massachusetts Constitution of 1780. Edited by Oscar and Mary Handlin. Cambridge, Mass.: Harvard University Press, 1966.
Portsmouth Journal
    Portsmouth Journal of Literature & Politics. A weekly newspaper published in Portsmouth, N.H.
Portsmouth Oracle
    The Portsmouth Oracle. A weekly newspaper published in Portsmouth, N.H.
Prakash and Yoo, "Origins of Judicial Review"
    Saikrishna B. Prakash and John C. Yoo, "The Origins of Judicial Review," *University of Chicago Law Review* 70 (2003): 887–974.
Proceedings of the Legislature
    Proceedings of the Legislature of New-Hampshire, on the Important Subjects Referred to in the Governor's Speech, at the Opening of the Special Session, October 27, 1813. . . . Concord, N.H.: George Hough, 1813.
Public Laws 1813
    The Public Laws of the State of New-Hampshire, Passed at a Session of the General Court, Begun and Holden at Concord, on Wednesday the Twenty-Seventh Day of October, 1813. Concord, 1813.
Publicola, *New Vade Mecum*
    Publicola, *New Vade Mecum: or a Pocket Companion for Lawyers, Deputy Sheriffs and Constables; Suggesting Many Grievous Abuses and Alarming Evils, which Attend the Present Mode of Administering the Laws of New Hampshire*. Concord, N.H.: Hews and Goss, and Isaac Hill, 1819.
Rakove, *Original Meanings*
    Jack N. Rakove, *Original Meanings: Politics and Ideas in the Making of the Constitution*. New York: Alfred A. Knopf, 1996.
Rakove, "Origins of Judicial Review"
    Jack N. Rakove, "The Origins of Judicial Review: A Plea for New Contexts," *Stanford Law Review* 49 (May 1997): 1031–64.
Rantoul, *Eulogy on Woodbury*
    Robert Rantoul, Jr., *Eulogy on the Hon. Levi Woodbury, Pronounced at Portsmouth, N. H. October 10, 1851, at the Request of the City Government*. Portsmouth, N.H.: C. W. Brewster & Son, 1852.

Reno, *Memoirs of the Judiciary*
Conrad Reno, *Memoirs of the Judiciary and the Bar of New England for the Nineteenth Century: With a History of the Judicial System of New England.* Boston: Century Memorial Publisher, 1900.

Report on Memorials
Report of Committee on Memorials, 5 November 1813, *House Journal* (October 1813), pp. 71–85.

Resch, *Suffering Soldiers*
John Resch, *Suffering Soldiers: Revolutionary War Veterans, Moral Sentiment, and Political Culture in the Early Republic.* Amherst: University of Massachusetts Press, 1999.

Resch, "Transformation of Peterborough"
John P. Resch, "The Transformation of a Frontier Community: Peterborough, New Hampshire," in *Themes in Rural History of the Western World.* Edited by Richard Herr. Ames: Iowa State University Press, 1993, pp. 227–48.

"Resolution of 29 November 1815"
Resolution of 29 November 1815, House of Representatives, *Acts of the General Assembly of the State of Georgia; Passed at Milledgeville; at an Annual Session, in November and December, 1815* (1815), pp. 132–33.

Richardson, *Oration at Groton*
William Merchant Richardson, *An Oration Pronounced at Groton, July 4, 1801; in Commemoration of the Anniversary of American Independence.* Amherst, N.H.: Samuel Preston, 1801.

Robinson, *Isaac Hill*
Francis E. Robinson, *Isaac Hill* (Master's Thesis, University of New Hampshire, 1933).

Rule of Law
John Phillip Reid, *Rule of Law: The Jurisprudence of Liberty in the Seventeenth and Eighteenth Centuries.* DeKalb: Northern Illinois University Press, 2004.

Second Address of the Convention
An *Address of the Convention for Framing a New Constitution or Form of Government for the State of New-Hampshire, to the Inhabitants of said State.* Exeter, N.H., 1782.

Selsam, "History of Judicial Tenure"
J. Paul Selsam, "A History of Judicial Tenure in Pennsylvania," *Dickinson Law Review* 38 (1934): 168–83.

Selsam, *Pennsylvania Constitution*
J. Paul Selsam, *The Pennsylvania Constitution of 1776: A Study of Revolutionary Democracy.* New York: Octagon Books, 1971.

Senate Debates on Judiciary
Debates in the Senate of the United States on the Judiciary, During the First Session of the Seventh Congress: also, the Several Motions, Resolutions, and Votes, taken upon that Momentous Subject; and a Complete List of the Yeas and Nays, as Entered on the Journals.* Philadelphia: E. Bronson, 1802.

Senate Journal (June 1789)
A *Journal of the Proceedings of the Honorable Senate of the State of New-Hampshire, at their Session of the General Court, holden at Concord, on Wednesday. June 3d, 1789.* Portsmouth, N.H.: J. Melcher, 1789.

Senate Journal (June 1790)
Journal of the Senate Containing the Proceedings from June 1 to June 19, 1790,* reprinted in *Early State Papers of New Hampshire Including the Journals of the Senate and House of Representatives and the Records of the President and Council, from June, 1790, to June, 1793.* Volume 22. Edited by Albert Stillman Batchellor. Concord, N.H.: Ira C. Evans Public Printer, 1893, pp. 5–31.

Senate Journal (January 1791)
Journal of the Senate Containing the Proceedings from January 5 to January 18, 1791,* reprinted in *Early State Papers of New Hampshire Including the Journals of the Senate

and House of Representatives and Records of the President and Council, from June, 1790, to June, 1793. Volume 22. Edited by Albert Stillman Batchellor. Concord, N.H.: Ira C. Evans Public Printer, 1893, pp. 95–137.

Senate Journal (June 1791)

Journal of the Senate Containing the Proceedings from June 1 to June 17, 1791, reprinted in *Early State Papers of New Hampshire Including the Journals of the Senate and House of Representatives and Records of the President and Council, from June, 1790, to June, 1793.* Volume 22. Edited by Albert Stillman Batchellor. Concord, N.H.: Ira C. Evans, 1893, pp. 279–304.

Senate Journal (November 1791)

Journal of the Senate Containing the Proceedings from November 30, 1791, to January 6, 1792, reprinted in *Early State Papers of New Hampshire Including the Journals of the Senate and House of Representatives and Records of the President and Council, from June, 1790, to June, 1793.* Volume 22. Edited by Albert Stillman Batchellor. Concord, N.H.: Ira C. Evans Public Printer, 1893, pp. 365–99.

Senate Journal (June 1792)

Journal of the Senate Containing the Proceedings from June 6 to June 22, 1792, reprinted in *Early State Papers of New Hampshire Including the Journals of the Senate and House of Representatives and Records of the President and Council, from June, 1790, to June, 1793.* Volume 22. Edited by Albert Stillman Batchellor. Concord, N.H.: Ira C. Evans Public Printer, 1893, pp. 517–39.

Senate Journal (November 1792)

Journal of the Senate Containing the Proceedings from November 21 to December 28, 1792, reprinted in *Early State Papers of New Hampshire Including the Journals of the Senate and House of Representatives and Records of the President and Council, from June, 1790, to June, 1793.* Volume 22. Edited by Albert Stillman Batchellor. Concord, N.H.: Ira C. Evans Public Printer, 1893, pp. 601–33.

Senate Journal (June 1793)

A Journal of the Proceedings of the Honorable Senate of the State of New-Hampshire, at a Session of the GENERAL COURT, Begun and Holden at CONCORD, on Wednesday the Fifth Day of June, 1793, Being the Day Appointed by the Constitution, for the Annual Meeting of Said Court. Portsmouth, N.H.: J. Melcher, 1893.

Senate Journal (December 1793)

A Journal of the Proceedings of the Honorable Senate of the State of New-Hampshire, at a Session of the General Court, Holden at Exeter, on Wednesday the Twenty-Fifth Day of December, Anno Domini, 1793. Portsmouth, N.H.: J. Melcher, 1794.

Senate Journal (November 1796)

A Journal of the Proceedings of the Honorable Senate of the State of New-Hampshire, at a Session of the General-Court, Holden at Concord, November, 1796. Portsmouth, N.H.: John Melcher, 1797.

Senate Journal (November 1797)

A Journal of the Proceedings of the Honorable Senate of the State of New-Hampshire, at a Session of the General-Court, Holden at Portsmouth, Nov. 1797. Portsmouth, N.H.: John Melcher, 1798.

Senate Journal (June 1798)

A Journal of the proceedings of the Honorable Senate of the State of New-Hampshire, at their Session begun and Holden at Hopkinton the 1st Wednesday in June, 1798. Portsmouth, N.H.: John Melcher, 1798.

Senate Journal (December 1799)

A Journal of the Proceedings of the Honorable Senate of the State of New-Hampshire begun and holden at Exeter, the first Wednesday of December, 1799. Portsmouth, N.H.: John Melcher, 1800.

Senate Journal (June 1809)

Journal of the Honorable Senate of the State of New-Hampshire, at their Session, Holden at Concord, on the first Wednesday of June, 1809. Concord, N.H., 1809.

Senate Journal (June 1810)

> *Journal of the Honorable Senate of the State of New-Hampshire, at their Session, Begun and Holden at Concord, on the first Wednesday of June, 1810.* Concord, N.H., 1810.

Senate Journal (June 1813)

> *Journal of the Honorable Senate of the State of New-Hampshire, at their Session, Holden at Concord, on the First Wednesday of June, 1813.* Concord, N.H.: George Hough, 1813.

Senate Journal (October 1813)

> *Journal of the Proceedings of the Honorable Senate of the State of New-Hampshire, at their Session, Begun and Holden at Concord, on Wednesday, October 27, 1813.* Concord, N.H.: George Hough, 1813.

Senate Journal (November 1816)

> *Journal of the Honorable Senate of the State of New-Hampshire, at their Session, Begun and Holden at Concord, on the third Wednesday of November, 1816.* Concord, N.H.: Isaac Hill, 1817.

Senate Journal (June 1856)

> *Journal of the Honorable Senate of the State of New Hampshire, June Session, 1856.* Concord, N.H.: Amos Hadley, State Printer, 1856.

Session Laws (June 1797)

> *The Laws of the State of New-Hampshire, Passed at a Session of the Honorable General-Court, June, 1797.* Portsmouth, N.H.: John Melcher, 1797.

Shankman, "Malcontents and Tertium Quids"

> Andrew Shankman, "Malcontents and Tertium Quids: The Battle to Define Democracy in Jeffersonian Philadelphia," *Journal of the Early Republic* 19 (1999): 43–72.

Shapiro, "Judicial Independence"

> Martin Shapiro, "Judicial Independence: The English Experience," *North Carolina Law Review* 55 (1977): 577–652.

Shimomura, "History of Claims"

> Floyd D. Shimomura, "The History of Claims Against the United States: The Evolution from a Legislative Toward a Judicial Model of Payment," *Louisiana Law Review* 45 (1985): 625–700.

Shipton, "Pickering"

> Clifford K. Shipton, "John Pickering," in Clifford K. Shipton, *Biographical Sketches of Those Who Attended Harvard College in the Classes 1761–1763, With Bibliographical and Other Notes (Sibley's Harvard Graduates, Vol. 15).* Boston: Massachusetts Historical Society, 1970, pp.91–96.

Shirley, *Early Jurisprudence*

> John M. Shirley, *The Early Jurisprudence of New Hampshire: An Address Delivered at the Annual Meeting of the N. H. Historical Society, June 13, 1883.* Concord, N.H.: Republican Press Association, 1885.

Shirley, "Reporter's Note"

> John Major Shirley, "Reporter's Note," 55 *N. H.* 6–8 (1876).

Simon, *What Kind of Nation*

> James F. Simon, *What Kind of a Nation: Thomas Jefferson, John Marshall, and the Epic Struggle to Create a United States.* New York: Simon & Schuster, 2002.

Smith, *Exeter Address*

> "An Address of Hon. Jeremiah Smith, LL. D., Delivered at the Celebration on the Close of the Second Century from the Time Exeter was Settled by John Wheelwright and Others, July 4, 1839," *Collections of the New-Hampshire Historical Society* 6 (1850): 167–204.

Smith, "Impeachment, Address, and Removal"

> Stephen A. Smith, "Impeachment, Address, and the Removal of Judges in Arkansas: An Historical Perspective," *Arkansas Law Review* 32 (1978): 253–68.

Smith, "Independent Judiciary"
> Joseph H. Smith, "An Independent Judiciary: The Colonial Background," *University of Pennsylvania Law Review* 124 (1976): 1104–56.

Smith, *Legal Manuscripts*
> "Extracts from Judge Smith's Legal Manuscripts," printed in *Smith's Reports*, pp. 521–31.

[Smith,] "New-Hampshire Law"
> [Jeremiah Smith,] "New-Hampshire Law—Its Sources," in *Collections Historical*, pp. 201–5.

Smith, *Probate Law*
> Jeremiah Smith, *Treatise on Probate Law* (mss), excerpts printed in *Smith's Reports*.

Smith's Reports
> *Decisions of the Superior and Supreme Courts of New Hampshire From 1802 to 1809, and from 1813 to 1816. Selected from the Manuscript Reports of the Late Jeremiah Smith, Chief Justice of those Courts. With Extracts from Judge Smith's Manuscript Treatise on Probate Law, and from his other Legal Manuscripts.* Boston: Little, Brown, and Company, 1879.

Smith, *Sketch of Ellis*
> Chief Justice [Jeremiah] Smith, *A Sketch of the Character of the Late Judge Ellis, as Delivered to the Grand Jury, after the usual Charge at the Opening of the Supreme Judicial Court, at Haverhill, on the 21st of May, 1816.* Portsmouth, N.H.: Charles Turell, 1816.

Sources and Documents
> *Sources and Documents of United States Constitutions [Volume] 2: Colorado, Connecticut, Delaware, Florida, Georgia.* Edited by William F. Swindler. Dobbs Ferry, N.Y.: Oceana Publications, 1973.

State Papers 20
> *Early State Papers of New Hampshire Including the Constitution of 1784, Journals of the Senate and House of Representatives, and Records of the President and Council from June 1784 to June 1787.* Volume 20. Edited by Albert Stillman Batchellor. Manchester, N.H.: John B. Clarke, 1891.

State Papers 21
> *Early State Papers of New Hampshire Including the Journals of the Senate and House of Representatives and Records of the President and Council, from June, 1787, to June, 1790. Volume 21.* Edited by Albert Stillman Batchellor. Concord, N.H.: Ira Evans, 1892.

Stearns, "Livermore"
> Ezra S. Stearns, "Hon. Arthur Livermore," *Proceedings of the Grafton and Coos Counties Bar Association at its Annual Meeting Held at Colebrook, September 2, 1892.* 9 (1893): 429–49.

Stimson, *American Revolution in Law*
> Shannon C. Stimson, *The American Revolution in the Law: Anglo-American Jurisprudence Before John Marshall.* Princeton, N.J.: Princeton University Press, 1990.

Stychin, "Commentaries of Kent"
> Carl F. Stychin, "The Commentaries of Chancellor James Kent and the Development of an American Common Law," *American Journal of Legal History* 37 (1993): 440–63.

Sullivan, *Speech at Rockingham Convention*
> George Sullivan, *Speech of the Hon. George Sullivan, at the Rockingham Convention, with the Memorial & Resolutions, and the Report of the Committee of Elections.* Concord, N.H.: George Hough, 1812.

Surrency, "Judiciary Act of 1801"
> Erwin C. Surrency, "The Judiciary Act of 1801," *American Journal of Legal History* 2 (1958): 53–65.

Swift, *System of Laws*
> Zephaniah Swift, *A System of the Laws of the State of Connecticut.* Windham, Conn.: John Byrne, 1795.

Swift, *Vindication*
> Zephaniah Swift, *A Vindication of the Calling of the Special Superior Court, at Middletown, on the 4th Tuesday of August, 1815, for the Trial of Peter Lung, Charged with the Crime of Murder. With Observations on the Constitutional Power of the Legislature to Interfere with the Judiciary in the Administration of Justice.* Windham, Conn.: J. Byrne, 1816.

Taishoff, "State Politics"
> Sue Taishoff, "New Hampshire State Politics and the Concept of a Party System, 1800–1840," *Historical New Hampshire* 31 (Spring-Summer 1976): 17–43.

Tenth Plumer Letterbook
> "Letters to & from William Plumer Volume 10. Beginning October 21. 1817 and Ending February 1. 1812." *Plumer Documents* (Library of Congress, Reel 4, Container 10).

Third Plumer Letterbook
> "Letters to & from William Plumer. Volume 3.5." *Plumer Documents* (Library of Congress, Reel 2, Container 5).

Thompson, "Adams and the Science of Politics"
> C. Bradley Thompson, "John Adams and the Science of Politics," in *John Adams and the Founding of the Republic.* Edited by Richard Alan Ryerson. Boston: Massachusetts Historical Society, 2001, pp. 237–59.

Thompson, *Thompson*
> Mary P. Thompson, *A Memoir of Judge Ebenezer Thompson of Durham, New Hampshire.* Concord, N.H.: Republican Press Association, 1886.

Thorpe, *Constitutions*
> Francis Newton Thorpe, *The Federal and State Constitutions: Colonial Charters, and Other Organic Laws of the States, Territories, and Colonies Now or Heretofore Forming the United States of America.* 7 volumes. Washington, DC.: Government Printing Office, 1909.

"Trial of Pickering"
> "Trial of Judge Pickering on a charge of High Crimes and Misdemeanors, exhibited to the Senate of the United States, in Senate of the United States," *Annals of Congress, Senate, 8th Congress, 1st Session,* pp. 315–68.

True, *Committees of Correspondence*
> Ransom B. True, *The New Hampshire Committees of Correspondence, 1773–1774* (Master's Thesis, University of New Hampshire, 1969).

Tucker's Blackstone
> St. George Tucker, *Blackstone's Commentaries: With Notes of Reference, to the Constitution and Laws, of the Federal Government of the United States; and of the Commonwealth of Virginia. In Five Volumes.* Volume 1. Philadelphia: William Young Birch and Abraham Small, 1803.

Turner, "Federalist Policy and Judiciary"
> Kathryn Turner, "Federalist Policy and the Judiciary Act of 1801," *William & Mary Quarterly* 22 (January 1965): 3–32.

Turner, "Impeachment of Pickering"
> Lynn W. Turner, "The Impeachment of John Pickering," *American Historical Review* 54 (April 1949): 485–507.

Turner, "Jefferson Through Plumer"
> Lynn W. Turner, "Thomas Jefferson Through the Eyes of a New Hampshire Politician," *Mississippi Valley Historical Review* 30 (September 1943): 205–14.

Turner, "Judiciary Act of 1801"
> Kathryn Turner, "Federalist Policy and the Judiciary Act of 1801," *William and Mary Quarterly* 22 (January 1965): 3–32.

Turner, "Midnight Judges"
    Kathryn Turner, "The Midnight Judges," *University of Pennsylvania Law Review* 109 (1961): 494–522.
Turner, *Ninth State*
    Lynn Warren Turner, *The Ninth State: New Hampshire's Formative Years*. Chapel Hill: University of North Carolina Press, 1983.
Turner, *Plumer*
    Lynn W. Turner, *William Plumer of New Hampshire 1759–1850*. Chapel Hill: University of North Carolina Press, 1962.
Upton, "Independence of Judiciary"
    Richard F. Upton, "The Independence of the Judiciary in New Hampshire," *New Hampshire Bar Journal* 1 (#4) (July 1959): 28–39.
Utter, "Ohio and Common Law"
    William T. Utter, "Ohio and the English Common Law," *Mississippi Valley Historical Review* 16 (December 1929): 321–33.
Wait, "William Plumer"
    Albert S. Wait, "William Plumer," in *Proceedings of the New Hampshire Historical Society*. Volume III, Part I. Concord, N.H.: Printed for the Society, 1897, pp. 119–42.
[Webster,] *Appeal to Old Whigs*
    [Daniel Webster,] *An Appeal to the Old Whigs of New-Hampshire*. no imprint, 1805.
Webster, "Comparative Study of Constitutions"
    William Clarence Webster, "Comparative Study of the State Constitutions of the American Revolutions," *Annals of the American Academy of Political Science* 9 (1899): 64–104.
Webster Legal Papers
    The Papers of Daniel Webster Legal Papers, Volume 1: The New Hampshire Practice. Edited by Alfred S. Konefsky and Andrew J. King. Hanover, N.H.: University Press of New England, 1982.
Webster Papers
    The Papers of Daniel Webster: Correspondence, Volume 1: 1798–1814. Edited by Charles M. Wiltse. Hanover, N.H.: University Press of New England, 1974.
Webster Papers Federal
    The Papers of Daniel Webster, Legal Papers, Volume 3: The Federal Practice. Part 1. Edited by Andrew J. King. Hanover, N.H.: University Press of New England, 1989.
Whittington, "Reconstructing the Judiciary"
    Keith E. Whittington, "Reconstructing the Federal Judiciary: The Chase Impeachment and the Constitution," *Studies in American Political Development* 9 (Spring 1995): 55–116.
Wingate, *Wingate*
    Charles E. L. Wingate, *Life and Letters of Paine Wingate, One of the Fathers of the Nation*. 2 volumes. Medford, Mass.: James D. P. Wingate, 1930.
Wood, *Creation of Republic*
    Gordon S. Wood, *The Creation of the American Republic, 1776–1787*. Chapel Hill: University of North Carolina Press, 1969.
Wood, "Judicial Review"
    Gordon S. Wood, "Judicial Review in the Era of the Founding," in *Is the Supreme Court the Guardian of the Constitution?* Edited by Robert A. Licht. Washington, D.C.: American Enterprise Institute Press, 1993, pp. 153–66.
Wood, "Launching"
    Gordon S. Wood, "Launching the 'Extended Republic': The Federalist Era," in *Launching the "Extended Republic": The Federalist Era*. Edited by Ronald Hoffman and Peter J. Albert. Charlottesville: University Press of Virginia, 1996, pp. 1–24.
Wood, "New Hampshire Constitution"
    Frederick A. Wood, "The New Hampshire Constitution," *New England Magazine* 29 (new series) (September 1903): 111–12.

Wood, "Origins of Judicial Review"
> Gordon S. Wood, "The Origins of Judicial Review," *Suffolk University Law Review* 22 (1988): 1293–1307.

Wood, "Origins of Vested Rights"
> Gordon S. Wood, "The Origins of Vested Rights in the Early Republic," *Virginia Law Review* 85 (1999): 1421–45.

Woodbury, *Memoir of Woodbury*
> Charles Levi Woodbury, *Memoir of Levi Woodbury*. Cambridge, Mass.: John Wilson and Son, 1881.

Woodman, *Election Sermon*
> Joseph Woodman, *A Sermon Preached at Concord, June 3d, 1802, on the Annual Election of the Governor, Council, Senate, and House of Representatives, of the State of New-Hampshire*. Concord, N.H.: George Hough, 1802.

Wootton, "Introduction"
> David Wootton, "Introduction," to *The Essential Federalist and Anti-Federalist Papers*. Edited by David Wootton. Indianapolis: Hackett Publishing Company, 2003, pp. ix–xliii.

Worcester, *Fast Day Sermon at Salisbury*
> Noah Worcester, *Abraham and Lot: A Sermon on the Way of Peace, and the Evils of War: Delivered at Salisbury, in New-Hampshire, on the Day of the National Fast, August 20, 1812*. Concord, N.H.: George Hough, 1812.

Works of Adams
> *The Works of John Adams, Second President of the United States*. Edited by Charles Francis Adams. 10 volumes. Boston: Little Brown, 1850–1856.

Works of Ames
> *Works of Fisher Ames with a Selection from his Speeches and Correspondence*. Edited by Seth Ames. 2 volumes. New York: William Gowans, 1869.

Works of Wilson
> *The Works of James Wilson*. 2 volumes. Edited by Robert Green McCloskey. Cambridge, Mass.: Harvard University Press, 1967.

Writings of Thomas Jefferson
> *The Writings of Thomas Jefferson*. Edited by Paul Leicester Ford. 10 volumes. New York: G.P. Putnam's Sons, 1892–1899.

Zuckert, "Founder of Natural Rights"
> Michael P. Zuckert, "Founder of the Natural Rights Republic," in *Thomas Jefferson and the Politics of Nature*. Edited by Thomas S. Engeman. Notre Dame, Ind.: University of Notre Dame Press, 2000, pp. 11–58.

Acknowledgments

Support for research was provided by the Filomen D'Agostino Greenberg and Max E. Greenberg Faculty Research Fund at New York University School of Law and by Richard L. Revesz, dean of the School of Law. Research was made easier and convenient by the professional competence, help, and good cheer of the staff of the Huntington Library, in San Marino, California. Much of this book was written at the Huntington Library where all activity is made pleasant by the encouragement of Alan Jutzi, Roy C. Ritchie, David Zeidberg, Susi Krasnoo, and Juan Gomez. The research was conducted chiefly in New York and New Hampshire. At New York University I owe special debts of gratitude to Calvin Hudson, who tracked many of the elusive and poorly indexed New Hampshire laws; to Kris Dalman, who obtained materials not readily available in New York; and to Gretchen Feltes, Conservation Librarian at the School of Law, who with her computer found material I otherwise would not have learned existed. Cite and substance checking was entrusted first to Barbara Kern and later to Jennifer Wertkin, who rescued a very difficult situation and without whose dedication and perseverance the publication of this book would have been very much further delayed. The index is the work of Barbara Kern. And finally, special heartfelt thanks are to be given to Annmarie Jean Zell, who spent hours tracking down the pictures of Jeremiah Smith, William Plumer, and Arthur Livermore and even more time making certain we obtained reproductions suitable for publication.

In some inexplicable manner this study may have benefitted from being read, discussed, and criticized by members of that most distinguished gathering of American legal historians, the members of the New York University School of Law colloquium in Legal History, led by William Edward Nelson, and including Richard Bruce Bernstein, William P. LaPiana, and Martin S. Flaherty.

Final appreciation is due to Daniel J. Hulsebosch whose careful read-ing of the text has prevented a serious factual error. It was he who pointed out that it was not Governor Benjamin Pierce but his son, Franklin Pierce, who in 1853 gave the following answer to William Rufus King's question about the difference between addressing a judge from of-fice and legislating a judge from office: "I don't think there is any differ-ence. Addressing and legislating out must be the same. We used both in a single session of the General Court to oust Jeremiah Smith. We only needed to enact one but we passed both to emphasize the hopeful expec-tation we were rid of him forever."

Index